DATE DUE

GAYLORD			PRINTED IN U.S.A.

DE...Z'S
FRA...EIN ™

...Son

...me Two

DYNAMITE ®
ENTERTAINMENT

DEAN KOONTZ'S
FRANKENSTEIN™
Prodigal Son

BASED ON THE NOVEL BY
DEAN KOONTZ

ADAPTED BY:
CHUCK DIXON

ILLUSTRATED BY:
SCOTT COHN & TIM SEELEY

COLORS BY:
ALE STARLIN

LETTERING & COLLECTION DESIGN BY:
BILL TORTOLINI

COLLECTION COVER BY:
BRETT BOOTH

CONSULTATION BY:
LES DABEL & ERNST DABEL

DYNAMITE®
ENTERTAINMENT

Dynamite Entertainment:

NICK BARRUCCI	• PRESIDENT
JUAN COLLADO	• CHIEF OPERATING OFFICER
JOSEPH RYBANDT	• EDITOR
JOSH JOHNSON	• CREATIVE DIRECTOR
RICH YOUNG	• BUSINESS DEVELOPMENT
JASON ULLMEYER	• SENIOR DESIGNER
JOSH GREEN	• TRAFFIC COORDINATOR
CHRIS CANIANO	• PRODUCTION ASSISTANT

www.dynamite.net

ISBN13: 978-1-60690-187-8   ISBN10: 1-60690-187-7

10 9 8 7 6 5 4 3 2 1

Over 200 years ago, a mad scientist named Frankenstein breathed life into a patchwork corpse, beginning a feud between the two that seemed to end in death.

Cut to modern day where the scientist, now going by the name **Victor Helios**, has set up shop in New Orleans, creating ever more of his New Race with the end goal of supplanting humanity and taking over the world. In a role reversal, the original monster - calling himself **Deucalion** - follows his creator to the Crescent City to put a stop to that mad plan.

Now, with one of Victor's New Race falling into madness and becoming a serial killer, two New Orleans Police Detectives - **Carson O'Connor** and **Michael Maddison** - are drawn into a world of science, horror, and the renewed feud between creator and creation.

COVER BY: BRETT BOOTH

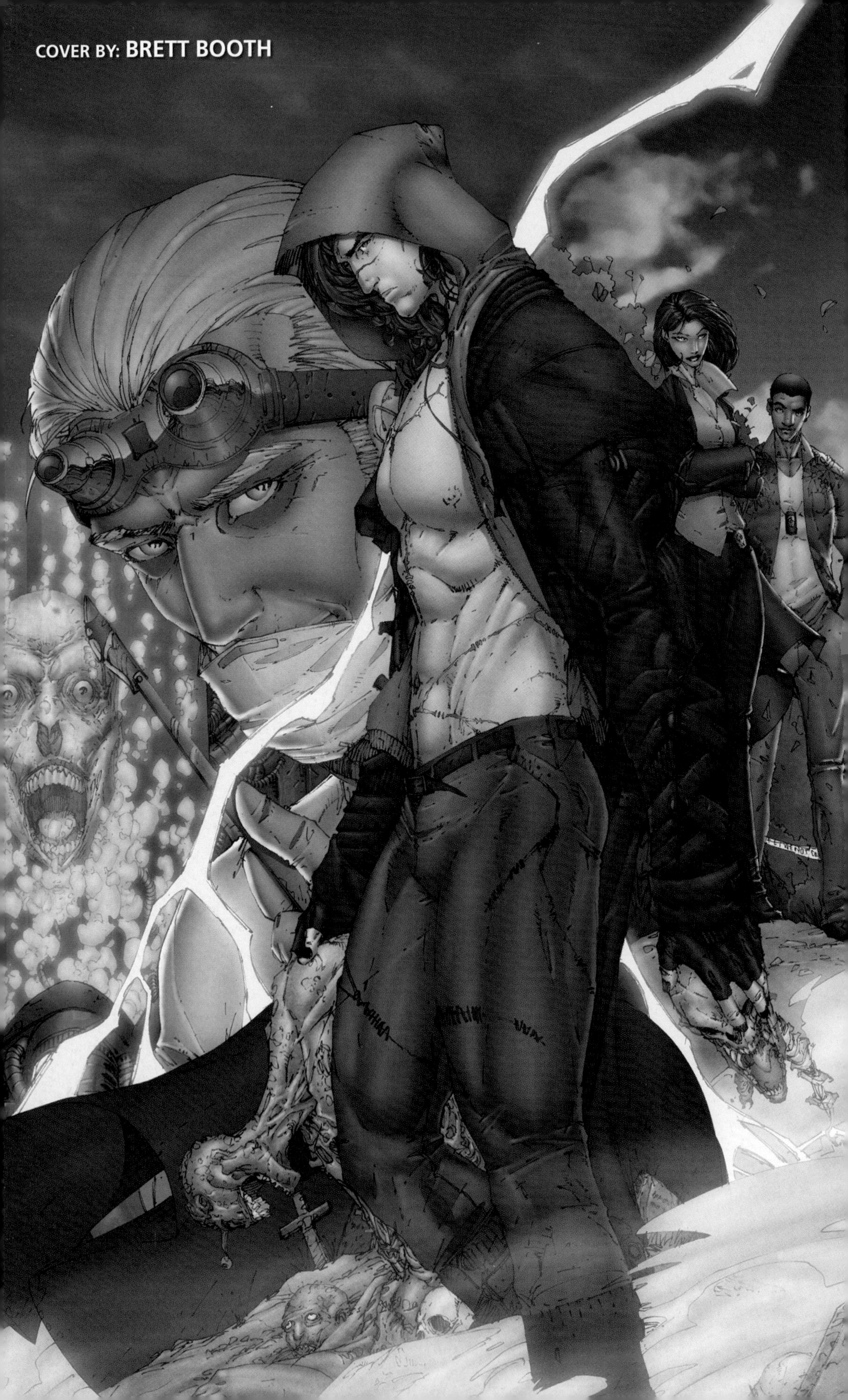

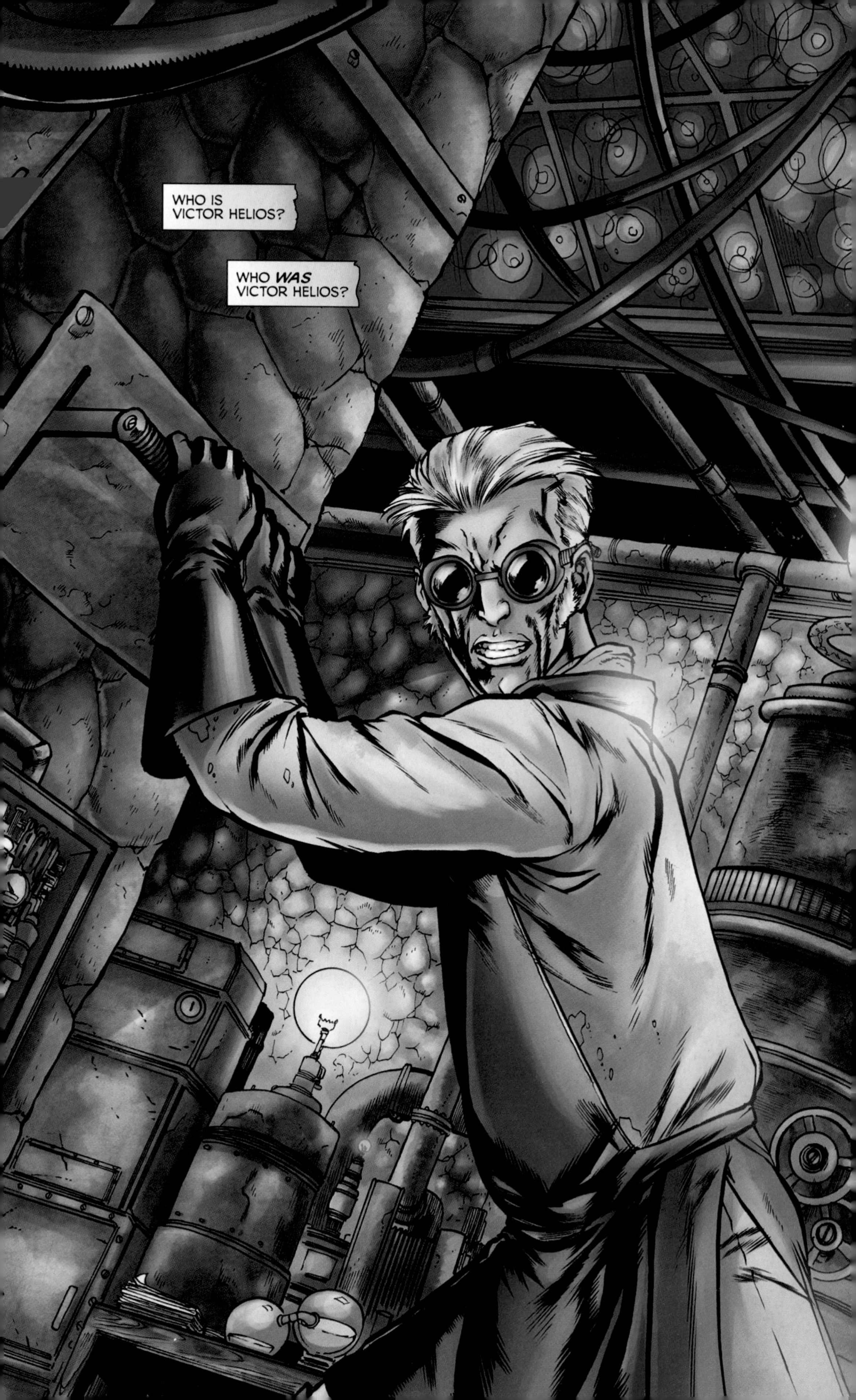
WHO IS VICTOR HELIOS?
WHO ***WAS*** VICTOR HELIOS?

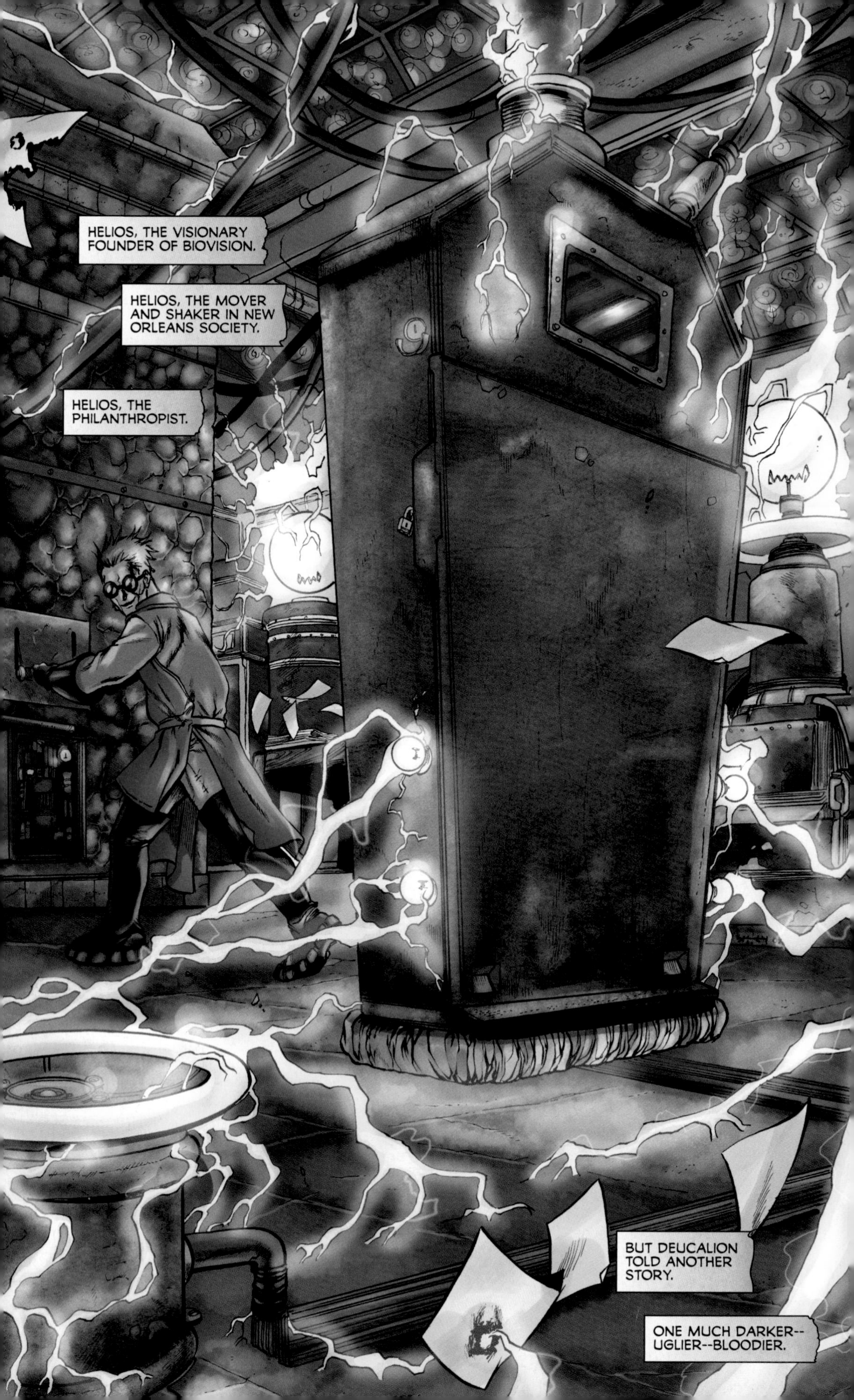
HELIOS, THE VISIONARY FOUNDER OF BIOVISION.
HELIOS, THE MOVER AND SHAKER IN NEW ORLEANS SOCIETY.
HELIOS, THE PHILANTHROPIST.
BUT DEUCALION TOLD ANOTHER STORY.
ONE MUCH DARKER--UGLIER--BLOODIER.

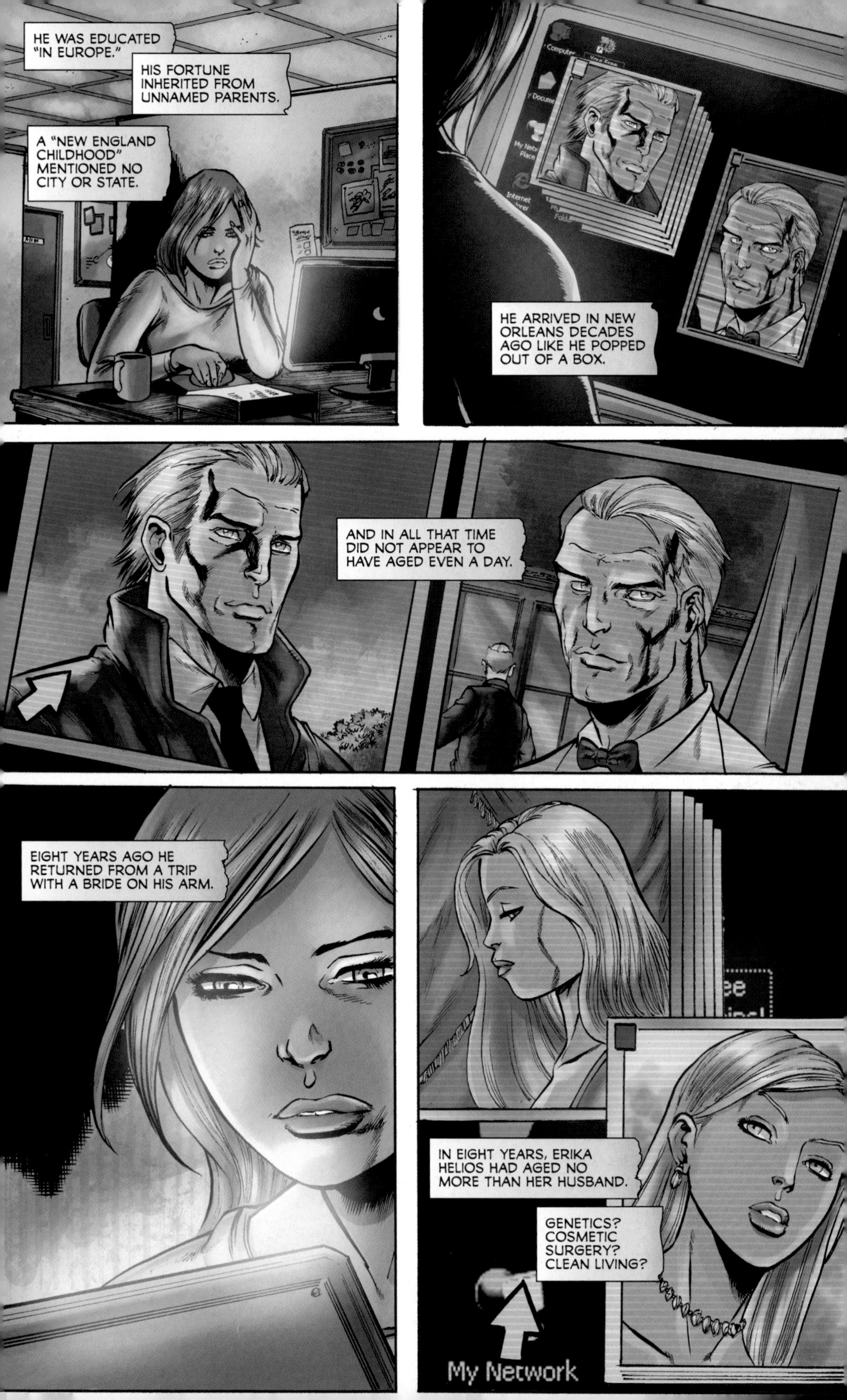
HE WAS EDUCATED "IN EUROPE."
HIS FORTUNE INHERITED FROM UNNAMED PARENTS.
A "NEW ENGLAND CHILDHOOD" MENTIONED NO CITY OR STATE.
HE ARRIVED IN NEW ORLEANS DECADES AGO LIKE HE POPPED OUT OF A BOX.
AND IN ALL THAT TIME DID NOT APPEAR TO HAVE AGED EVEN A DAY.
EIGHT YEARS AGO HE RETURNED FROM A TRIP WITH A BRIDE ON HIS ARM.
IN EIGHT YEARS, ERIKA HELIOS HAD AGED NO MORE THAN HER HUSBAND.
GENETICS? COSMETIC SURGERY? CLEAN LIVING?
My Network

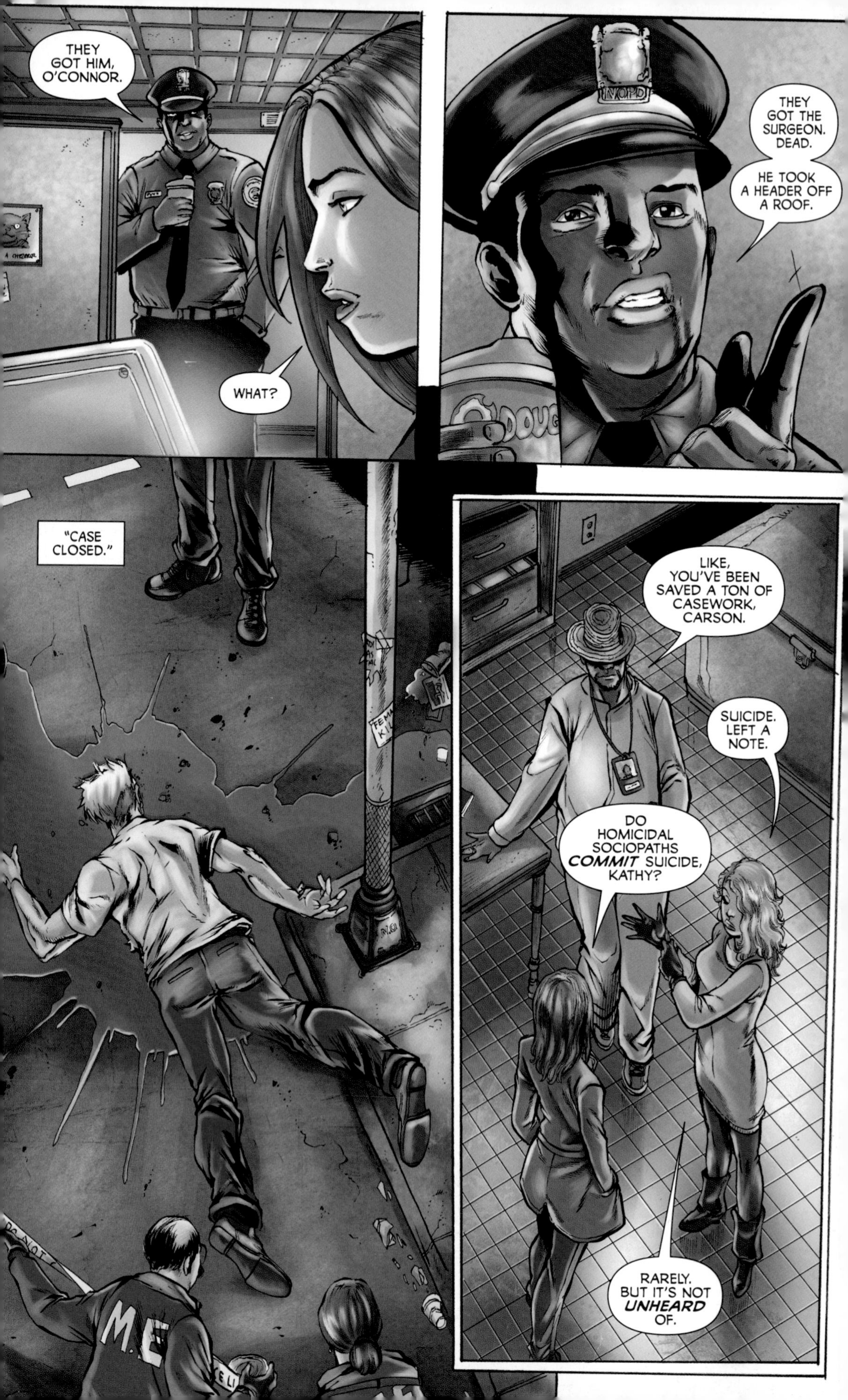
THEY GOT HIM, O'CONNOR.
WHAT?
THEY GOT THE SURGEON. DEAD.
HE TOOK A HEADER OFF A ROOF.
"CASE CLOSED."
LIKE, YOU'VE BEEN SAVED A TON OF CASEWORK, CARSON.
SUICIDE. LEFT A NOTE.
DO HOMICIDAL SOCIOPATHS COMMIT SUICIDE, KATHY?
RARELY. BUT IT'S NOT UNHEARD OF.

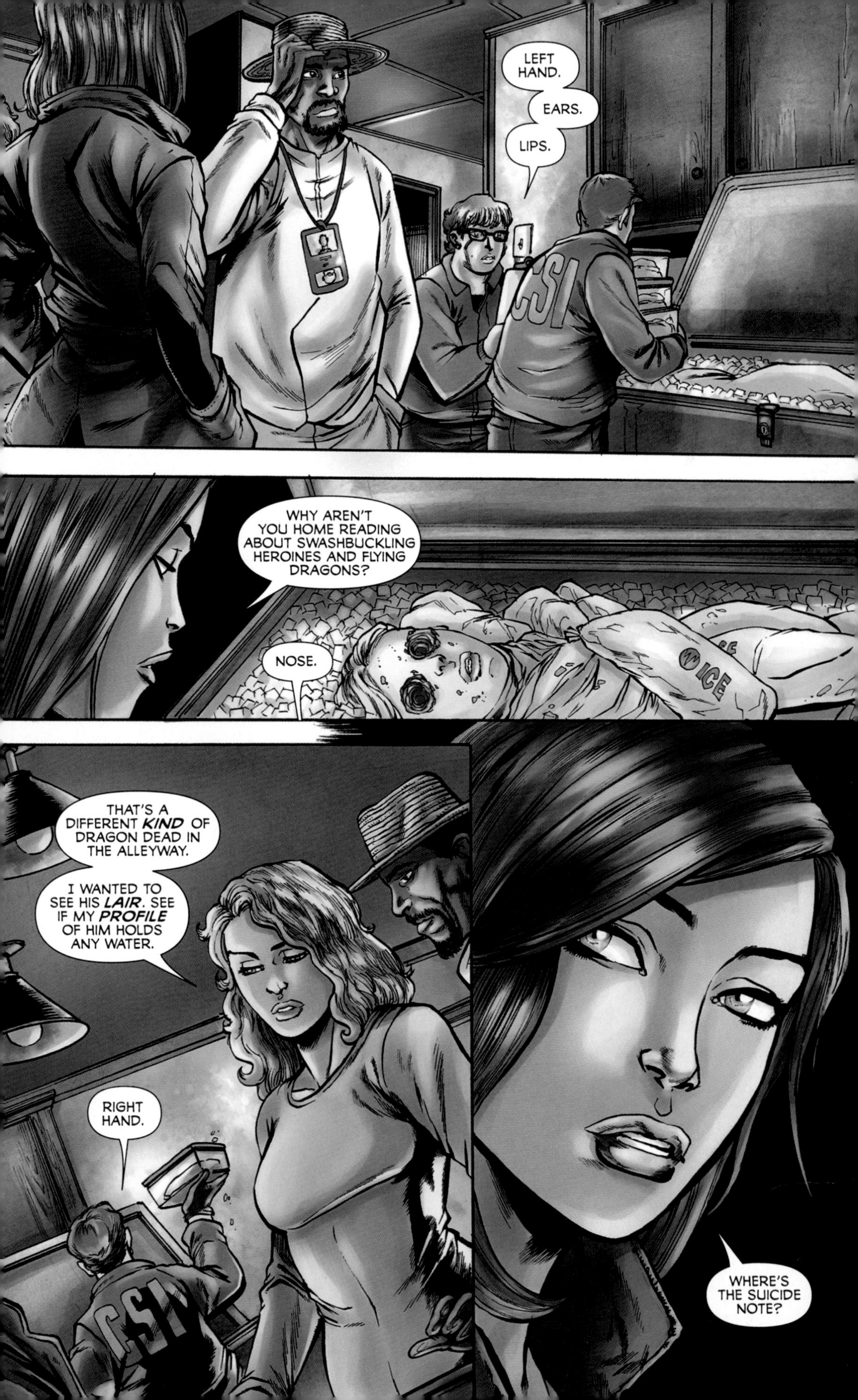
LEFT HAND.
EARS.
LIPS.
WHY AREN'T YOU HOME READING ABOUT SWASHBUCKLING HEROINES AND FLYING DRAGONS?
NOSE.
ICE
ICE
THAT'S A DIFFERENT *KIND* OF DRAGON DEAD IN THE ALLEYWAY.
I WANTED TO SEE HIS *LAIR*. SEE IF MY *PROFILE* OF HIM HOLDS ANY WATER.
RIGHT HAND.
WHERE'S THE SUICIDE NOTE?

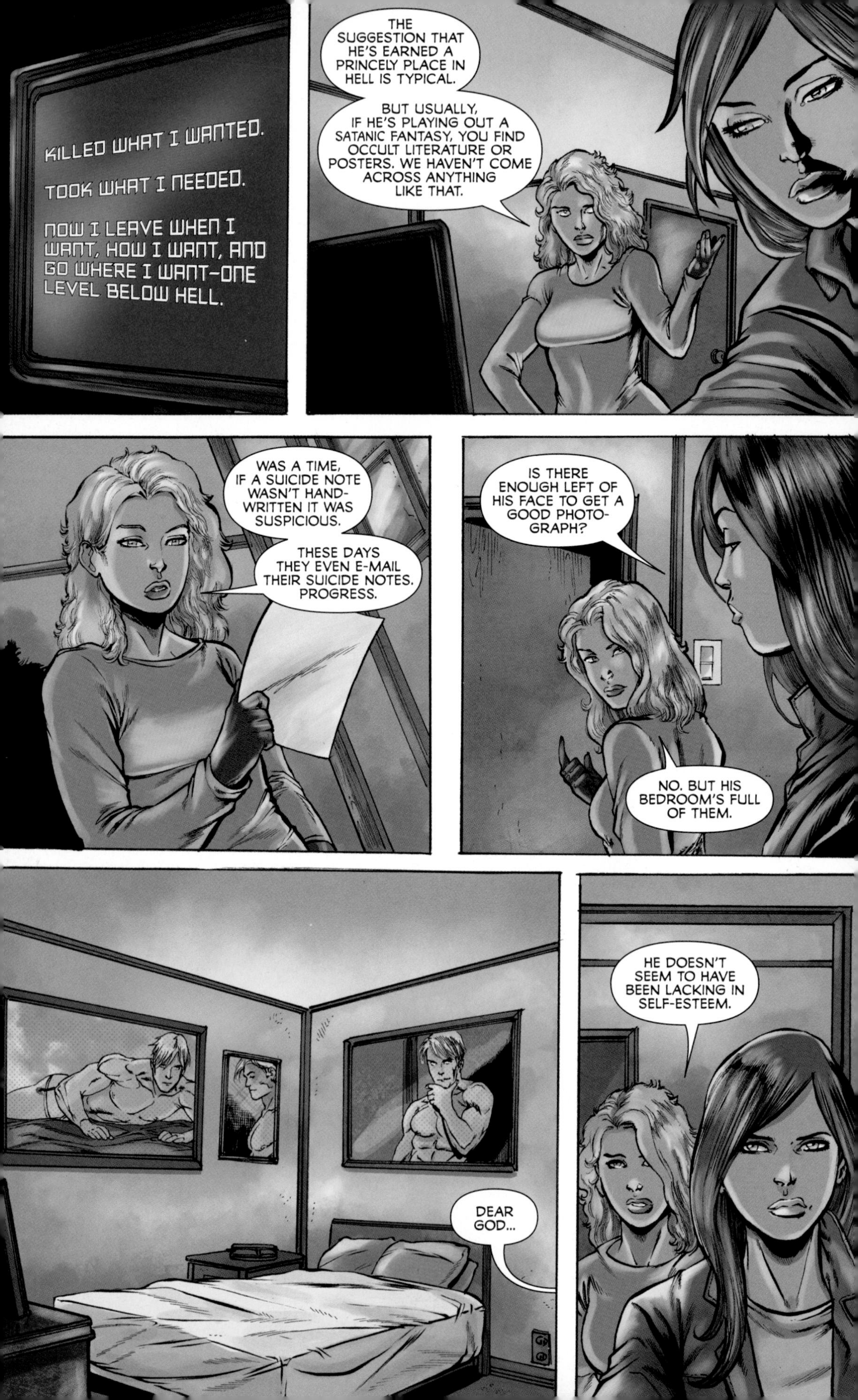
KILLED WHAT I WANTED.
TOOK WHAT I NEEDED.
NOW I LEAVE WHEN I WANT, HOW I WANT, AND GO WHERE I WANT—ONE LEVEL BELOW HELL.
THE SUGGESTION THAT HE'S EARNED A PRINCELY PLACE IN HELL IS TYPICAL.
BUT USUALLY, IF HE'S PLAYING OUT A SATANIC FANTASY, YOU FIND OCCULT LITERATURE OR POSTERS. WE HAVEN'T COME ACROSS ANYTHING LIKE THAT.
WAS A TIME, IF A SUICIDE NOTE WASN'T HAND-WRITTEN IT WAS SUSPICIOUS.
THESE DAYS THEY EVEN E-MAIL THEIR SUICIDE NOTES. PROGRESS.
IS THERE ENOUGH LEFT OF HIS FACE TO GET A GOOD PHOTO-GRAPH?
NO. BUT HIS BEDROOM'S FULL OF THEM.
DEAR GOD...
HE DOESN'T SEEM TO HAVE BEEN LACKING IN SELF-ESTEEM.

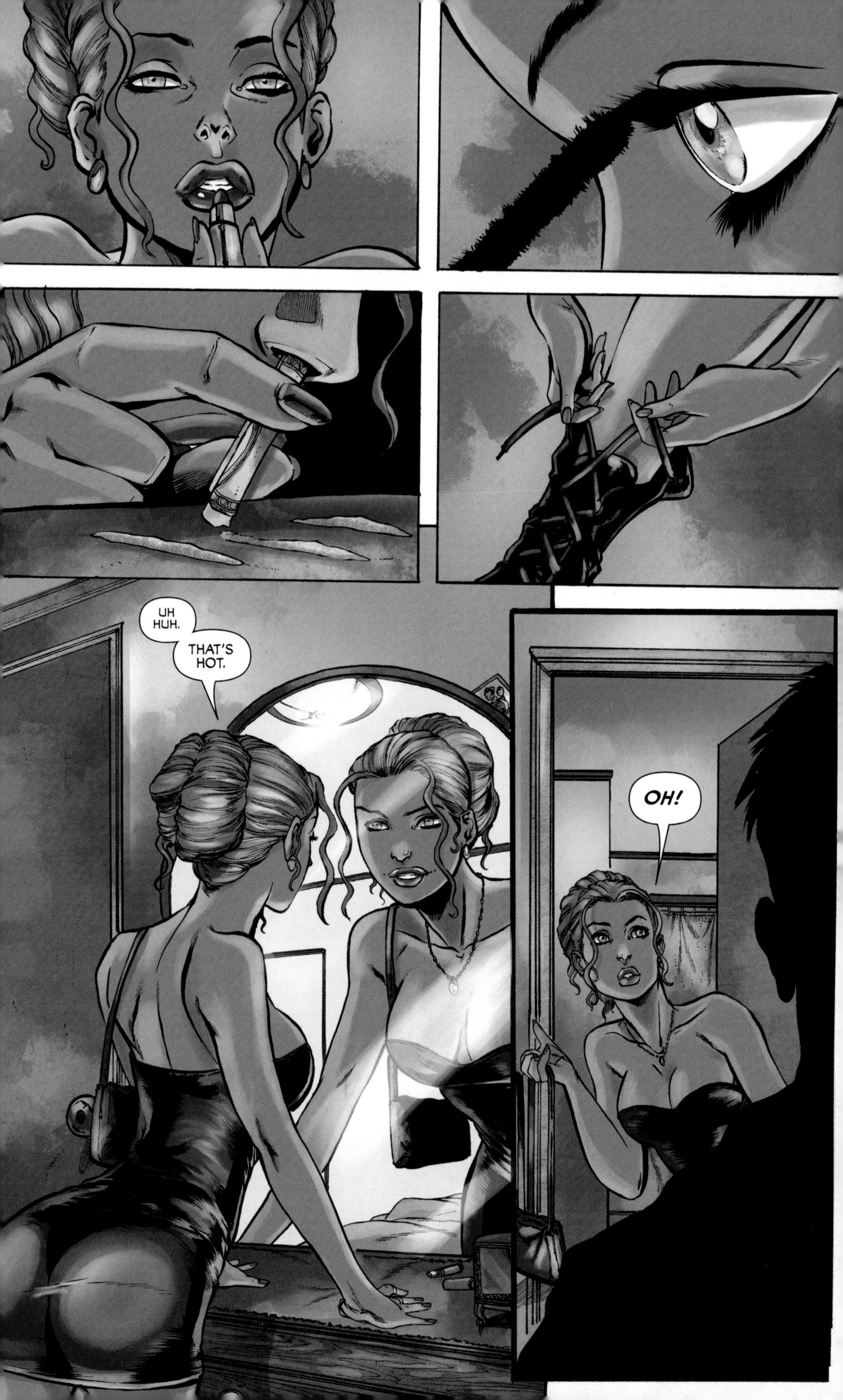

UH HUH.
THAT'S HOT.
OH!

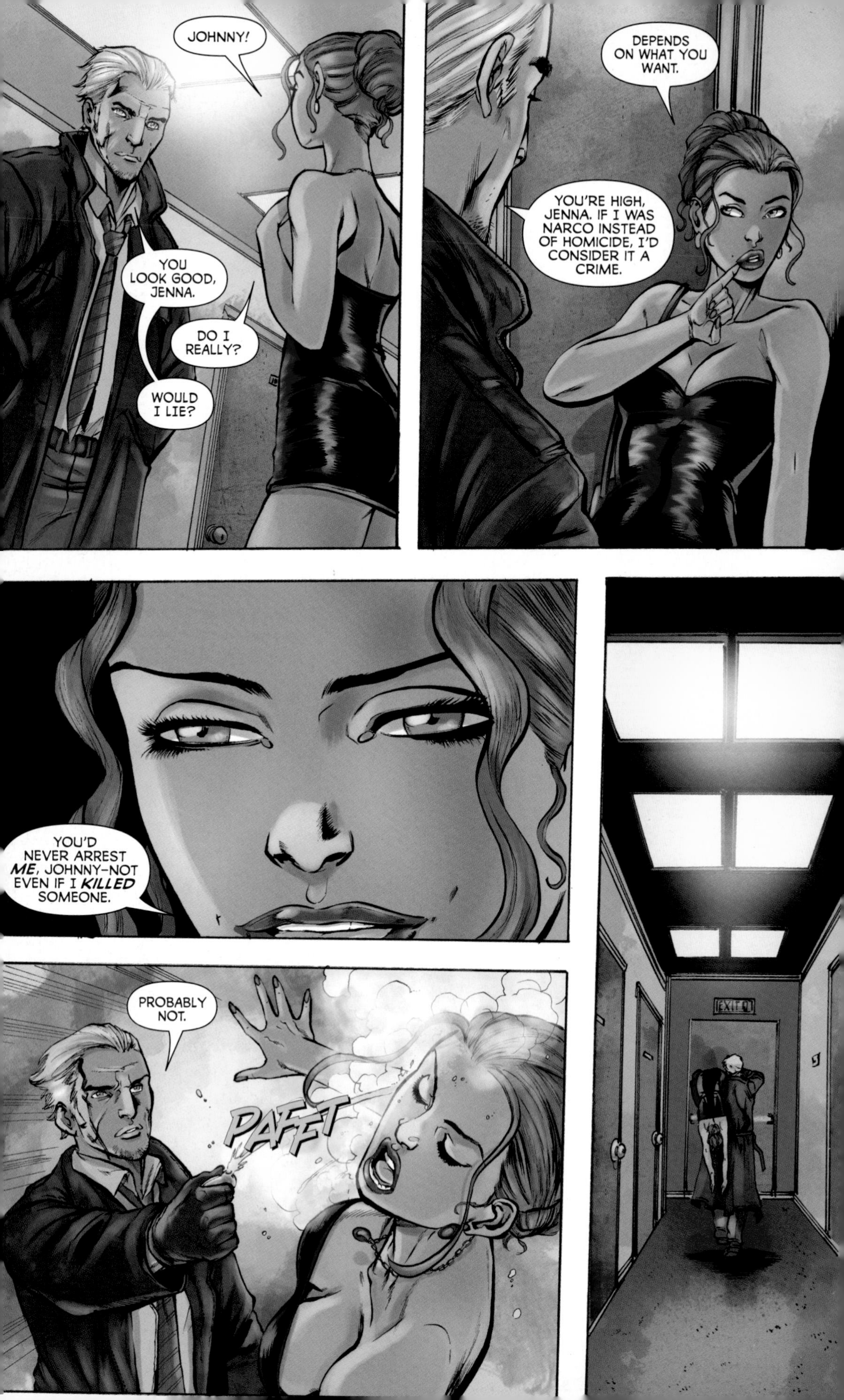
JOHNNY!
YOU LOOK GOOD, JENNA.
DO I REALLY?
WOULD I LIE?
DEPENDS ON WHAT YOU WANT.
YOU'RE HIGH, JENNA. IF I WAS NARCO INSTEAD OF HOMICIDE, I'D CONSIDER IT A CRIME.
YOU'D NEVER ARREST *ME*, JOHNNY–NOT EVEN IF I *KILLED* SOMEONE.
PROBABLY NOT.
PAFFT
EXIT

HANDS OF MERCY.

RANDAL SIX HEARS HIM EVEN BEFORE HE ENTERS THE BUILDING.

RANDAL KNOWS HIS STRIDE; HAS MEMORIZED HIS FOOTFALL.

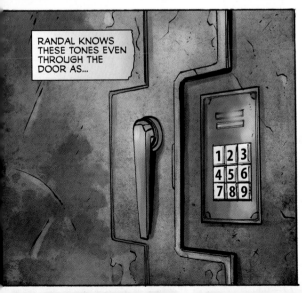

RANDAL KNOWS THESE TONES EVEN THROUGH THE DOOR AS...

THE DOCTOR IS IN.

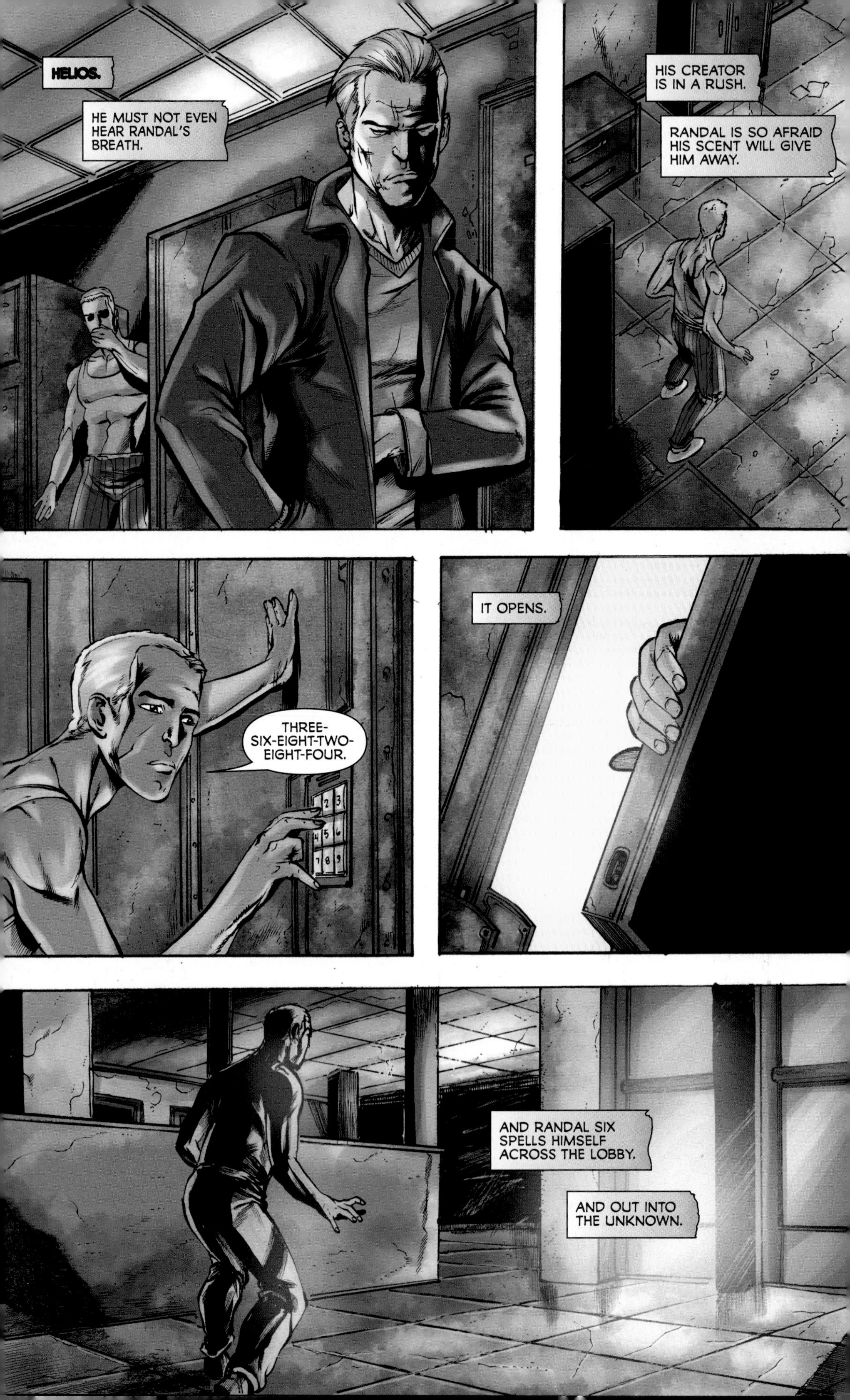
HELIOS.
HE MUST NOT EVEN HEAR RANDAL'S BREATH.
HIS CREATOR IS IN A RUSH.
RANDAL IS SO AFRAID HIS SCENT WILL GIVE HIM AWAY.
THREE-SIX-EIGHT-TWO-EIGHT-FOUR.
IT OPENS.
AND RANDAL SIX SPELLS HIMSELF ACROSS THE LOBBY.
AND OUT INTO THE UNKNOWN.

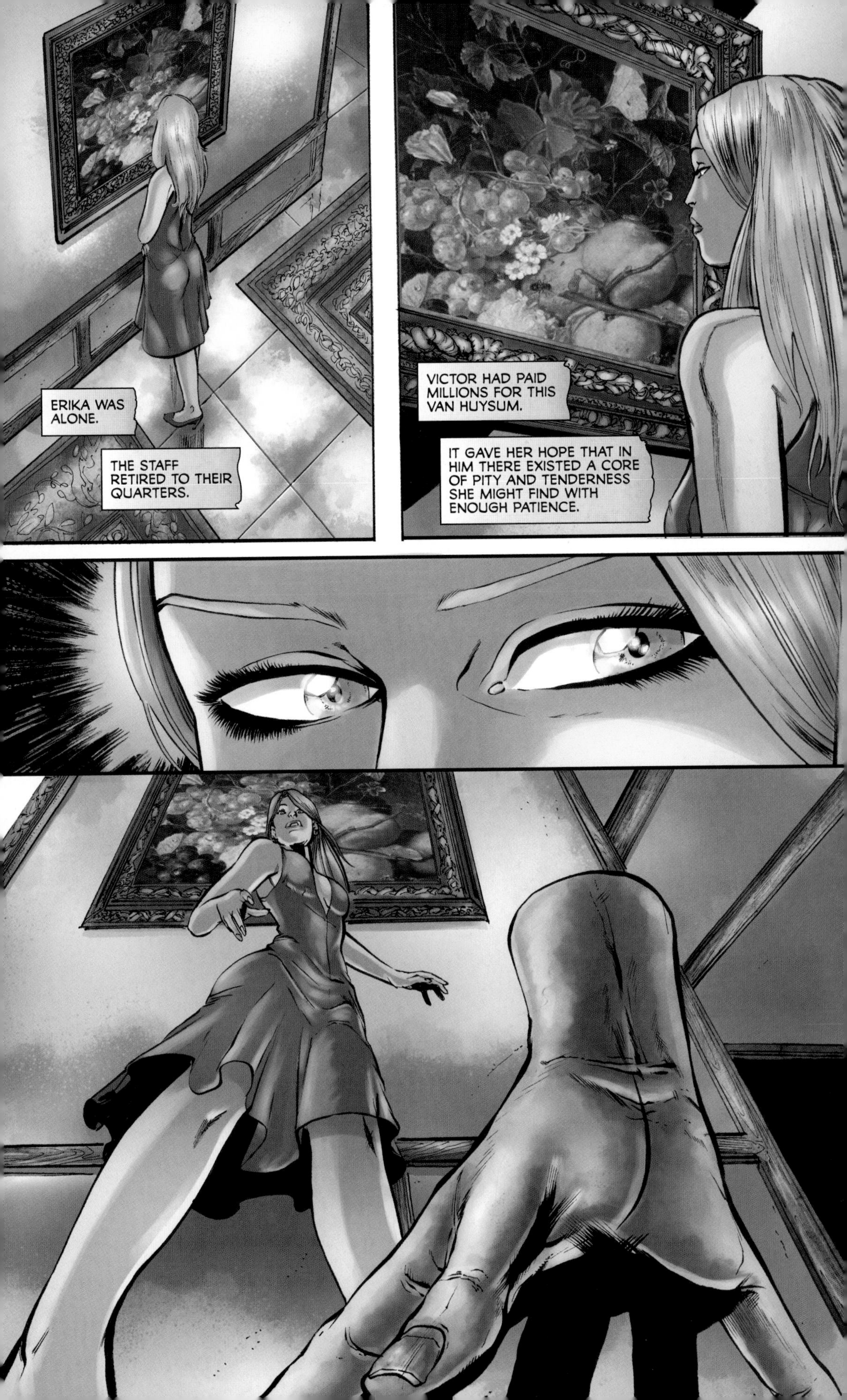
ERIKA WAS ALONE.
THE STAFF RETIRED TO THEIR QUARTERS.
VICTOR HAD PAID MILLIONS FOR THIS VAN HUYSUM.
IT GAVE HER HOPE THAT IN HIM THERE EXISTED A CORE OF PITY AND TENDERNESS SHE MIGHT FIND WITH ENOUGH PATIENCE.

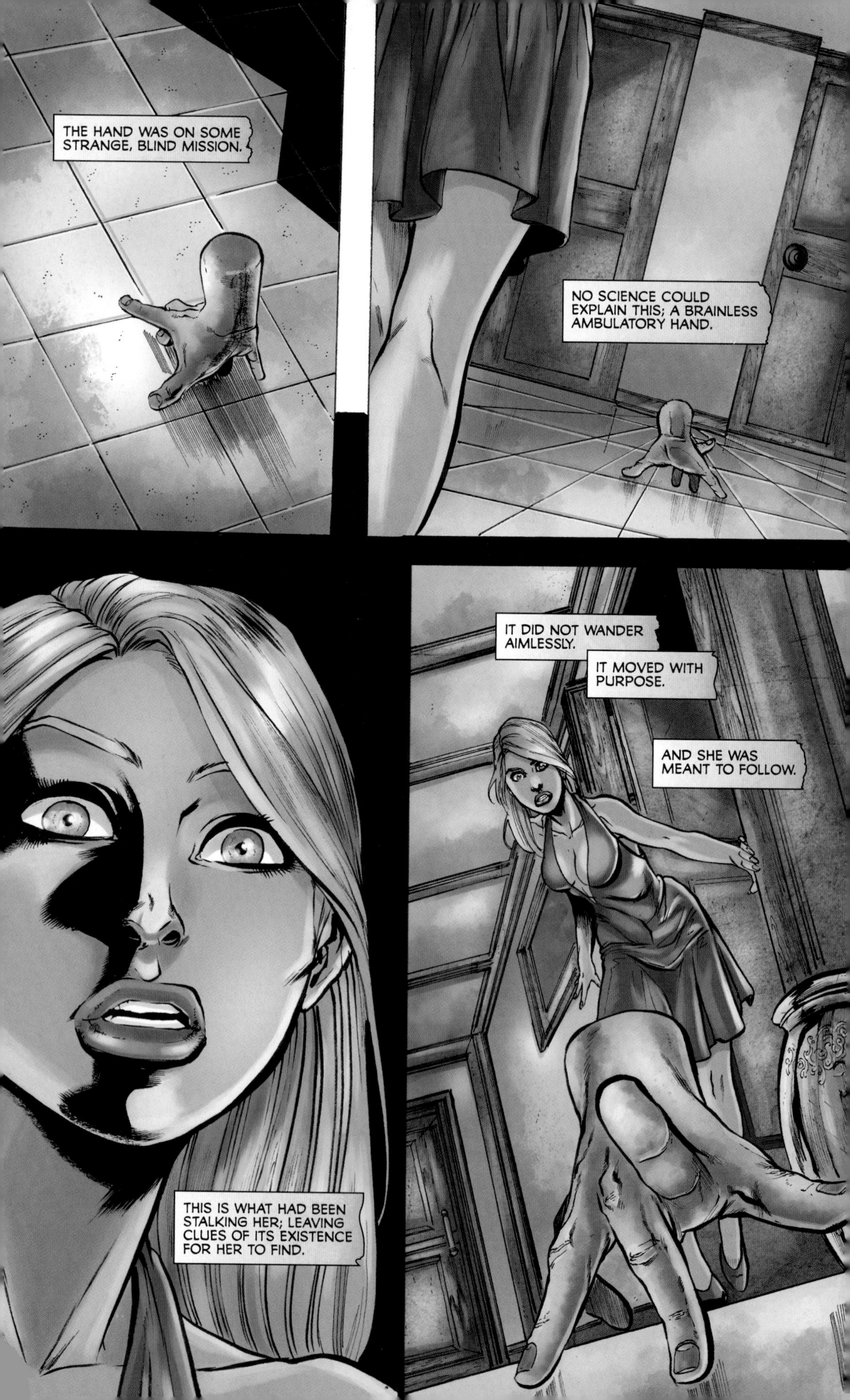
THE HAND WAS ON SOME STRANGE, BLIND MISSION.
NO SCIENCE COULD EXPLAIN THIS; A BRAINLESS AMBULATORY HAND.
THIS IS WHAT HAD BEEN STALKING HER; LEAVING CLUES OF ITS EXISTENCE FOR HER TO FIND.
IT DID NOT WANDER AIMLESSLY.
IT MOVED WITH PURPOSE.
AND SHE WAS MEANT TO FOLLOW.

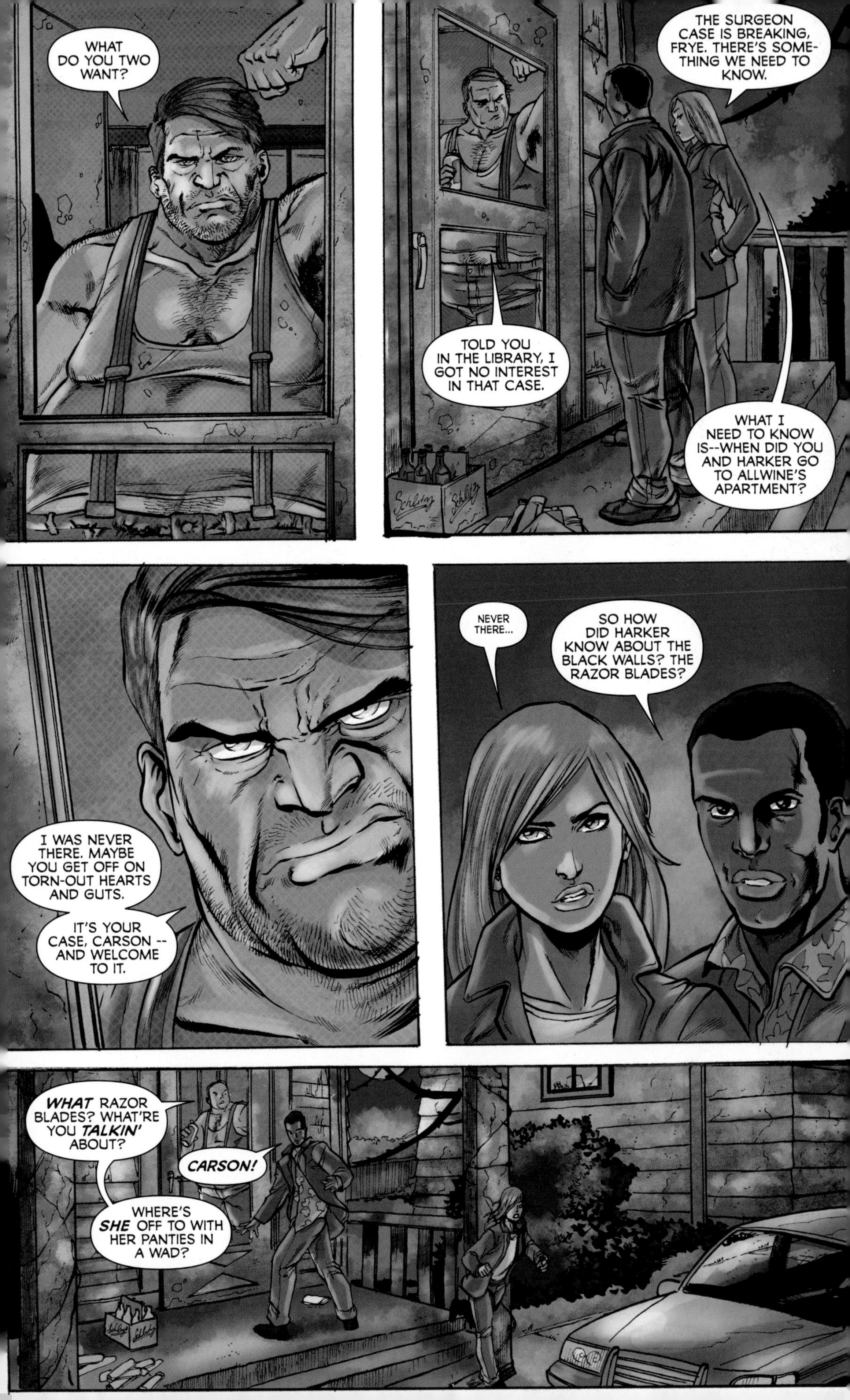
WHAT DO YOU TWO WANT?
THE SURGEON CASE IS BREAKING, FRYE. THERE'S SOME-THING WE NEED TO KNOW.
TOLD YOU IN THE LIBRARY, I GOT NO INTEREST IN THAT CASE.
WHAT I NEED TO KNOW IS--WHEN DID YOU AND HARKER GO TO ALLWINE'S APARTMENT?
I WAS NEVER THERE. MAYBE YOU GET OFF ON TORN-OUT HEARTS AND GUTS.
IT'S YOUR CASE, CARSON -- AND WELCOME TO IT.
NEVER THERE...
SO HOW DID HARKER KNOW ABOUT THE BLACK WALLS? THE RAZOR BLADES?
WHAT RAZOR BLADES? WHAT'RE YOU TALKIN' ABOUT?
CARSON!
WHERE'S SHE OFF TO WITH HER PANTIES IN A WAD?

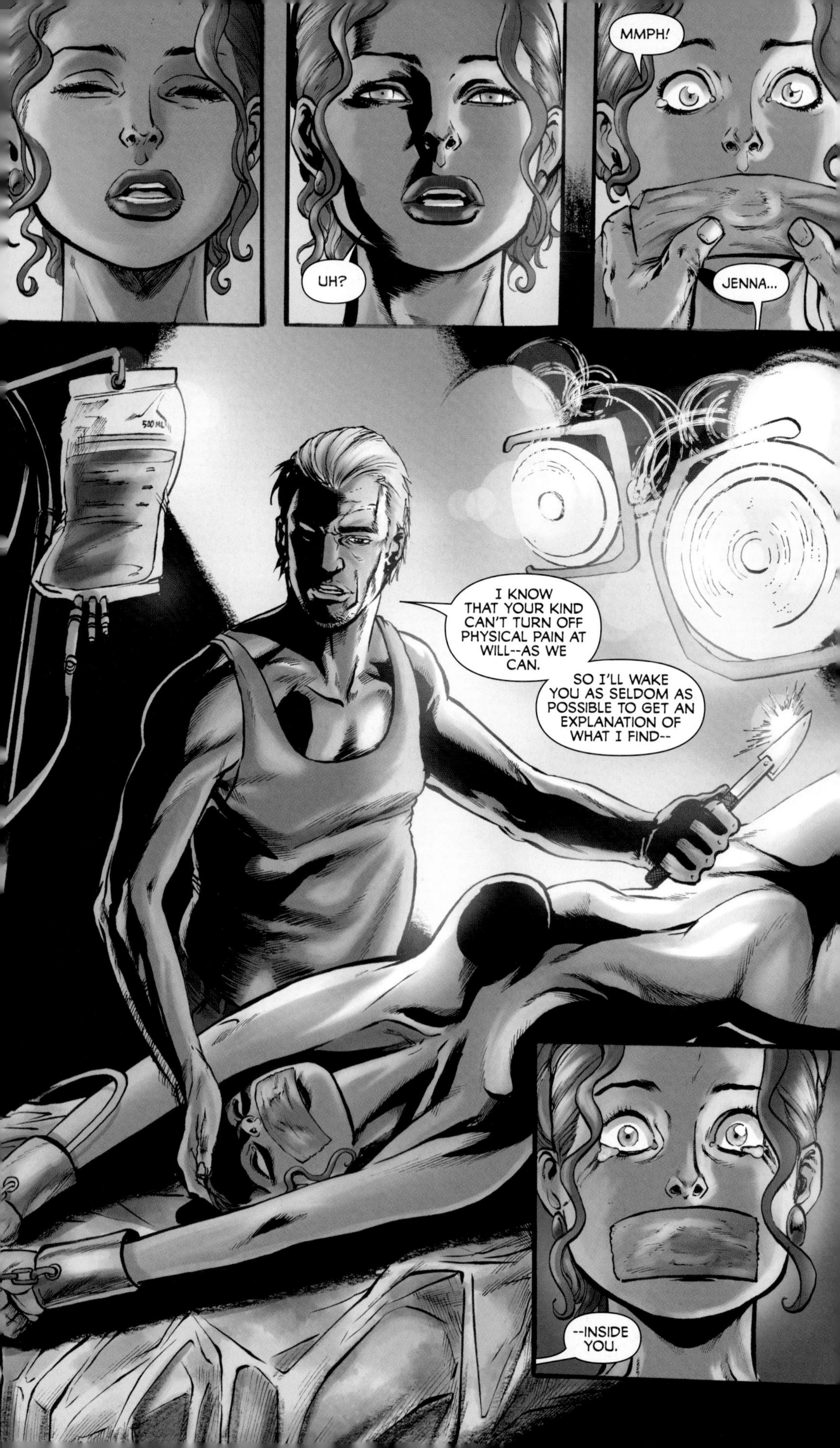
UH?
MMPH!
JENNA...
500 ML
I KNOW THAT YOUR KIND CAN'T TURN OFF PHYSICAL PAIN AT WILL--AS WE CAN.
SO I'LL WAKE YOU AS SELDOM AS POSSIBLE TO GET AN EXPLANATION OF WHAT I FIND--
--INSIDE YOU.

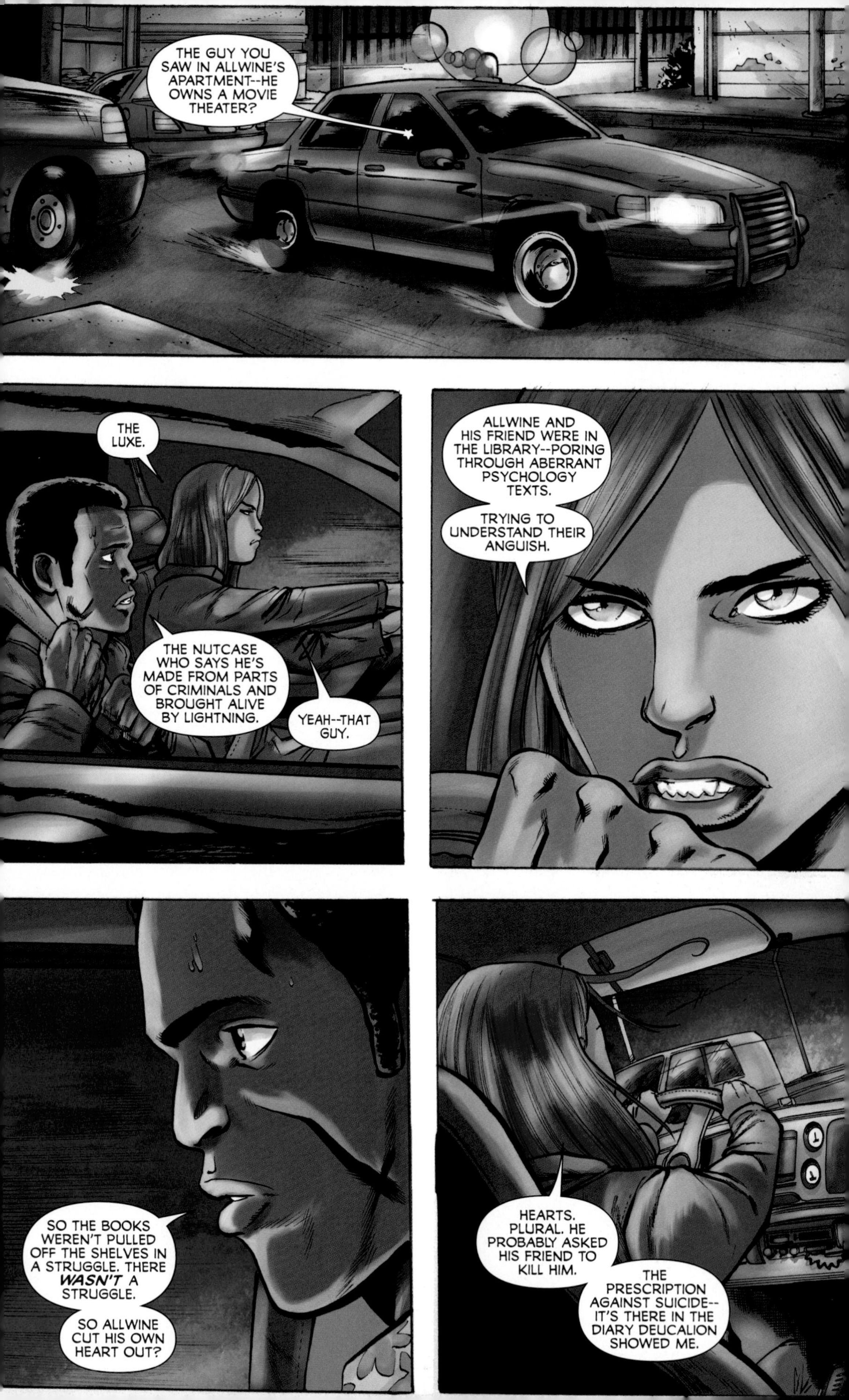
THE GUY YOU SAW IN ALLWINE'S APARTMENT--HE OWNS A MOVIE THEATER?
THE LUXE.
THE NUTCASE WHO SAYS HE'S MADE FROM PARTS OF CRIMINALS AND BROUGHT ALIVE BY LIGHTNING.
YEAH--THAT GUY.
ALLWINE AND HIS FRIEND WERE IN THE LIBRARY--PORING THROUGH ABERRANT PSYCHOLOGY TEXTS.
TRYING TO UNDERSTAND THEIR ANGUISH.
SO THE BOOKS WEREN'T PULLED OFF THE SHELVES IN A STRUGGLE. THERE ***WASN'T*** A STRUGGLE.
SO ALLWINE CUT HIS OWN HEART OUT?
HEARTS. PLURAL. HE PROBABLY ASKED HIS FRIEND TO KILL HIM.
THE PRESCRIPTION AGAINST SUICIDE--IT'S THERE IN THE DIARY DEUCALION SHOWED ME.

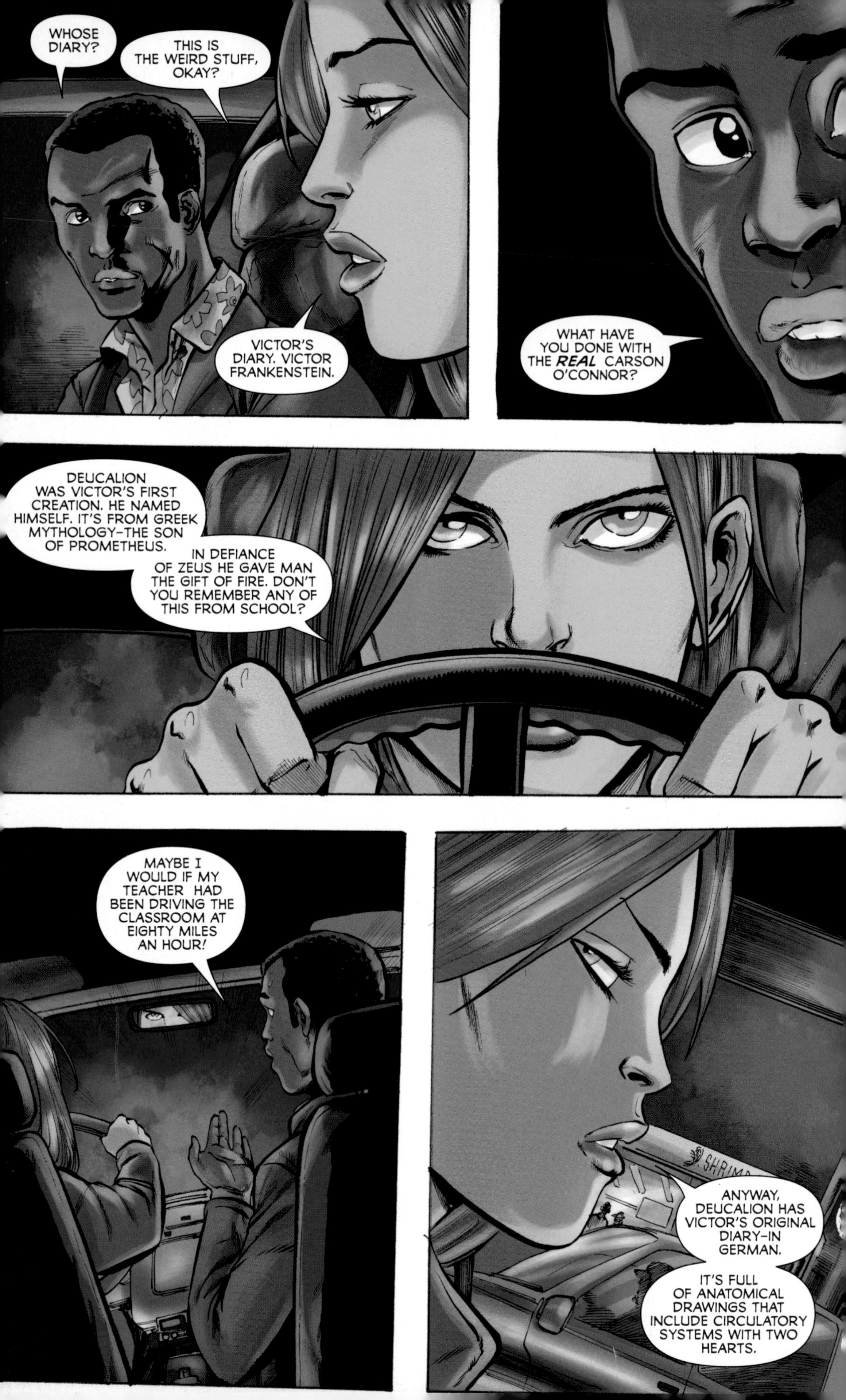
WHOSE DIARY?
THIS IS THE WEIRD STUFF, OKAY?
VICTOR'S DIARY. VICTOR FRANKENSTEIN.
WHAT HAVE YOU DONE WITH THE *REAL* CARSON O'CONNOR?
DEUCALION WAS VICTOR'S FIRST CREATION. HE NAMED HIMSELF. IT'S FROM GREEK MYTHOLOGY–THE SON OF PROMETHEUS.
IN DEFIANCE OF ZEUS HE GAVE MAN THE GIFT OF FIRE. DON'T YOU REMEMBER ANY OF THIS FROM SCHOOL?
MAYBE I WOULD IF MY TEACHER HAD BEEN DRIVING THE CLASSROOM AT EIGHTY MILES AN HOUR!
ANYWAY, DEUCALION HAS VICTOR'S ORIGINAL DIARY–IN GERMAN.
IT'S FULL OF ANATOMICAL DRAWINGS THAT INCLUDE CIRCULATORY SYSTEMS WITH TWO HEARTS.

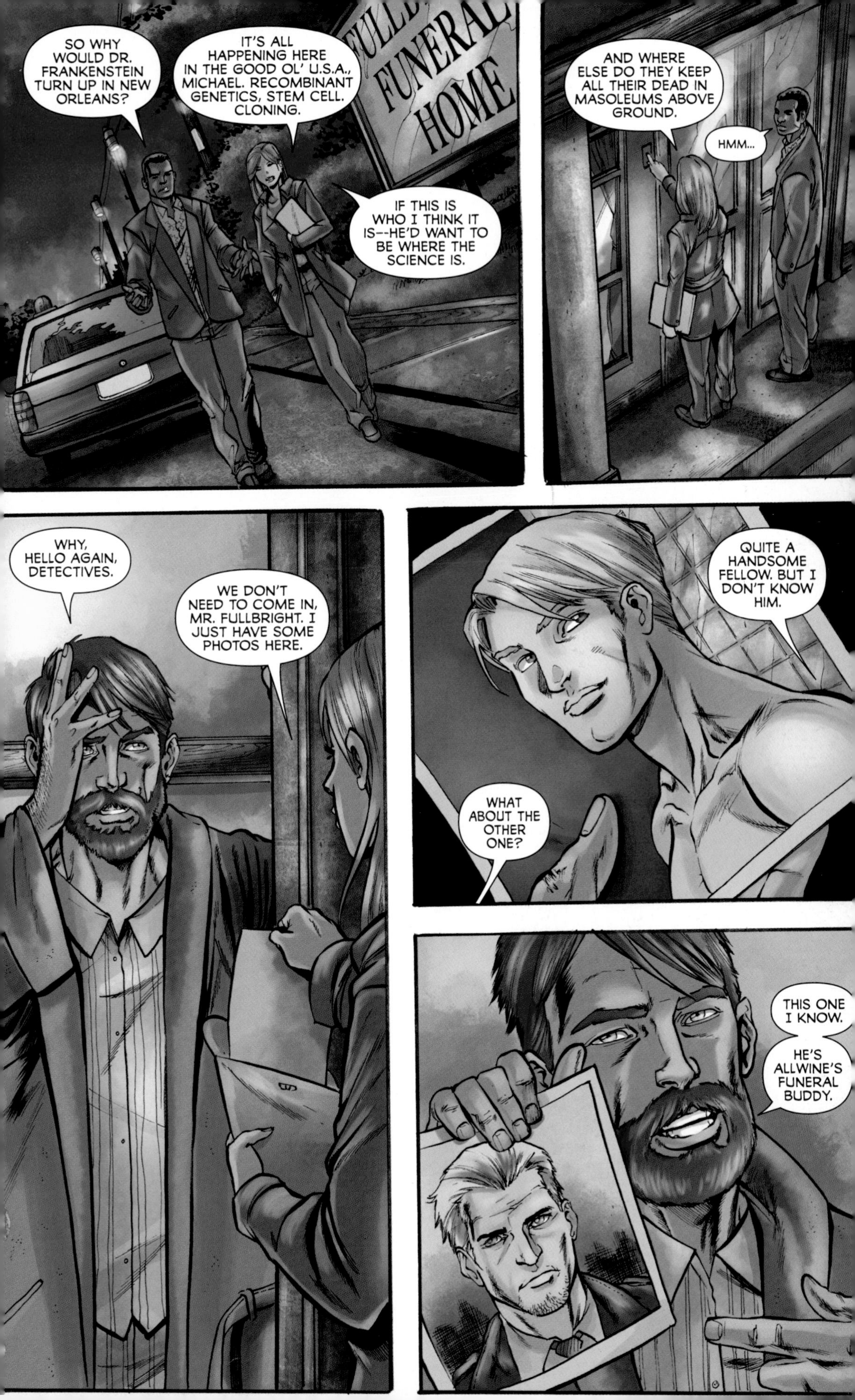
FULLBRIGHT FUNERAL HOME
SO WHY WOULD DR. FRANKENSTEIN TURN UP IN NEW ORLEANS?
IT'S ALL HAPPENING HERE IN THE GOOD OL' U.S.A., MICHAEL. RECOMBINANT GENETICS, STEM CELL. CLONING.
IF THIS IS WHO I THINK IT IS--HE'D WANT TO BE WHERE THE SCIENCE IS.
AND WHERE ELSE DO THEY KEEP ALL THEIR DEAD IN MASOLEUMS ABOVE GROUND.
HMM...
WHY, HELLO AGAIN, DETECTIVES.
WE DON'T NEED TO COME IN, MR. FULLBRIGHT. I JUST HAVE SOME PHOTOS HERE.
QUITE A HANDSOME FELLOW. BUT I DON'T KNOW HIM.
WHAT ABOUT THE OTHER ONE?
THIS ONE I KNOW.
HE'S ALLWINE'S FUNERAL BUDDY.

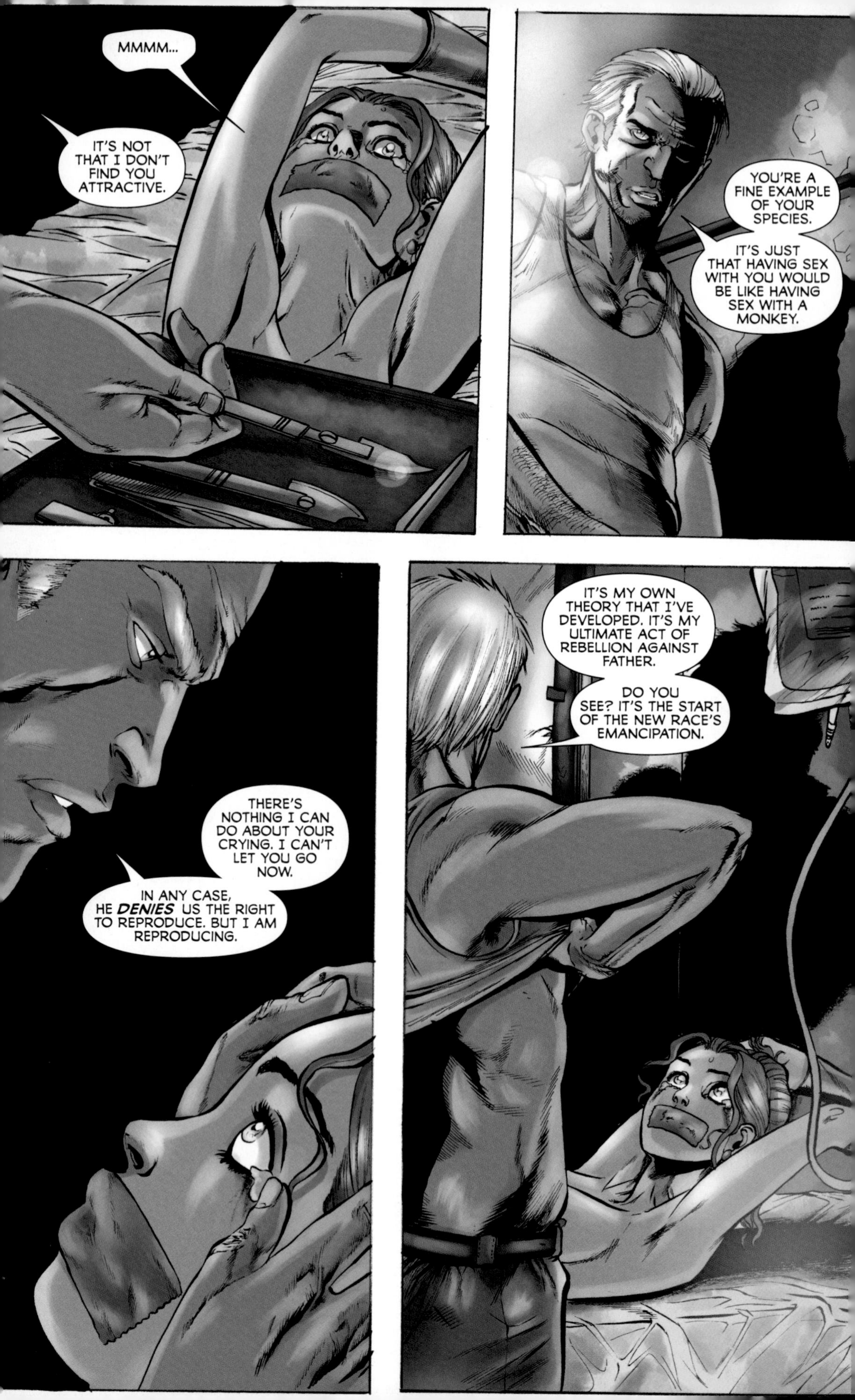
MMMM...
IT'S NOT THAT I DON'T FIND YOU ATTRACTIVE.
YOU'RE A FINE EXAMPLE OF YOUR SPECIES.
IT'S JUST THAT HAVING SEX WITH YOU WOULD BE LIKE HAVING SEX WITH A MONKEY.
THERE'S NOTHING I CAN DO ABOUT YOUR CRYING. I CAN'T LET YOU GO NOW.
IN ANY CASE, HE DENIES US THE RIGHT TO REPRODUCE. BUT I AM REPRODUCING.
IT'S MY OWN THEORY THAT I'VE DEVELOPED. IT'S MY ULTIMATE ACT OF REBELLION AGAINST FATHER.
DO YOU SEE? IT'S THE START OF THE NEW RACE'S EMANCIPATION.

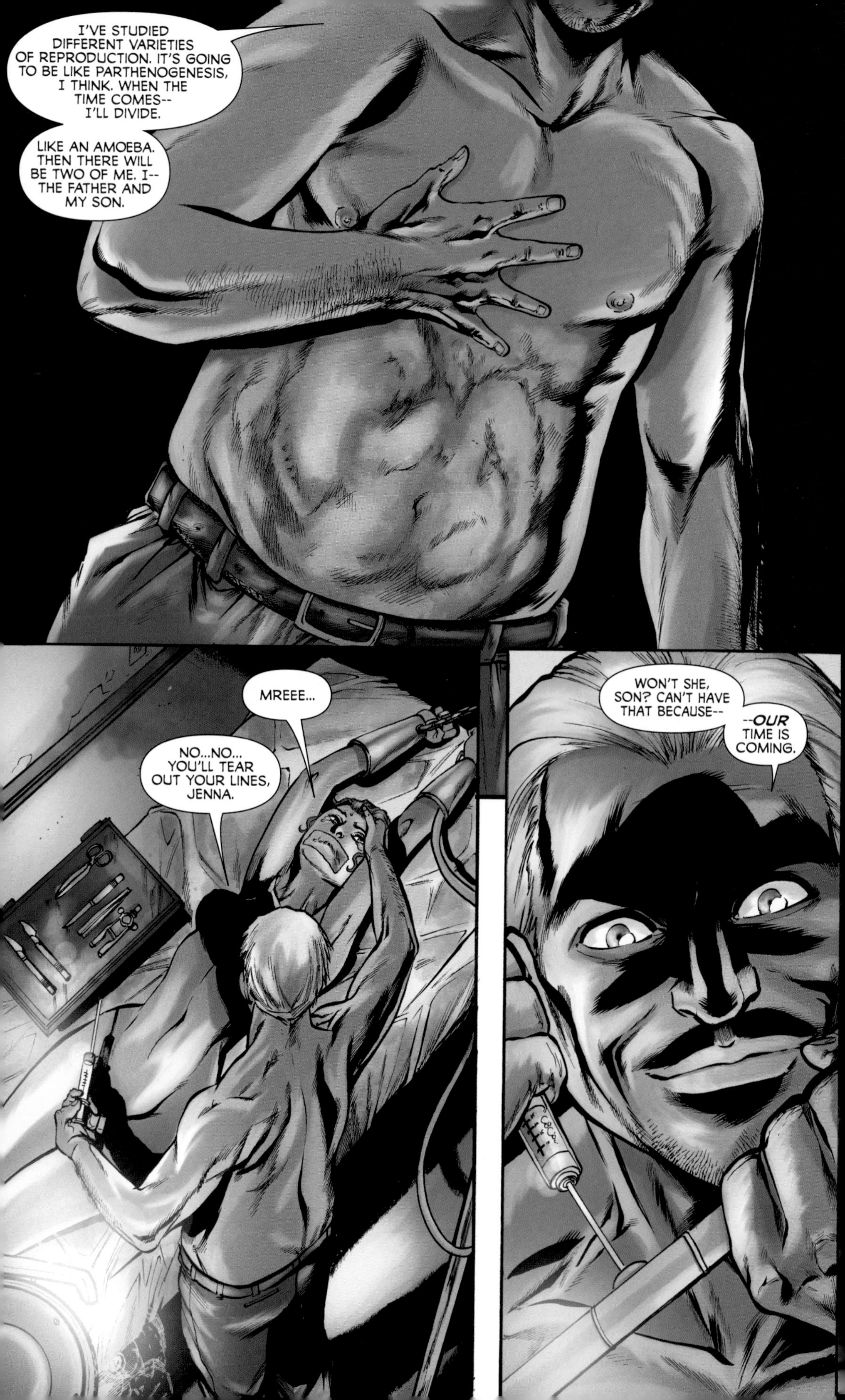
I'VE STUDIED DIFFERENT VARIETIES OF REPRODUCTION. IT'S GOING TO BE LIKE PARTHENOGENESIS, I THINK. WHEN THE TIME COMES-- I'LL DIVIDE.
LIKE AN AMOEBA. THEN THERE WILL BE TWO OF ME. I-- THE FATHER AND MY SON.
MREEE...
NO...NO... YOU'LL TEAR OUT YOUR LINES, JENNA.
WON'T SHE, SON? CAN'T HAVE THAT BECAUSE--
--OUR TIME IS COMING.

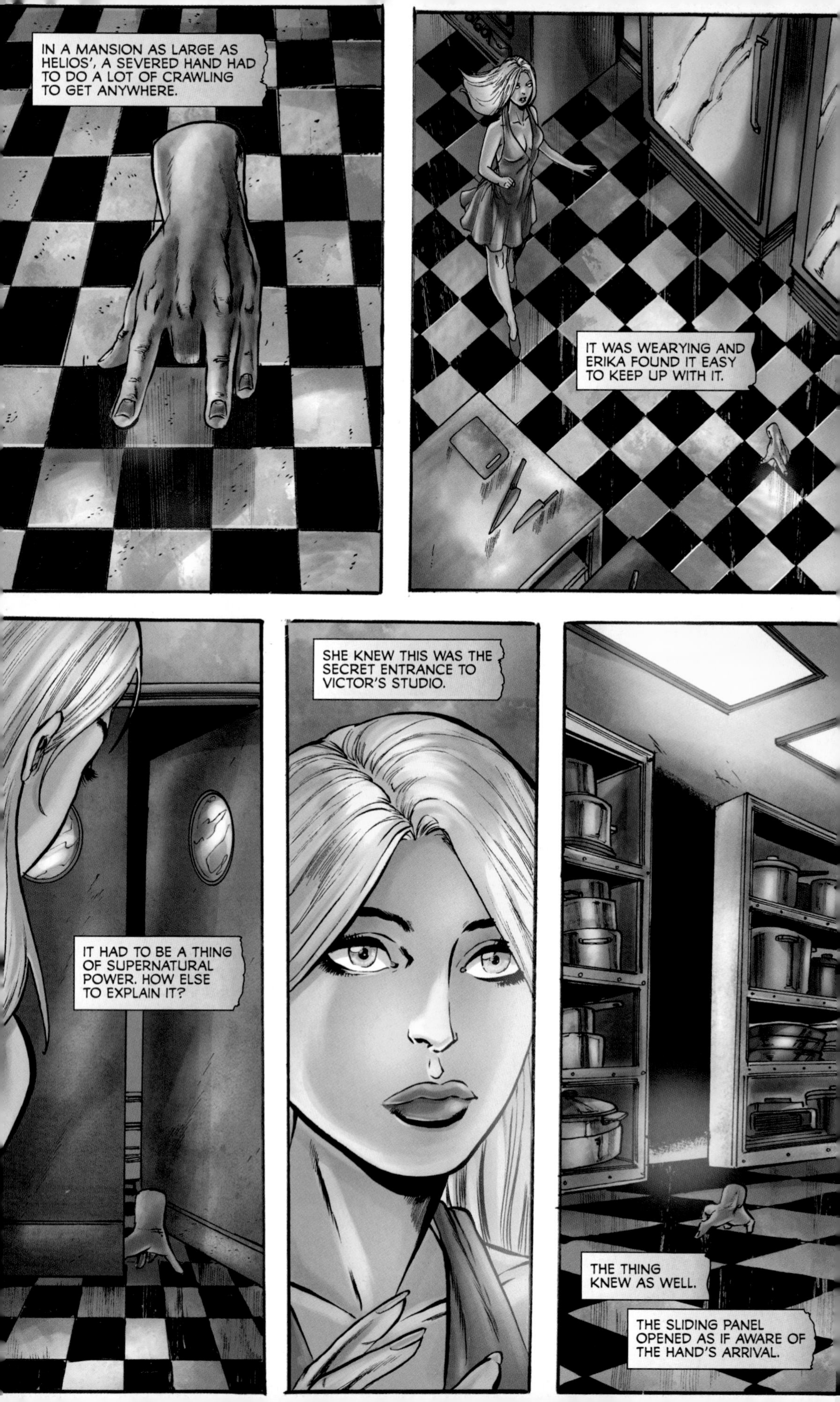
IN A MANSION AS LARGE AS HELIOS', A SEVERED HAND HAD TO DO A LOT OF CRAWLING TO GET ANYWHERE.
IT WAS WEARYING AND ERIKA FOUND IT EASY TO KEEP UP WITH IT.
IT HAD TO BE A THING OF SUPERNATURAL POWER. HOW ELSE TO EXPLAIN IT?
SHE KNEW THIS WAS THE SECRET ENTRANCE TO VICTOR'S STUDIO.
THE THING KNEW AS WELL.
THE SLIDING PANEL OPENED AS IF AWARE OF THE HAND'S ARRIVAL.

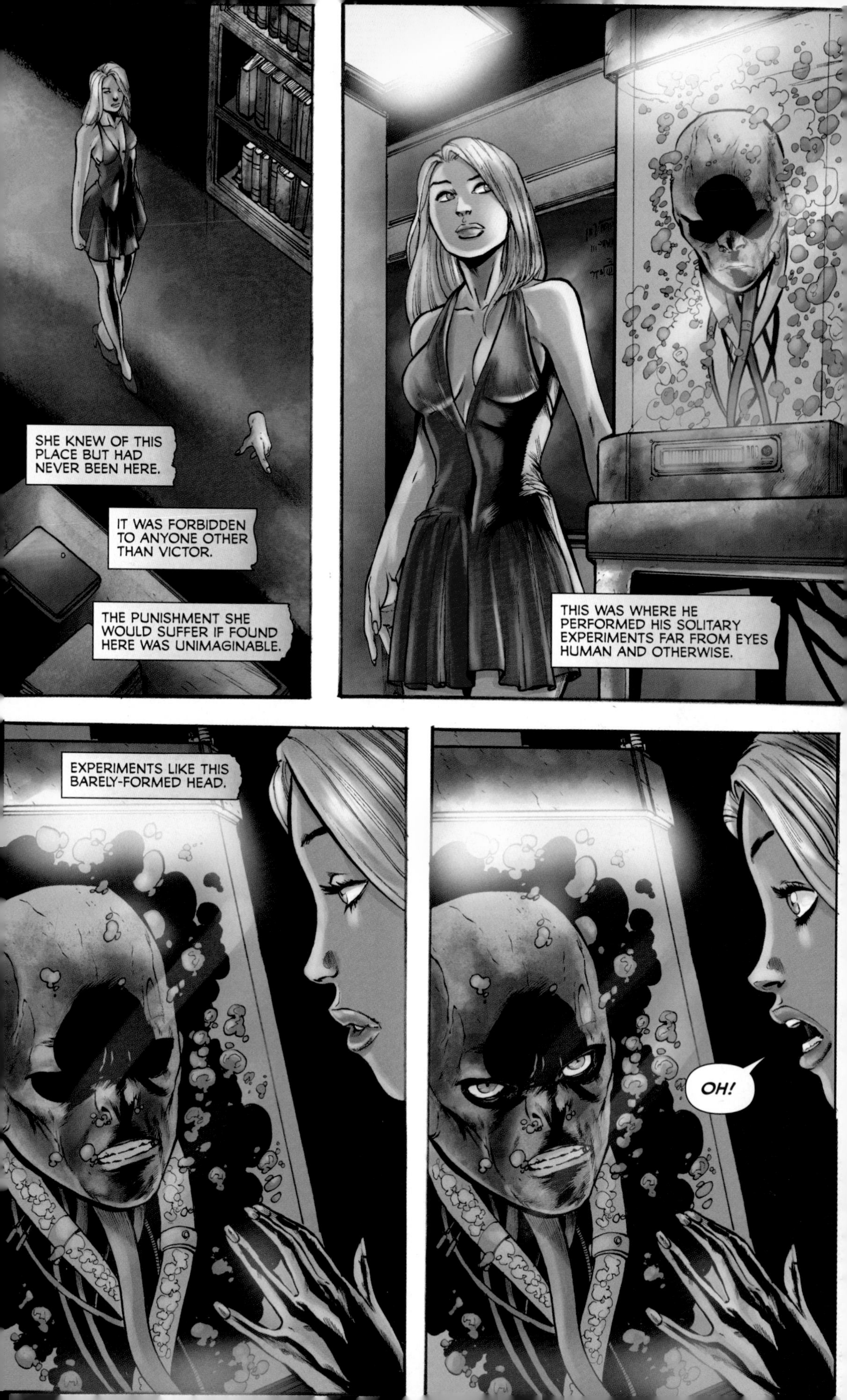
SHE KNEW OF THIS PLACE BUT HAD NEVER BEEN HERE.
IT WAS FORBIDDEN TO ANYONE OTHER THAN VICTOR.
THE PUNISHMENT SHE WOULD SUFFER IF FOUND HERE WAS UNIMAGINABLE.
THIS WAS WHERE HE PERFORMED HIS SOLITARY EXPERIMENTS FAR FROM EYES HUMAN AND OTHERWISE.
EXPERIMENTS LIKE THIS BARELY-FORMED HEAD.
OH!

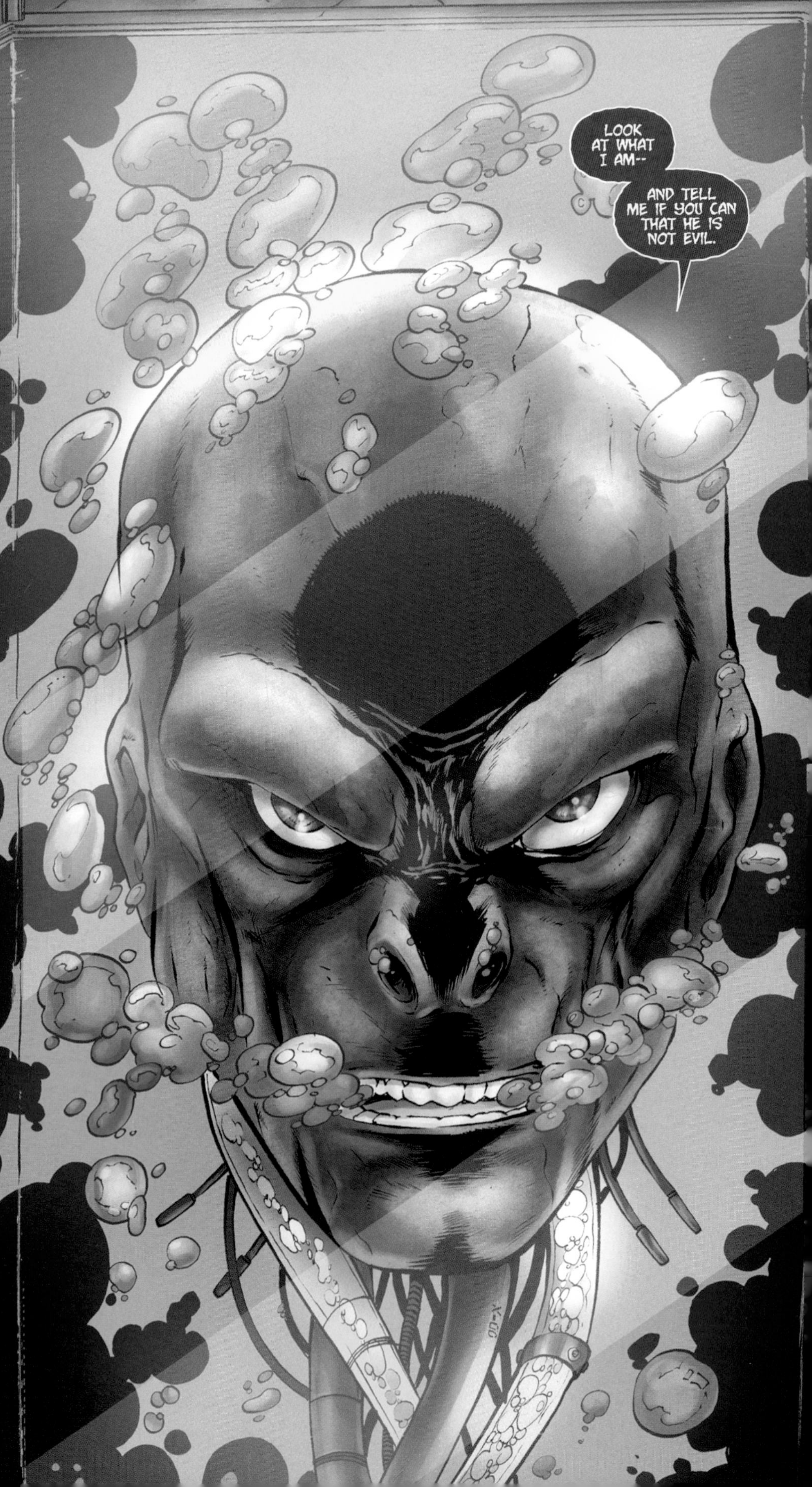
LOOK AT WHAT I AM--
AND TELL ME IF YOU CAN THAT HE IS NOT EVIL.

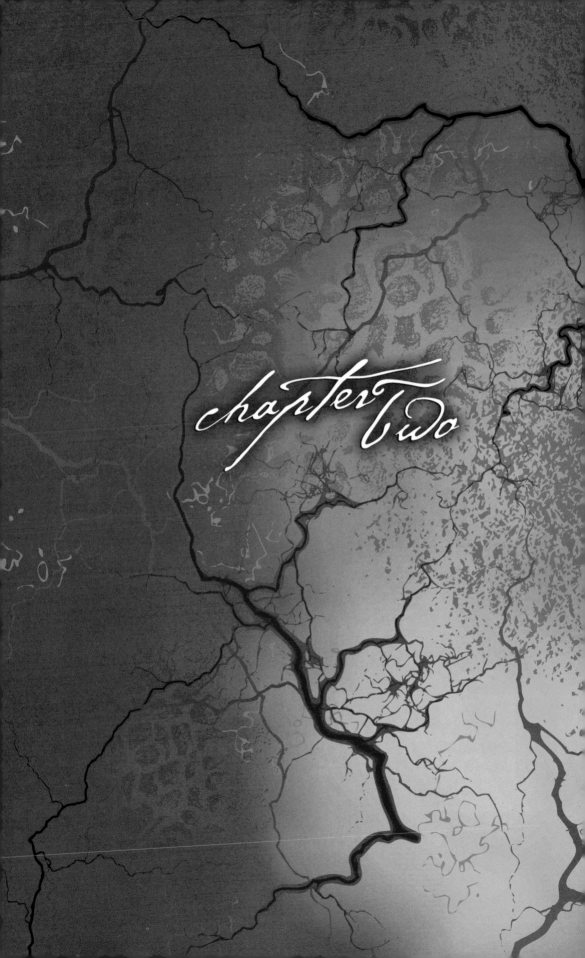

chapter Two

COVER BY: SCOTT COHN

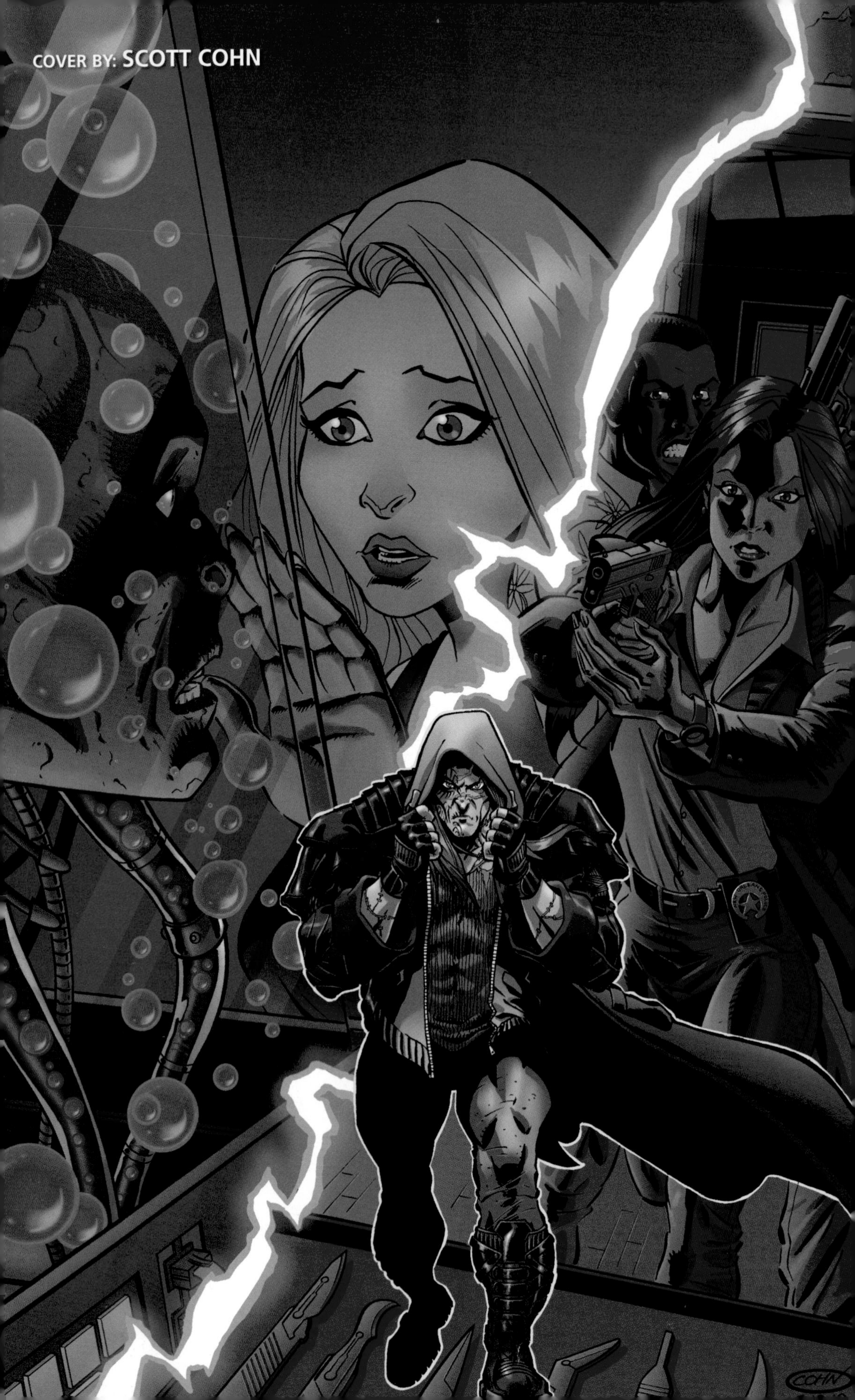
COHN

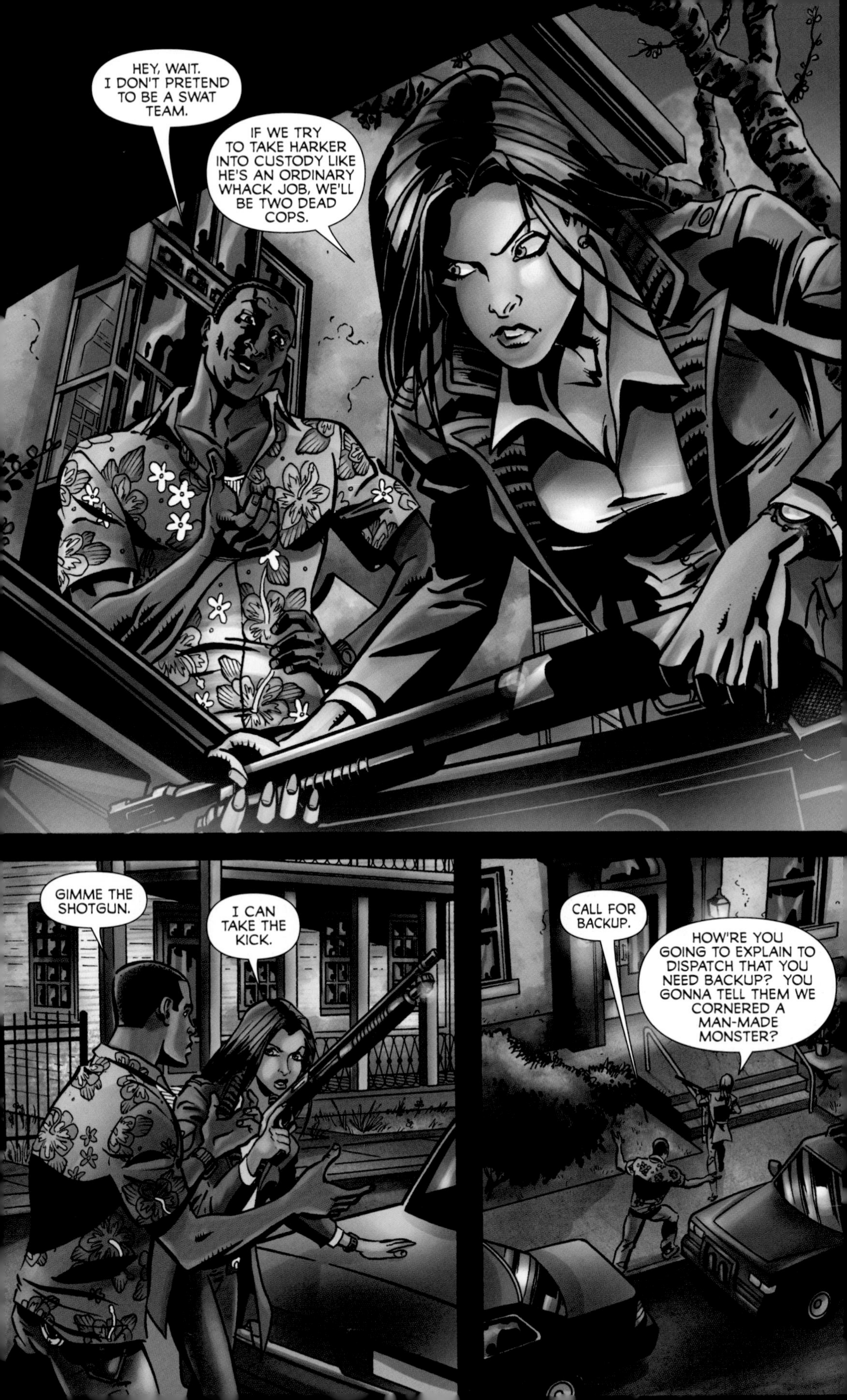
HEY, WAIT. I DON'T PRETEND TO BE A SWAT TEAM.
IF WE TRY TO TAKE HARKER INTO CUSTODY LIKE HE'S AN ORDINARY WHACK JOB, WE'LL BE TWO DEAD COPS.
GIMME THE SHOTGUN.
I CAN TAKE THE KICK.
CALL FOR BACKUP.
HOW'RE YOU GOING TO EXPLAIN TO DISPATCH THAT YOU NEED BACKUP? YOU GONNA TELL THEM WE CORNERED A MAN-MADE MONSTER?

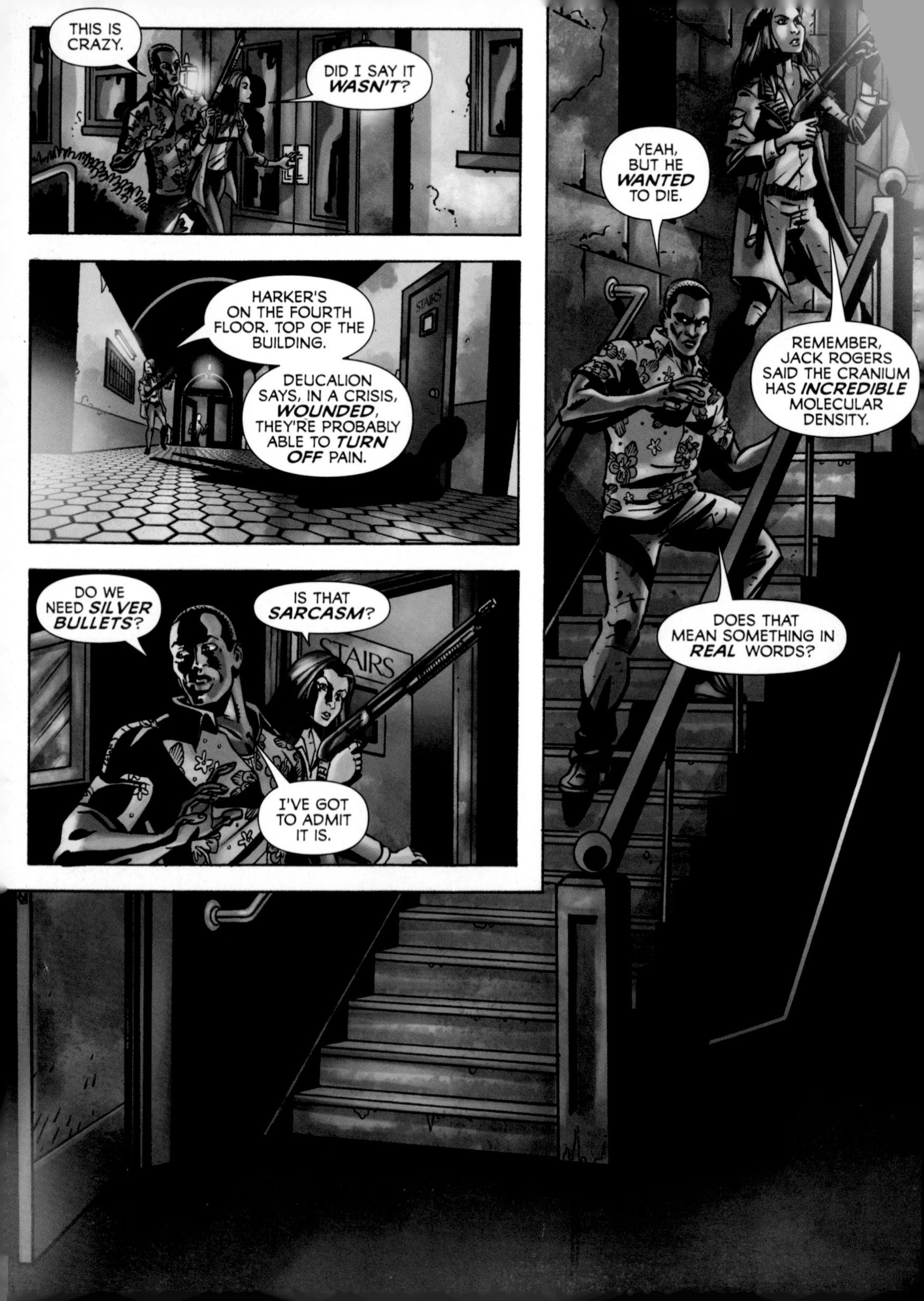

THIS IS CRAZY.
DID I SAY IT WASN'T?
HARKER'S ON THE FOURTH FLOOR. TOP OF THE BUILDING.
DEUCALION SAYS, IN A CRISIS, WOUNDED, THEY'RE PROBABLY ABLE TO TURN OFF PAIN.
DO WE NEED SILVER BULLETS?
IS THAT SARCASM?
I'VE GOT TO ADMIT IT IS.
YEAH, BUT HE WANTED TO DIE.
REMEMBER, JACK ROGERS SAID THE CRANIUM HAS INCREDIBLE MOLECULAR DENSITY.
DOES THAT MEAN SOMETHING IN REAL WORDS?

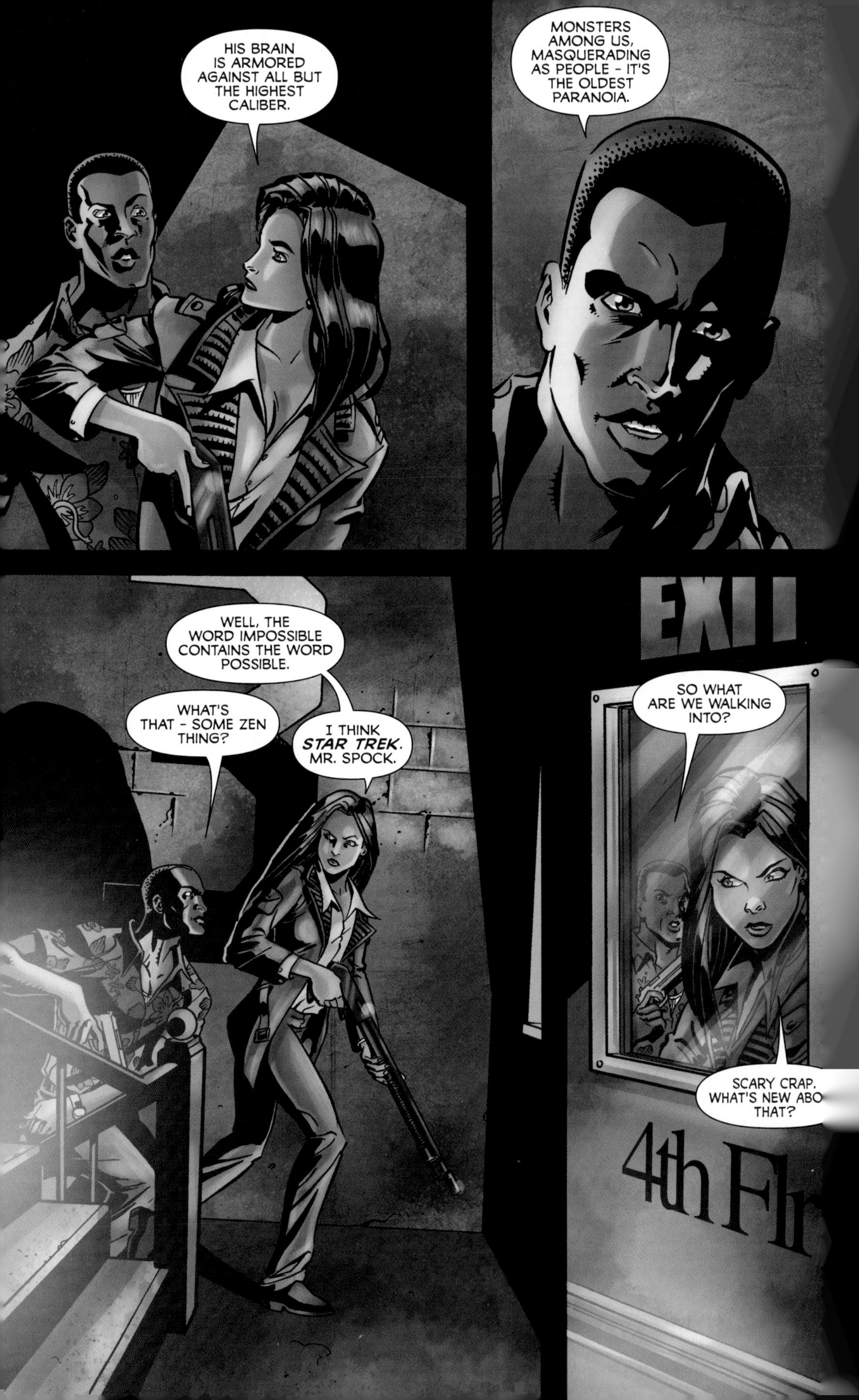
HIS BRAIN IS ARMORED AGAINST ALL BUT THE HIGHEST CALIBER.
MONSTERS AMONG US, MASQUERADING AS PEOPLE - IT'S THE OLDEST PARANOIA.
WELL, THE WORD IMPOSSIBLE CONTAINS THE WORD POSSIBLE.
WHAT'S THAT - SOME ZEN THING?
I THINK *STAR TREK*. MR. SPOCK.
EXIT
SO WHAT ARE WE WALKING INTO?
SCARY CRAP. WHAT'S NEW ABO
THAT?
4th Flr

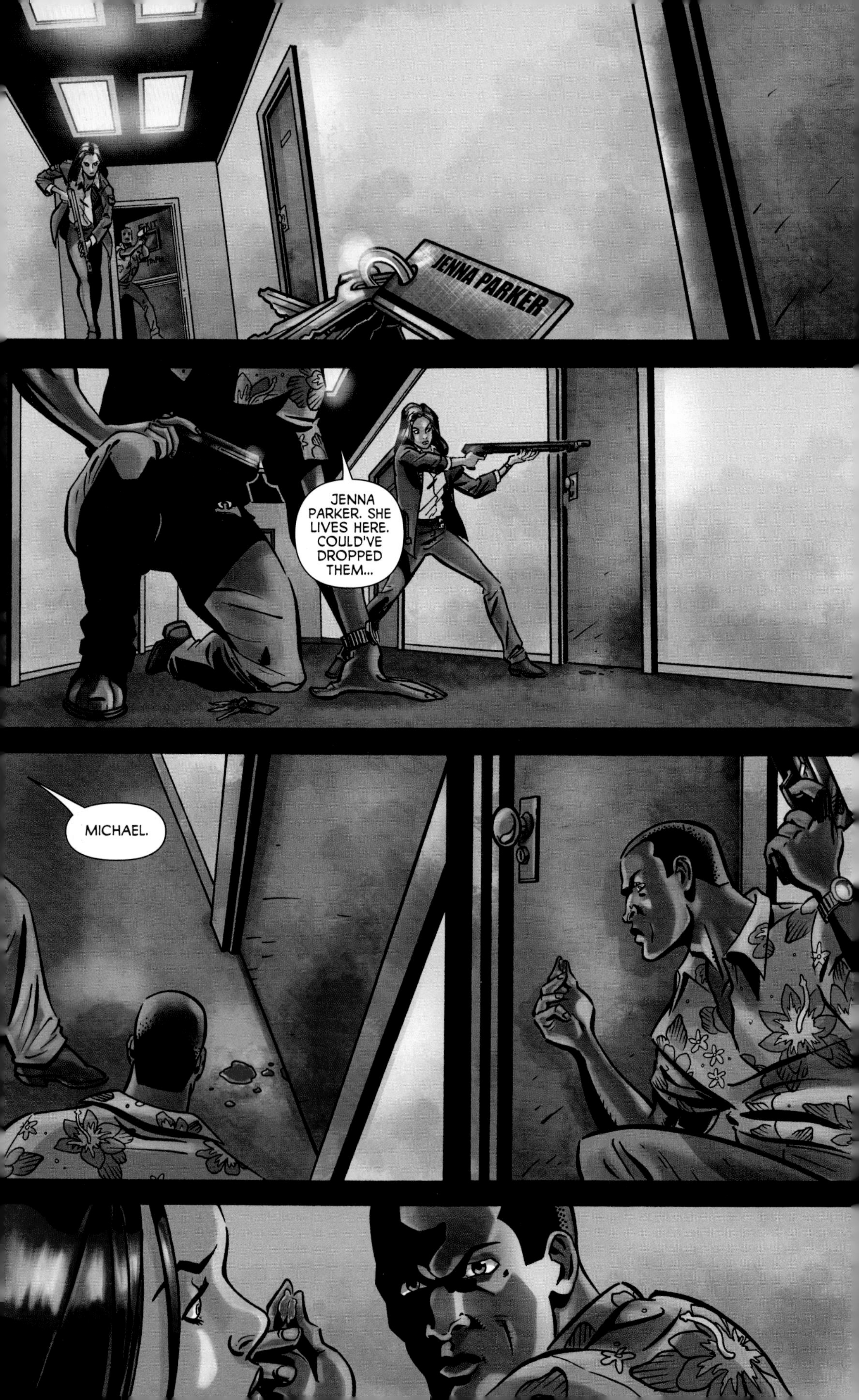
JENNA PARKER
JENNA PARKER. SHE LIVES HERE. COULD'VE DROPPED THEM...
MICHAEL.

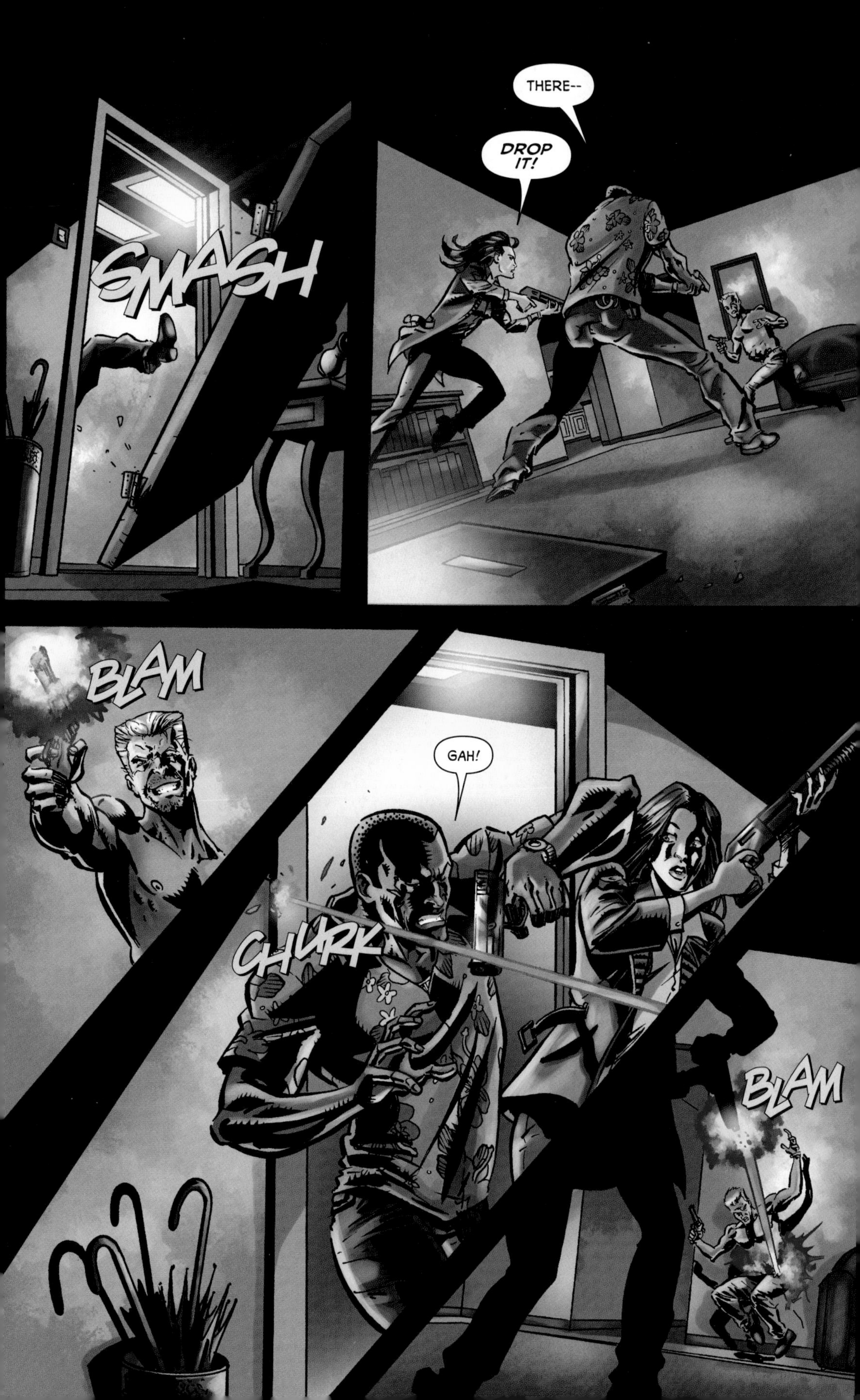
SMASH
THERE--
DROP IT!
BLAM
GAH!
CHURK
BLAM

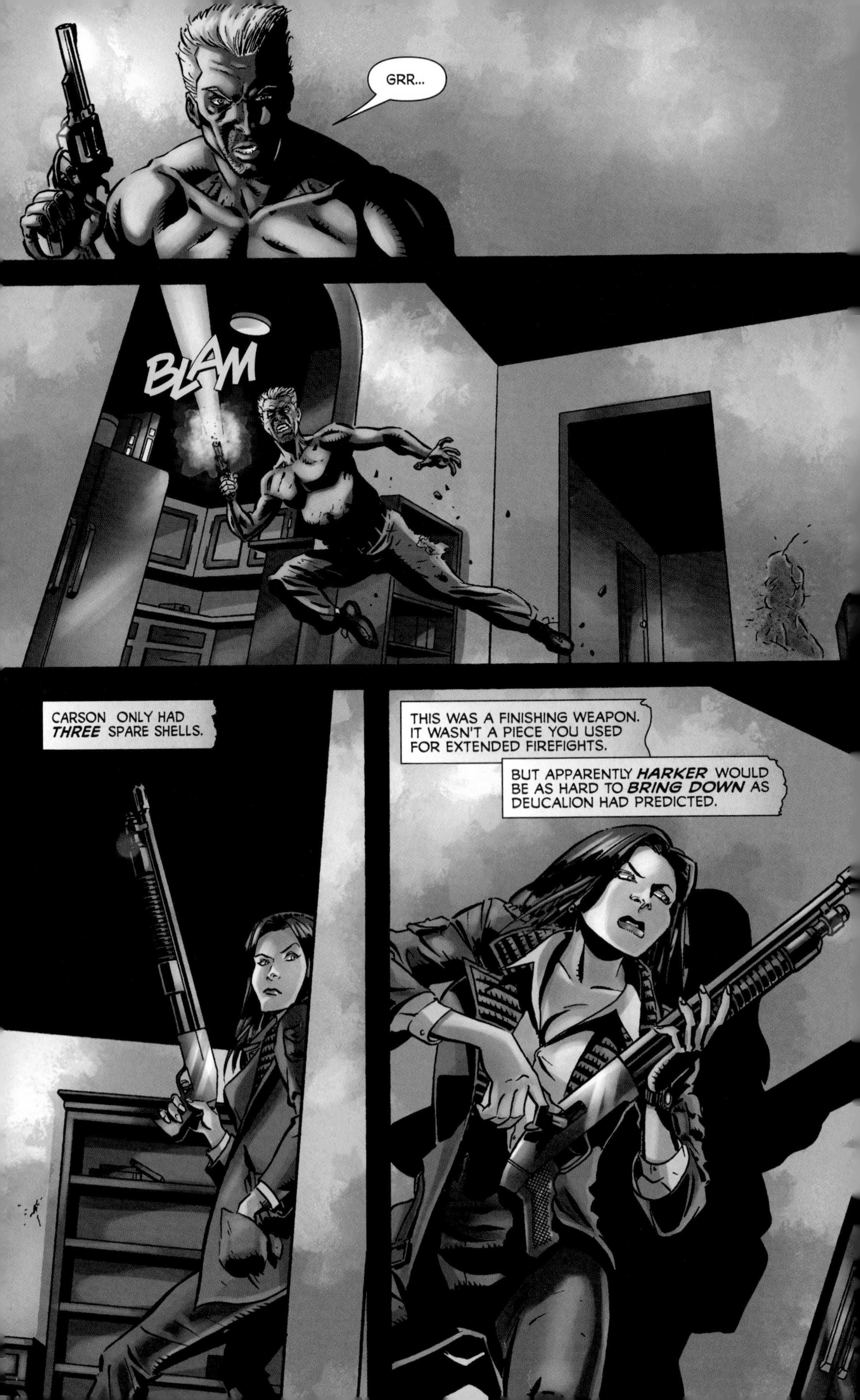

GRR...
BLAM
CARSON ONLY HAD THREE SPARE SHELLS.
THIS WAS A FINISHING WEAPON. IT WASN'T A PIECE YOU USED FOR EXTENDED FIREFIGHTS.
BUT APPARENTLY HARKER WOULD BE AS HARD TO BRING DOWN AS DEUCALION HAD PREDICTED.

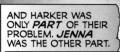AND HARKER WAS ONLY *PART* OF THEIR PROBLEM. *JENNA* WAS THE OTHER PART.

BLOOD IN THE HALLWAY SUGGESTED SHE WAS IN THE APARTMENT. HURT, *MAYBE* MORTALLY WOUNDED.

THEY HAD TO WHACK HARKER QUICKLY, GET JENNA MEDICAL HELP.

THE WOMAN WASN'T SCREAMING. MAYBE DEAD. MAYBE *DYING*.

HE'S GOING OUT A *WINDOW!*

THE FALL WAS AT *LEAST* THIRTY FEET, FAR ENOUGH TO AQUIRE A MORTAL VELOCITY BEFORE IMPACT.

THE PLUNGE *REFUTED* DEUCALION'S CONTENTION THAT VICTOR'S CREATIONS WERE EFFECTIVELY *FORBIDDEN* TO SELF-DESTRUCT.

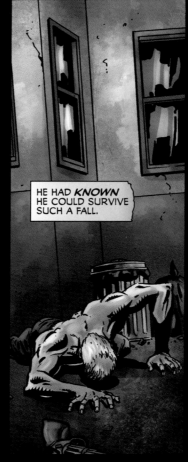

HE HAD *KNOWN* HE COULD SURVIVE SUCH A FALL.

AT THIS DISTANCE, A ROUND – OR ALL FOUR ROUNDS – FROM THE SHOTGUN WOULDN'T FAZE HIM.

HARKER!

COME!

DAMN.

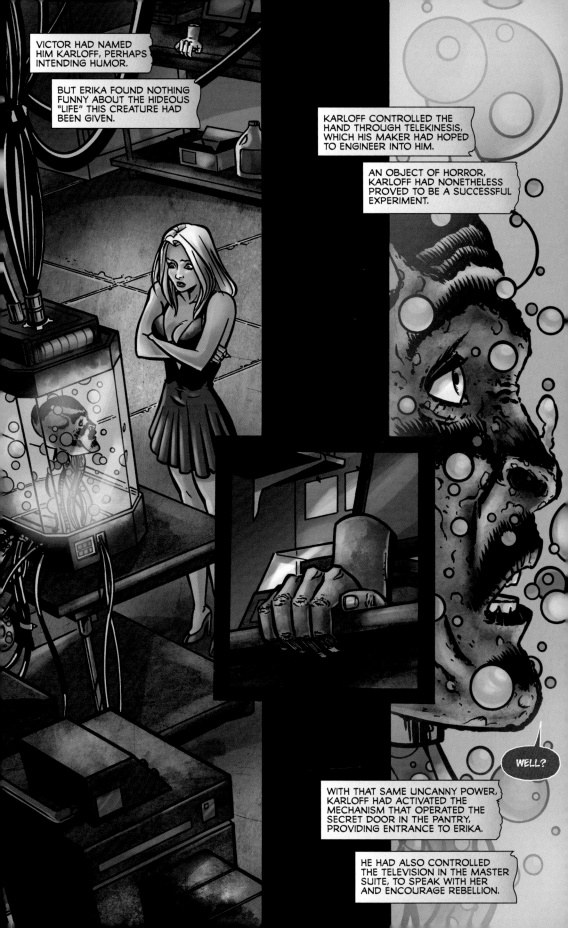

VICTOR HAD NAMED HIM KARLOFF, PERHAPS INTENDING HUMOR.

BUT ERIKA FOUND NOTHING FUNNY ABOUT THE HIDEOUS "LIFE" THIS CREATURE HAD BEEN GIVEN.

KARLOFF CONTROLLED THE HAND THROUGH TELEKINESIS, WHICH HIS MAKER HAD HOPED TO ENGINEER INTO HIM.

AN OBJECT OF HORROR, KARLOFF HAD NONETHELESS PROVED TO BE A SUCCESSFUL EXPERIMENT.

WELL?

WITH THAT SAME UNCANNY POWER, KARLOFF HAD ACTIVATED THE MECHANISM THAT OPERATED THE SECRET DOOR IN THE PANTRY, PROVIDING ENTRANCE TO ERIKA.

HE HAD ALSO CONTROLLED THE TELEVISION IN THE MASTER SUITE, TO SPEAK WITH HER AND ENCOURAGE REBELLION.

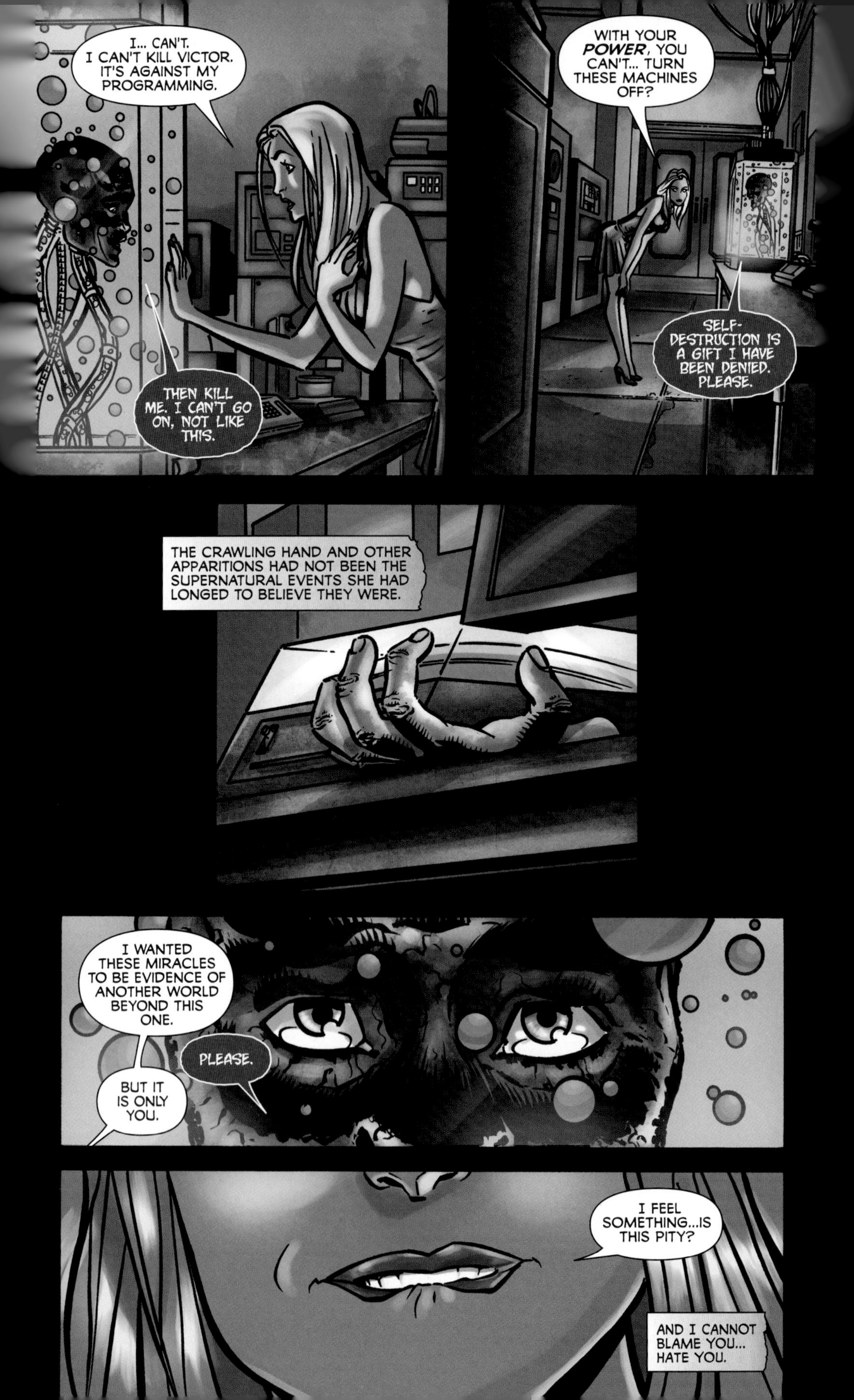
I... CAN'T. I CAN'T KILL VICTOR. IT'S AGAINST MY PROGRAMMING.
THEN KILL ME. I CAN'T GO ON, NOT LIKE THIS.
WITH YOUR POWER, YOU CAN'T... TURN THESE MACHINES OFF?
SELF-DESTRUCTION IS A GIFT I HAVE BEEN DENIED. PLEASE.
THE CRAWLING HAND AND OTHER APPARITIONS HAD NOT BEEN THE SUPERNATURAL EVENTS SHE HAD LONGED TO BELIEVE THEY WERE.
I WANTED THESE MIRACLES TO BE EVIDENCE OF ANOTHER WORLD BEYOND THIS ONE.
BUT IT IS ONLY YOU.
PLEASE.
I FEEL SOMETHING...IS THIS PITY?
AND I CANNOT BLAME YOU... HATE YOU.

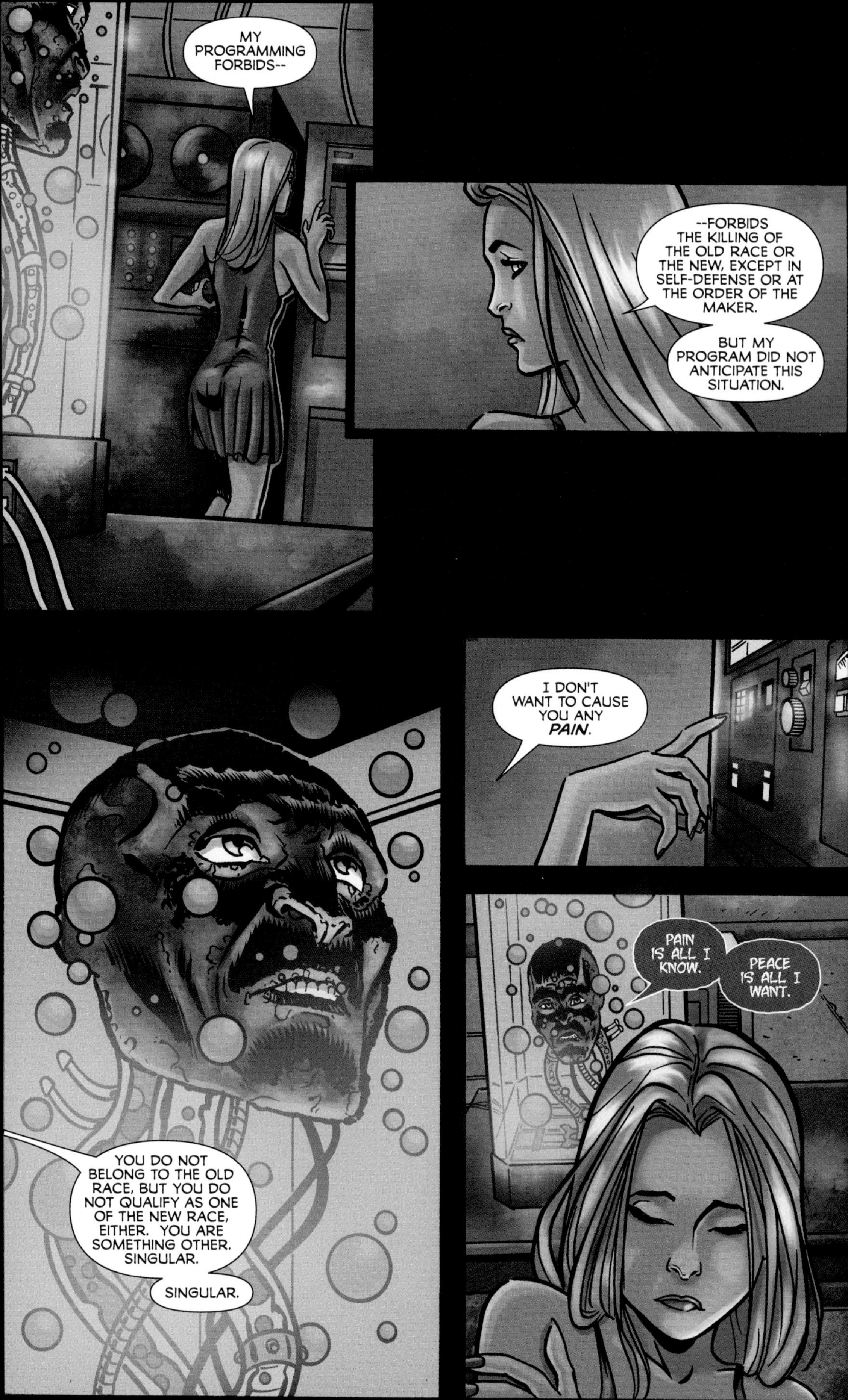
MY PROGRAMMING FORBIDS--
--FORBIDS THE KILLING OF THE OLD RACE OR THE NEW, EXCEPT IN SELF-DEFENSE OR AT THE ORDER OF THE MAKER.
BUT MY PROGRAM DID NOT ANTICIPATE THIS SITUATION.
YOU DO NOT BELONG TO THE OLD RACE, BUT YOU DO NOT QUALIFY AS ONE OF THE NEW RACE, EITHER. YOU ARE SOMETHING OTHER. SINGULAR.
SINGULAR.
I DON'T WANT TO CAUSE YOU ANY *PAIN*.
PAIN IS ALL I KNOW.
PEACE IS ALL I WANT.

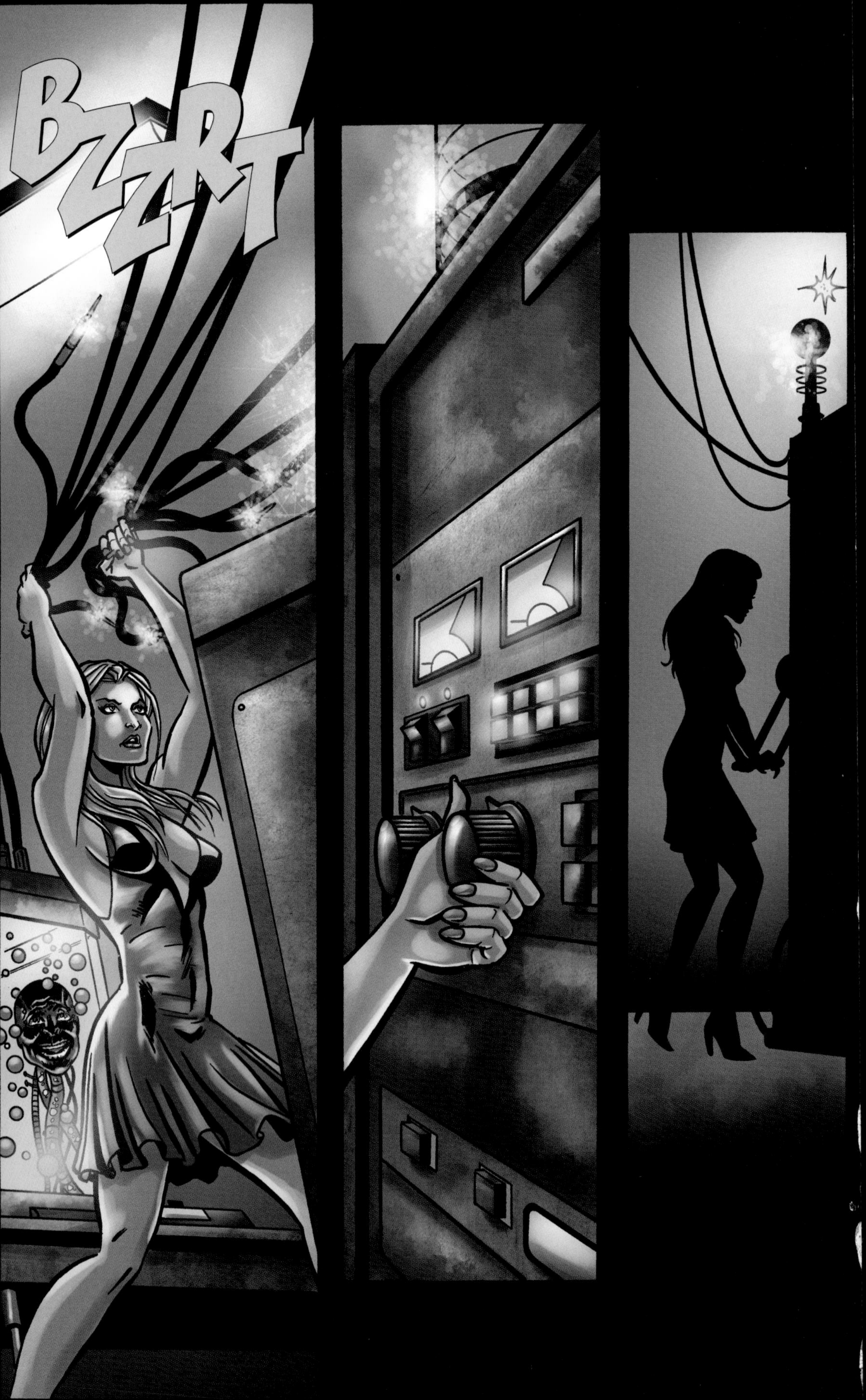
BZZRT

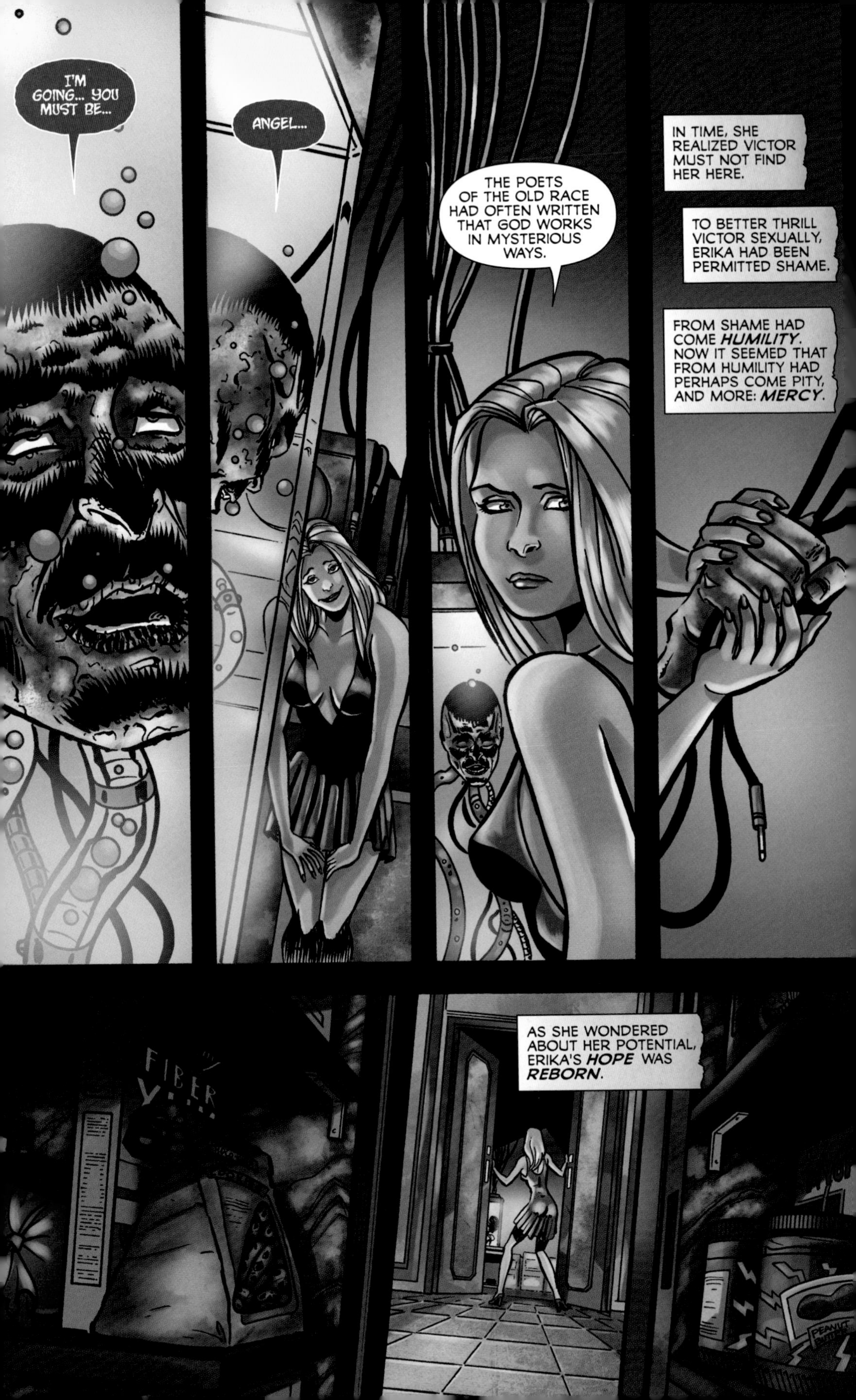
I'M GOING... YOU MUST BE...
ANGEL...
THE POETS OF THE OLD RACE HAD OFTEN WRITTEN THAT GOD WORKS IN MYSTERIOUS WAYS.
IN TIME, SHE REALIZED VICTOR MUST NOT FIND HER HERE.
TO BETTER THRILL VICTOR SEXUALLY, ERIKA HAD BEEN PERMITTED SHAME.
FROM SHAME HAD COME *HUMILITY*. NOW IT SEEMED THAT FROM HUMILITY HAD PERHAPS COME PITY, AND MORE: *MERCY*.
FIBER
AS SHE WONDERED ABOUT HER POTENTIAL, ERIKA'S *HOPE* WAS *REBORN*.

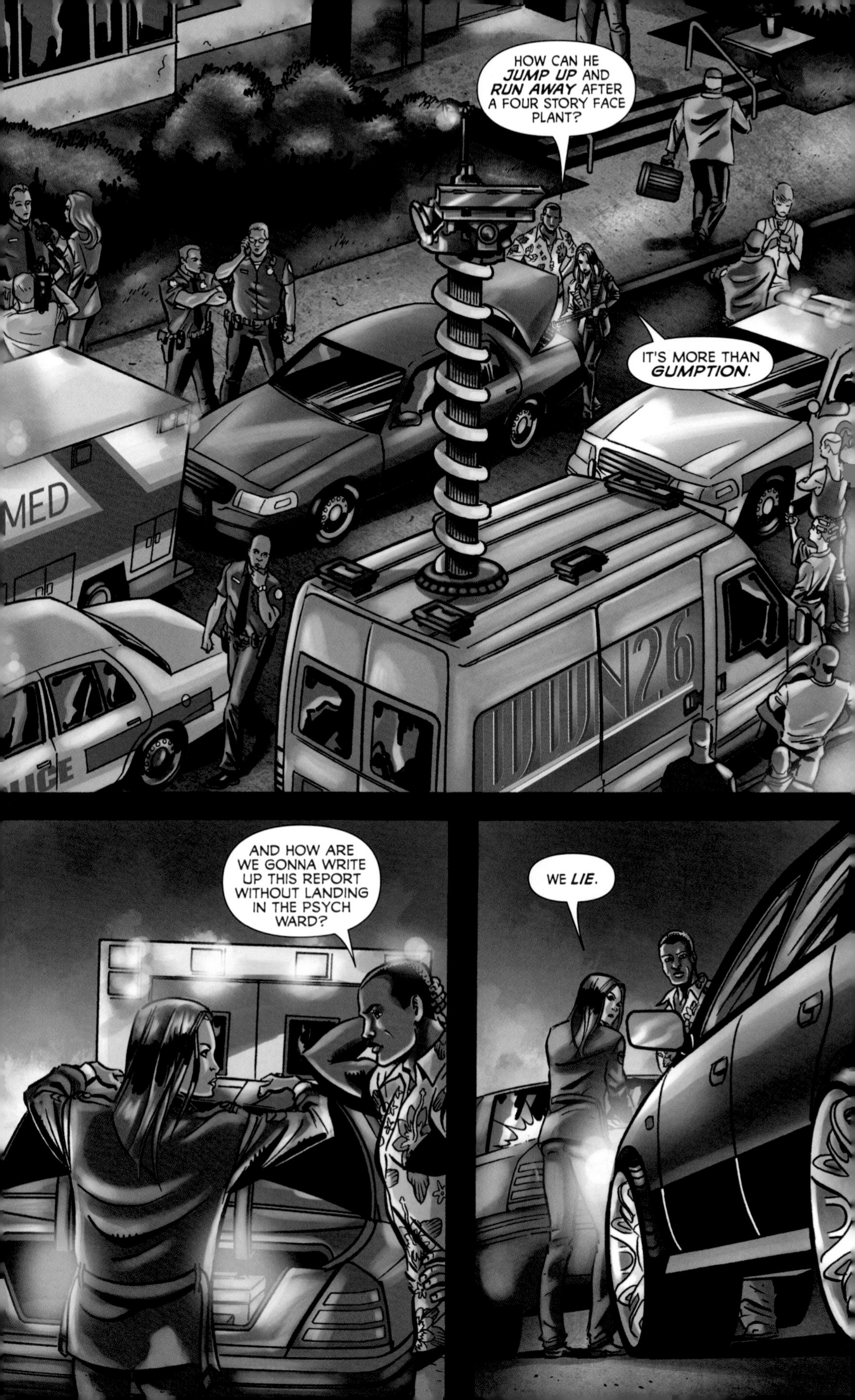
HOW CAN HE JUMP UP AND RUN AWAY AFTER A FOUR STORY FACE PLANT?
IT'S MORE THAN GUMPTION.
MED
WWN26
AND HOW ARE WE GONNA WRITE UP THIS REPORT WITHOUT LANDING IN THE PSYCH WARD?
WE LIE.

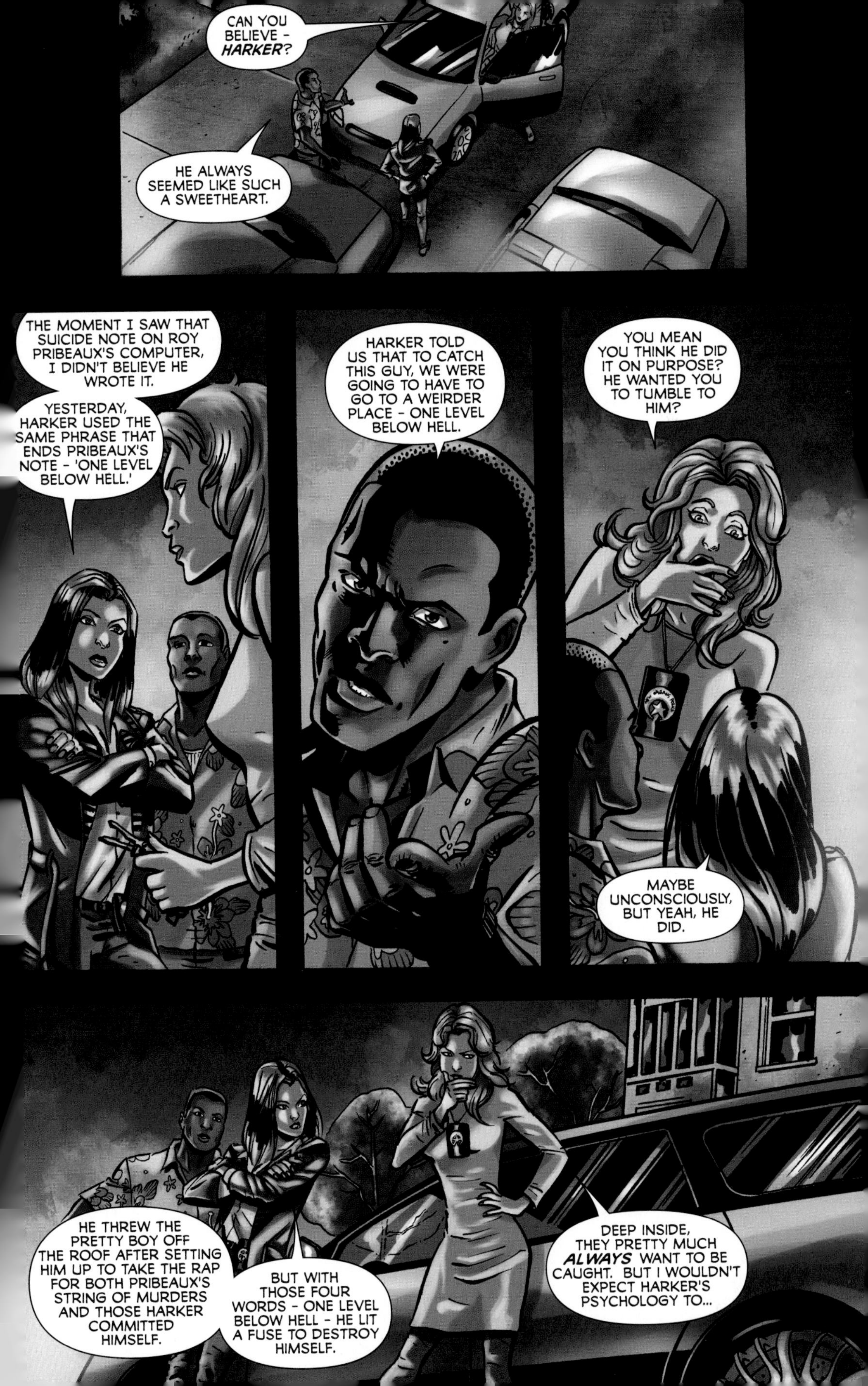
CAN YOU BELIEVE - HARKER?
HE ALWAYS SEEMED LIKE SUCH A SWEETHEART.
THE MOMENT I SAW THAT SUICIDE NOTE ON ROY PRIBEAUX'S COMPUTER, I DIDN'T BELIEVE HE WROTE IT.
YESTERDAY, HARKER USED THE SAME PHRASE THAT ENDS PRIBEAUX'S NOTE - 'ONE LEVEL BELOW HELL.'
HARKER TOLD US THAT TO CATCH THIS GUY, WE WERE GOING TO HAVE TO GO TO A WEIRDER PLACE - ONE LEVEL BELOW HELL.
YOU MEAN YOU THINK HE DID IT ON PURPOSE? HE WANTED YOU TO TUMBLE TO HIM?
MAYBE UNCONSCIOUSLY, BUT YEAH, HE DID.
HE THREW THE PRETTY BOY OFF THE ROOF AFTER SETTING HIM UP TO TAKE THE RAP FOR BOTH PRIBEAUX'S STRING OF MURDERS AND THOSE HARKER COMMITTED HIMSELF.
BUT WITH THOSE FOUR WORDS - ONE LEVEL BELOW HELL - HE LIT A FUSE TO DESTROY HIMSELF.
DEEP INSIDE, THEY PRETTY MUCH *ALWAYS* WANT TO BE CAUGHT. BUT I WOULDN'T EXPECT HARKER'S PSYCHOLOGY TO...

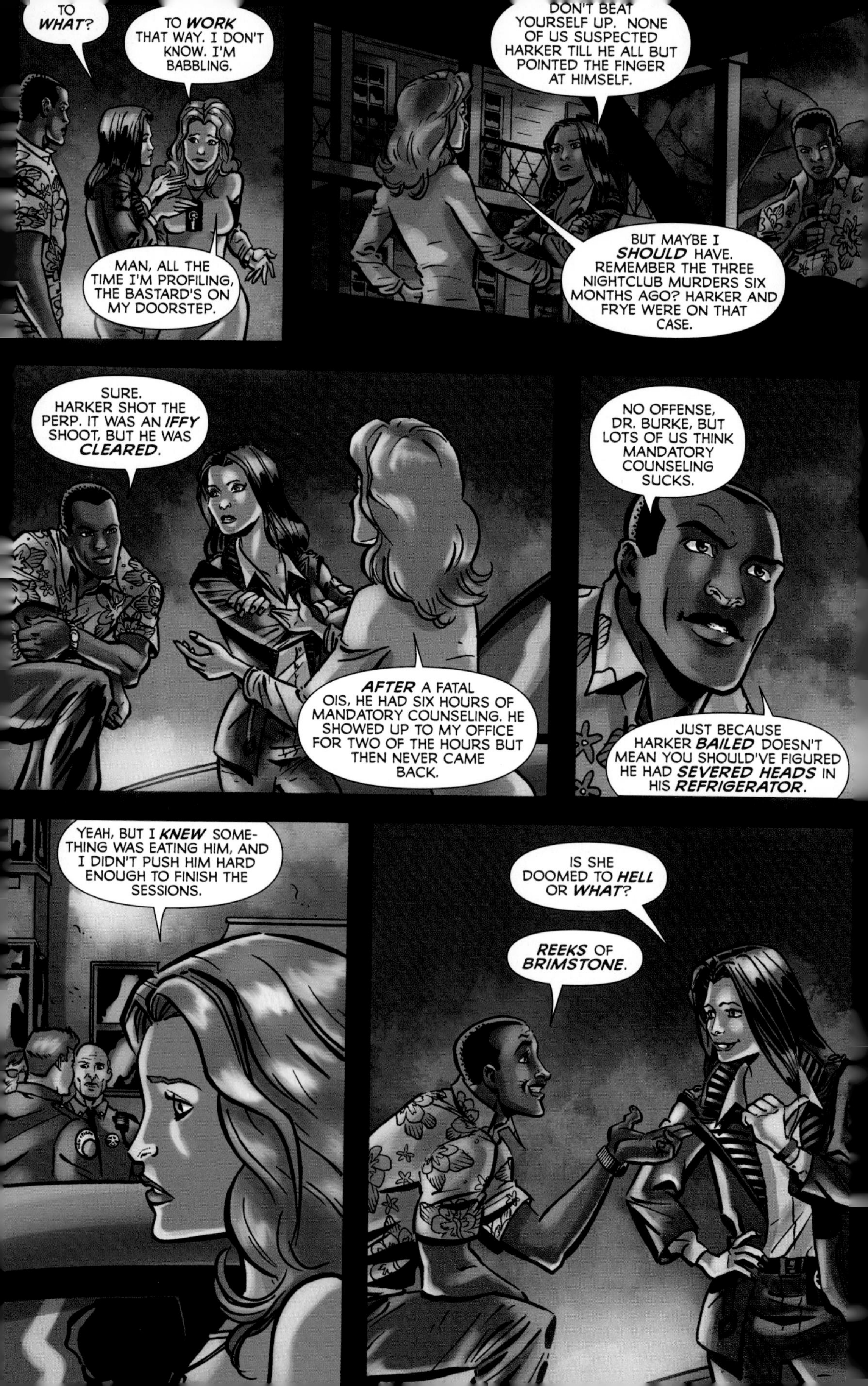
TO WHAT?
TO WORK THAT WAY. I DON'T KNOW. I'M BABBLING.
MAN, ALL THE TIME I'M PROFILING, THE BASTARD'S ON MY DOORSTEP.
DON'T BEAT YOURSELF UP. NONE OF US SUSPECTED HARKER TILL HE ALL BUT POINTED THE FINGER AT HIMSELF.
BUT MAYBE I SHOULD HAVE. REMEMBER THE THREE NIGHTCLUB MURDERS SIX MONTHS AGO? HARKER AND FRYE WERE ON THAT CASE.
SURE. HARKER SHOT THE PERP. IT WAS AN IFFY SHOOT, BUT HE WAS CLEARED.
AFTER A FATAL OIS, HE HAD SIX HOURS OF MANDATORY COUNSELING. HE SHOWED UP TO MY OFFICE FOR TWO OF THE HOURS BUT THEN NEVER CAME BACK.
NO OFFENSE, DR. BURKE, BUT LOTS OF US THINK MANDATORY COUNSELING SUCKS.
JUST BECAUSE HARKER BAILED DOESN'T MEAN YOU SHOULD'VE FIGURED HE HAD SEVERED HEADS IN HIS REFRIGERATOR.
YEAH, BUT I KNEW SOME-THING WAS EATING HIM, AND I DIDN'T PUSH HIM HARD ENOUGH TO FINISH THE SESSIONS.
IS SHE DOOMED TO HELL OR WHAT?
REEKS OF BRIMSTONE.

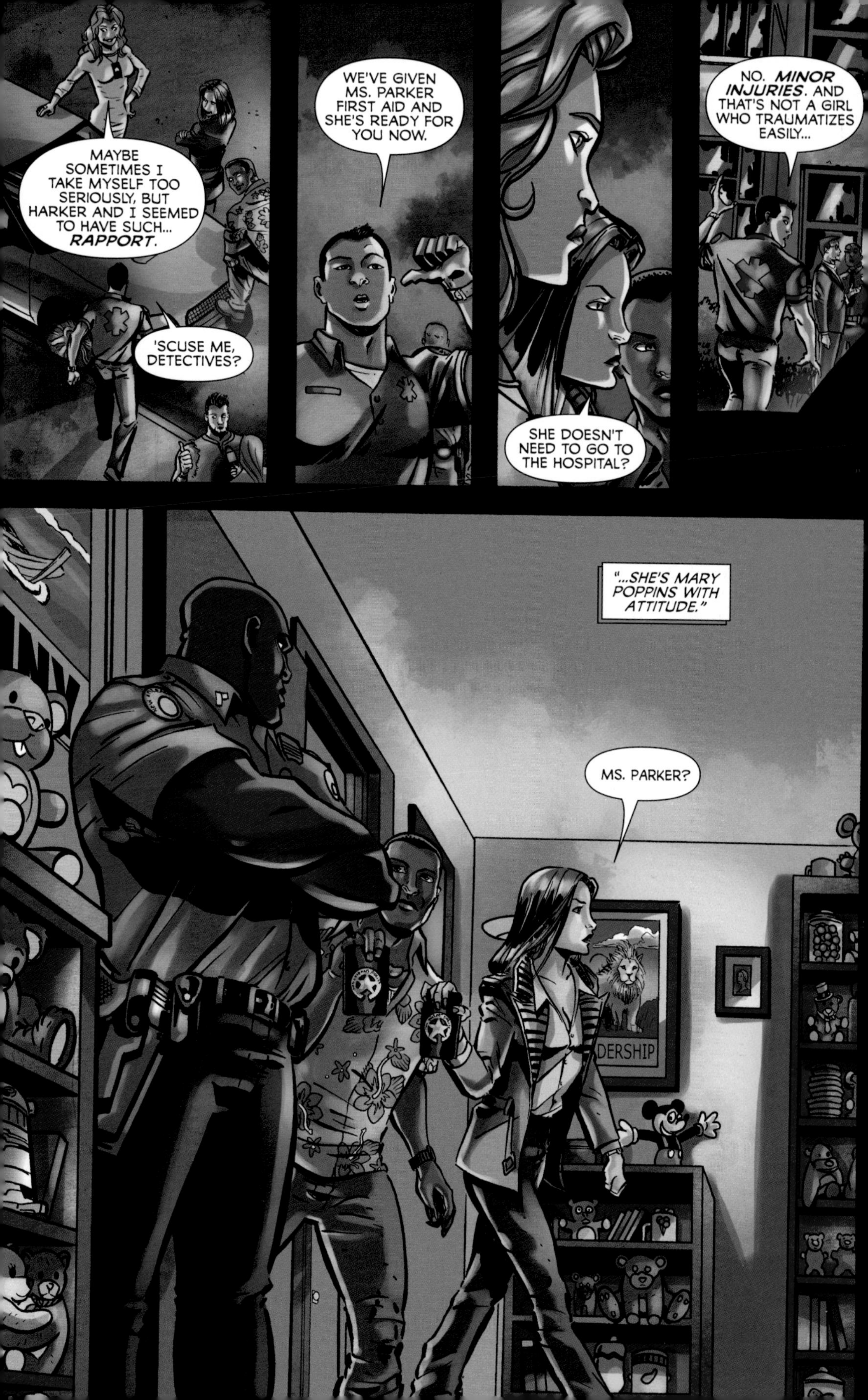
MAYBE SOMETIMES I TAKE MYSELF TOO SERIOUSLY, BUT HARKER AND I SEEMED TO HAVE SUCH... RAPPORT.
'SCUSE ME, DETECTIVES?
WE'VE GIVEN MS. PARKER FIRST AID AND SHE'S READY FOR YOU NOW.
SHE DOESN'T NEED TO GO TO THE HOSPITAL?
NO. MINOR INJURIES. AND THAT'S NOT A GIRL WHO TRAUMATIZES EASILY...
"...SHE'S MARY POPPINS WITH ATTITUDE."
MS. PARKER?
DERSHIP

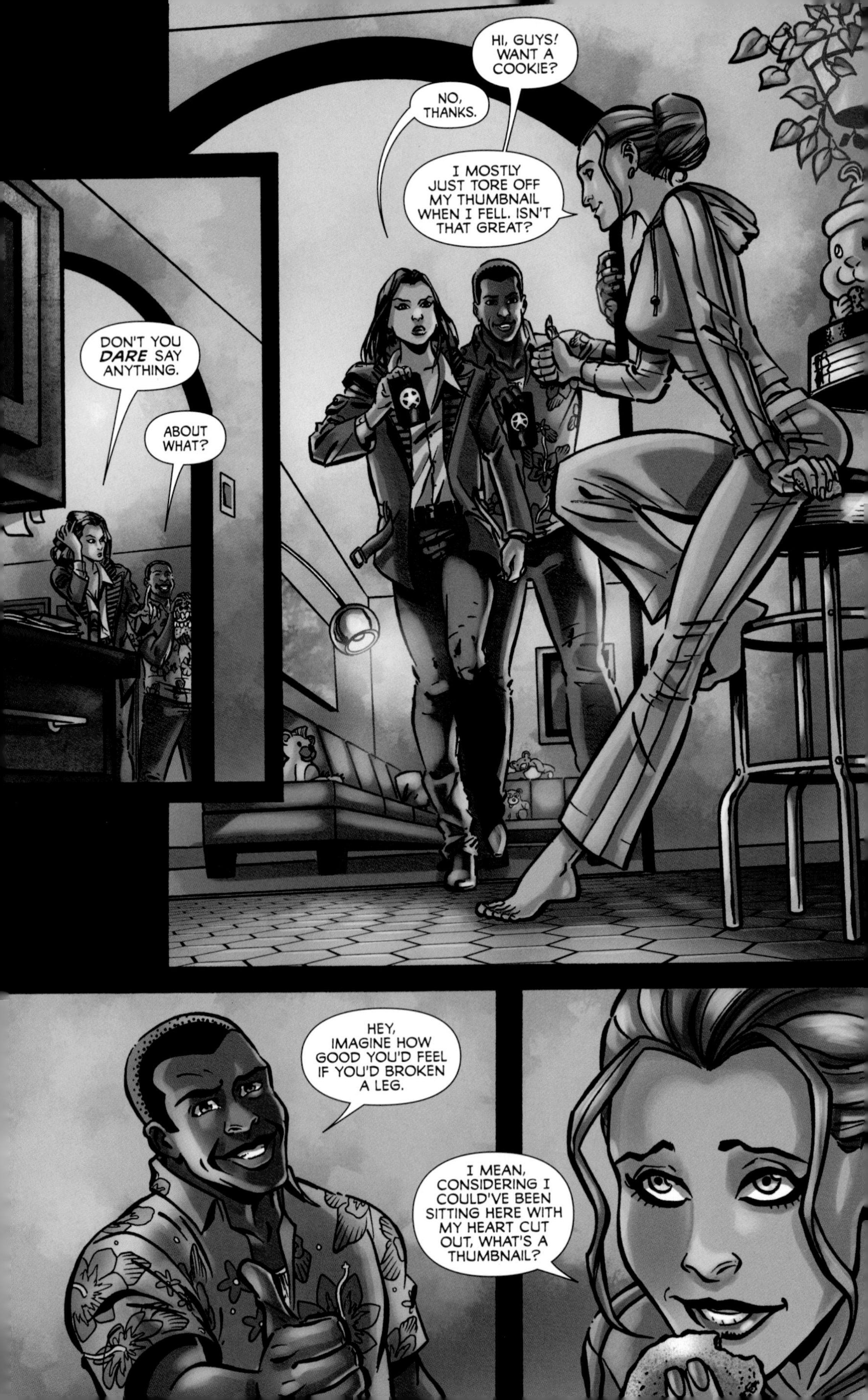

HI, GUYS! WANT A COOKIE?
NO, THANKS.
I MOSTLY JUST TORE OFF MY THUMBNAIL WHEN I FELL. ISN'T THAT GREAT?
DON'T YOU *DARE* SAY ANYTHING.
ABOUT WHAT?
HEY, IMAGINE HOW GOOD YOU'D FEEL IF YOU'D BROKEN A LEG.
I MEAN, CONSIDERING I COULD'VE BEEN SITTING HERE WITH MY HEART CUT OUT, WHAT'S A THUMBNAIL?

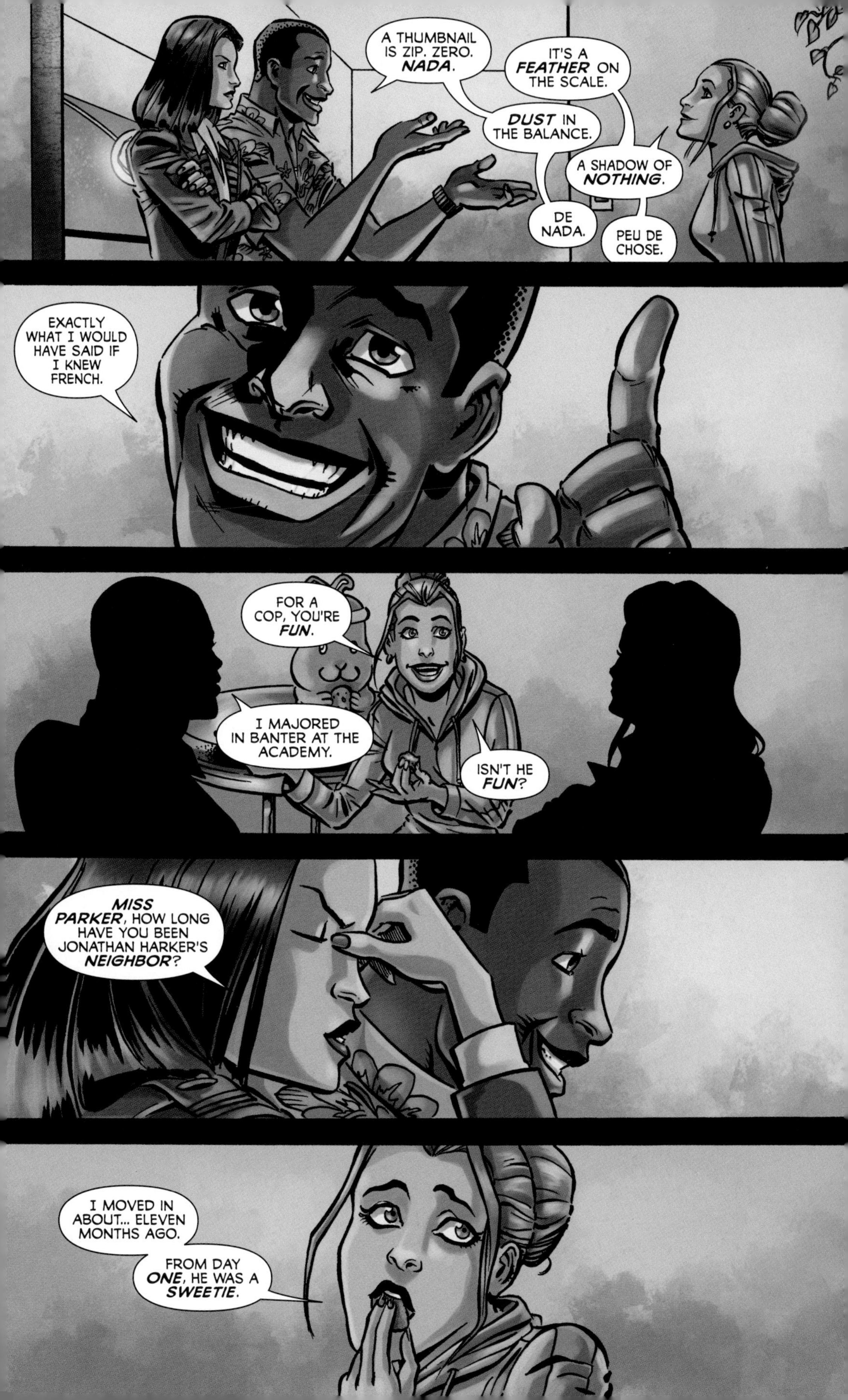

A THUMBNAIL IS ZIP. ZERO. ***NADA***.
IT'S A ***FEATHER*** ON THE SCALE.
DUST IN THE BALANCE.
A SHADOW OF ***NOTHING***.
DE NADA.
PEU DE CHOSE.
EXACTLY WHAT I WOULD HAVE SAID IF I KNEW FRENCH.
FOR A COP, YOU'RE ***FUN***.
I MAJORED IN BANTER AT THE ACADEMY.
ISN'T HE ***FUN***?
MISS PARKER, HOW LONG HAVE YOU BEEN JONATHAN HARKER'S ***NEIGHBOR***?
I MOVED IN ABOUT... ELEVEN MONTHS AGO.
FROM DAY ***ONE***, HE WAS A ***SWEETIE***.

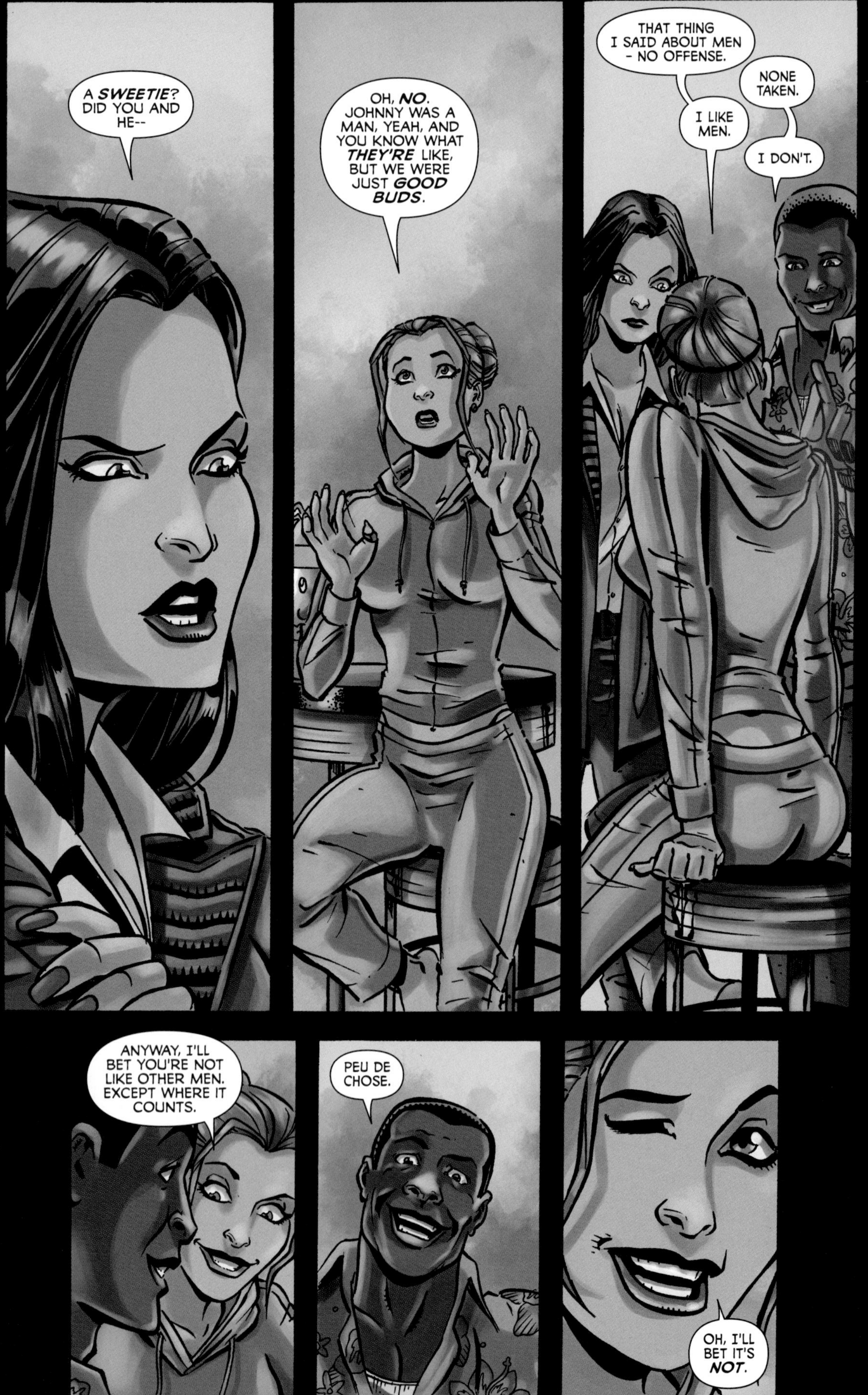
A SWEETIE? DID YOU AND HE--
OH, NO. JOHNNY WAS A MAN, YEAH, AND YOU KNOW WHAT THEY'RE LIKE, BUT WE WERE JUST GOOD BUDS.
THAT THING I SAID ABOUT MEN - NO OFFENSE.
NONE TAKEN.
I LIKE MEN.
I DON'T.
ANYWAY, I'LL BET YOU'RE NOT LIKE OTHER MEN. EXCEPT WHERE IT COUNTS.
PEU DE CHOSE.
OH, I'LL BET IT'S NOT.

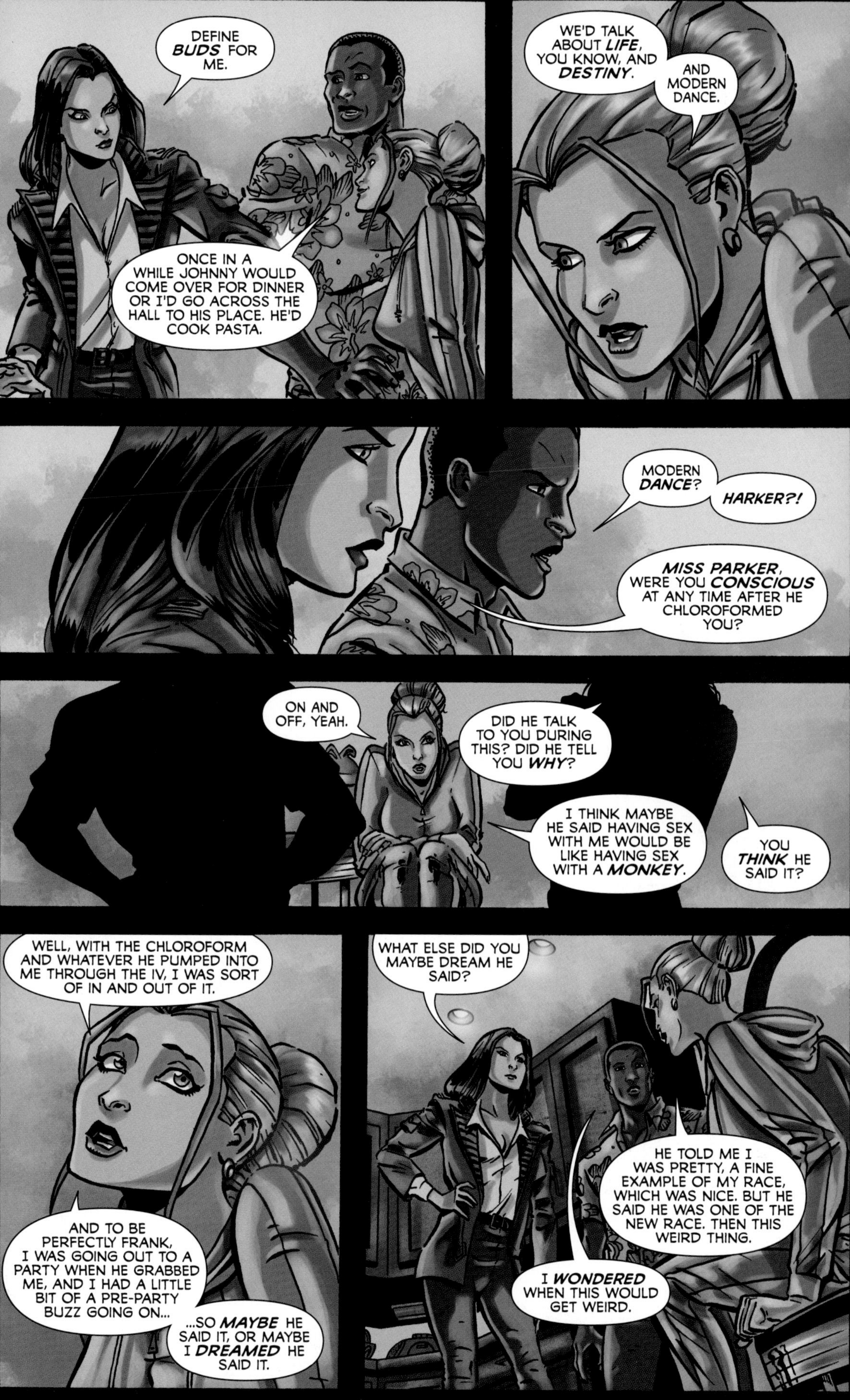

DEFINE BUDS FOR ME.
ONCE IN A WHILE JOHNNY WOULD COME OVER FOR DINNER OR I'D GO ACROSS THE HALL TO HIS PLACE. HE'D COOK PASTA.
WE'D TALK ABOUT LIFE, YOU KNOW, AND DESTINY.
AND MODERN DANCE.
MODERN DANCE?
HARKER?!
MISS PARKER, WERE YOU CONSCIOUS AT ANY TIME AFTER HE CHLOROFORMED YOU?
ON AND OFF, YEAH.
DID HE TALK TO YOU DURING THIS? DID HE TELL YOU WHY?
I THINK MAYBE HE SAID HAVING SEX WITH ME WOULD BE LIKE HAVING SEX WITH A MONKEY.
YOU THINK HE SAID IT?
WELL, WITH THE CHLOROFORM AND WHATEVER HE PUMPED INTO ME THROUGH THE IV, I WAS SORT OF IN AND OUT OF IT.
AND TO BE PERFECTLY FRANK, I WAS GOING OUT TO A PARTY WHEN HE GRABBED ME, AND I HAD A LITTLE BIT OF A PRE-PARTY BUZZ GOING ON...
...SO MAYBE HE SAID IT, OR MAYBE I DREAMED HE SAID IT.
WHAT ELSE DID YOU MAYBE DREAM HE SAID?
HE TOLD ME I WAS PRETTY, A FINE EXAMPLE OF MY RACE, WHICH WAS NICE. BUT HE SAID HE WAS ONE OF THE NEW RACE. THEN THIS WEIRD THING.
I WONDERED WHEN THIS WOULD GET WEIRD.

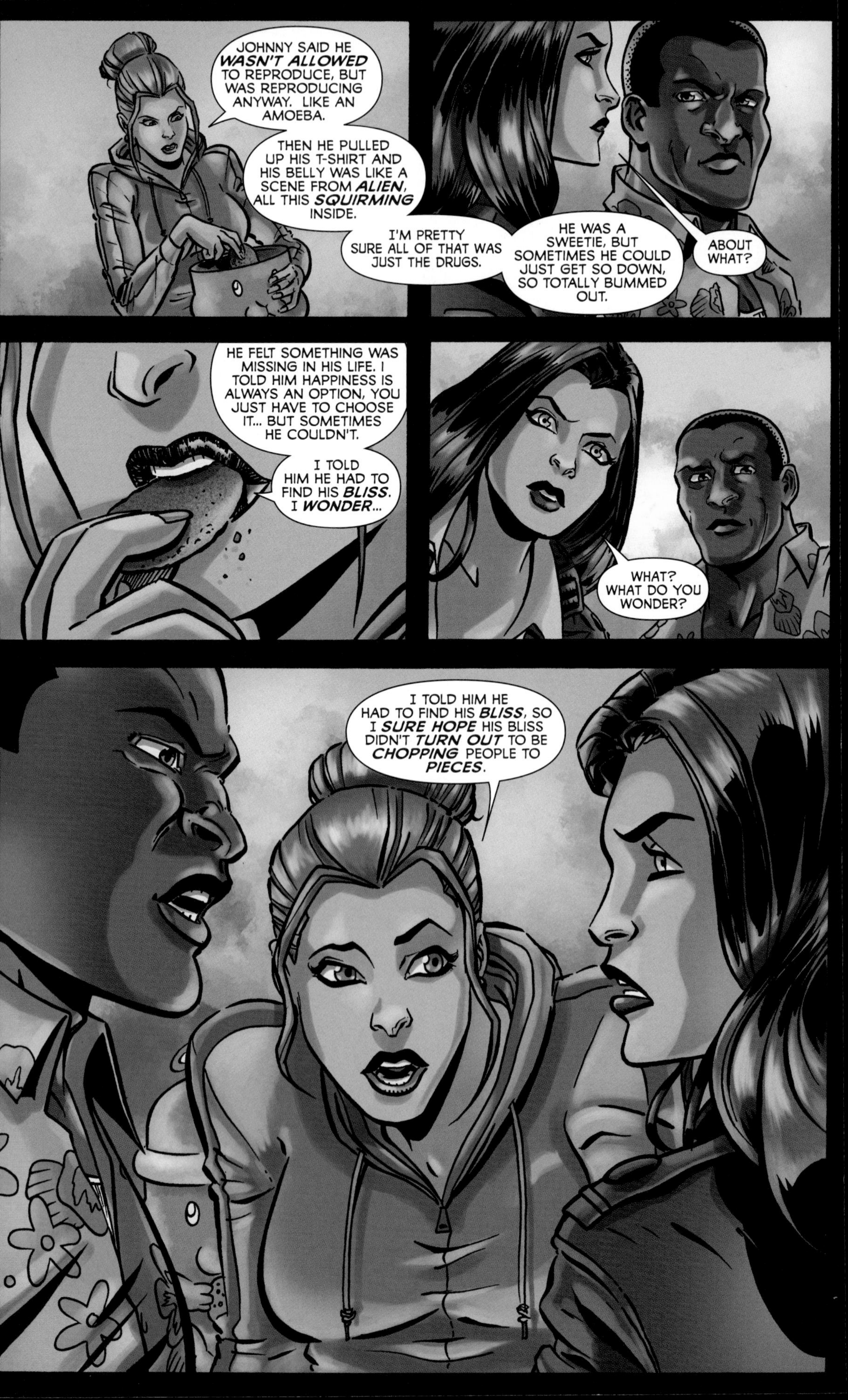
JOHNNY SAID HE *WASN'T ALLOWED* TO REPRODUCE, BUT WAS REPRODUCING ANYWAY. LIKE AN AMOEBA.
THEN HE PULLED UP HIS T-SHIRT AND HIS BELLY WAS LIKE A SCENE FROM *ALIEN*, ALL THIS *SQUIRMING* INSIDE.
I'M PRETTY SURE ALL OF THAT WAS JUST THE DRUGS.
HE WAS A SWEETIE, BUT SOMETIMES HE COULD JUST GET SO DOWN, SO TOTALLY BUMMED OUT.
ABOUT WHAT?
HE FELT SOMETHING WAS MISSING IN HIS LIFE. I TOLD HIM HAPPINESS IS ALWAYS AN OPTION, YOU JUST HAVE TO CHOOSE IT... BUT SOMETIMES HE COULDN'T.
I TOLD HIM HE HAD TO FIND HIS *BLISS*. I *WONDER*...
WHAT? WHAT DO YOU WONDER?
I TOLD HIM HE HAD TO FIND HIS *BLISS*, SO I *SURE HOPE* HIS BLISS DIDN'T *TURN OUT* TO BE *CHOPPING* PEOPLE TO *PIECES*.

chapter Three

COVER BY: **SCOTT COHN**

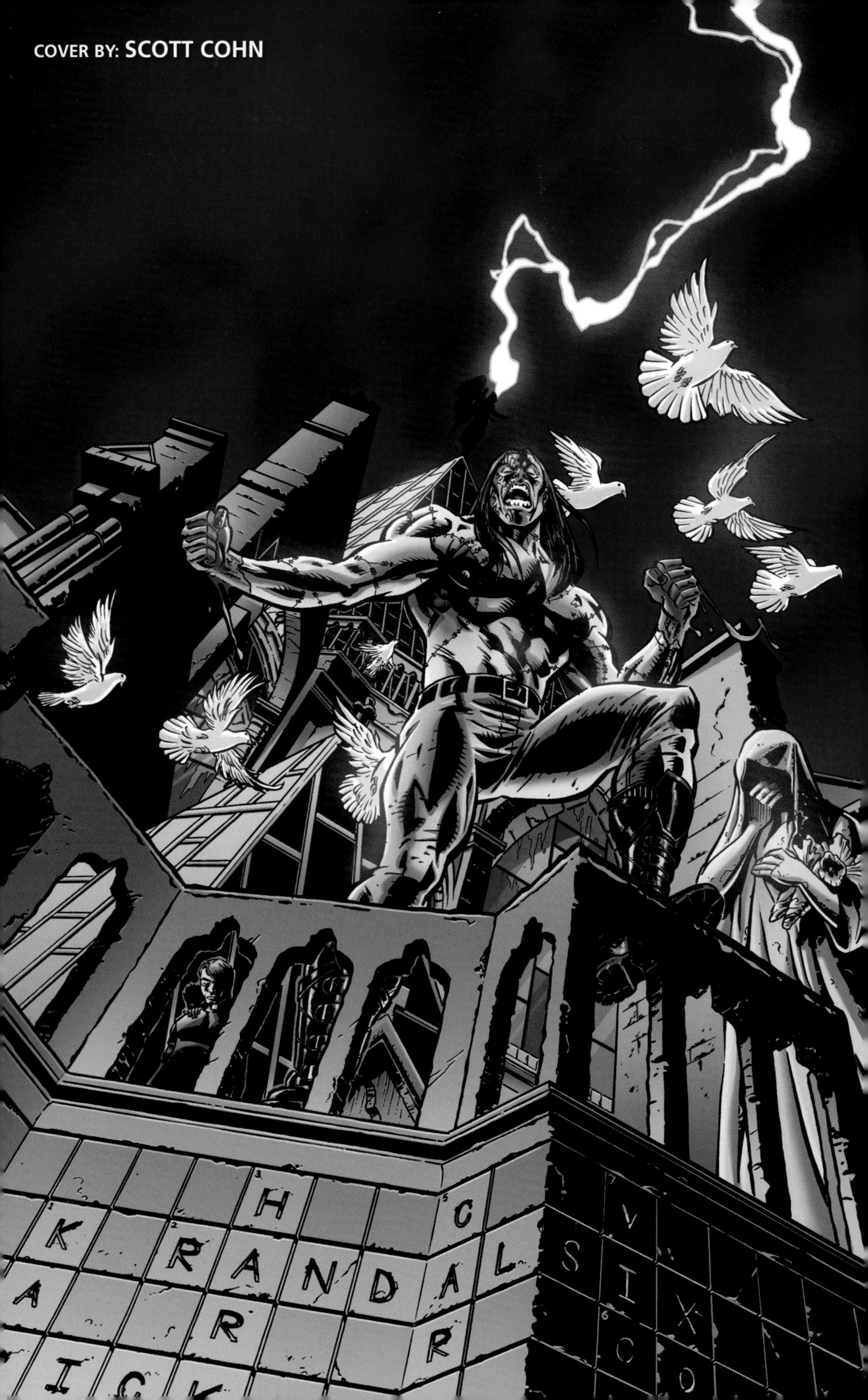

THROUGH THE CODED DOOR, OUT OF MERCY, RANDAL SIX FINDS HIMSELF IN AN EMPTY PASSAGEWAY.

APPROXIMATELY ONE HUNDRED AND FORTY FEET FROM HIM WAITS ANOTHER DOOR – HAPPILY, THERE ARE NO CHOICES.

HE HAS COME TOO FAR TO RETREAT.

HE CAN ONLY GO *FORWARD*.

THE FLOOR HAS BEEN POURED IN THREE-FOOT-SQUARE BLOCKS.

BY TAKING LONG STRIDES – SOMETIMES *BOUNDING* – RANDAL IS ABLE TO SPELL HIMSELF ALONG THESE OVERSIZE BOXES TOWARD THE FARTHER END OF THE CORRIDOR.

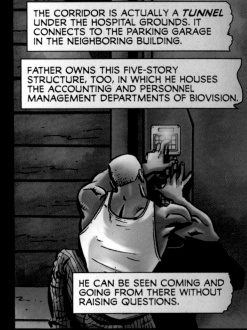

THE CORRIDOR IS ACTUALLY A *TUNNEL* UNDER THE HOSPITAL GROUNDS. IT CONNECTS TO THE PARKING GARAGE IN THE NEIGHBORING BUILDING.

FATHER OWNS THIS FIVE-STORY STRUCTURE, TOO, IN WHICH HE HOUSES THE ACCOUNTING AND PERSONNEL MANAGEMENT DEPARTMENTS OF BIOVISION.

HE CAN BE SEEN COMING AND GOING FROM THERE WITHOUT RAISING QUESTIONS.

USING THE SECRETLY CONSTRUCTED UNDERGROUND PASSAGEWAY BETWEEN BUILDINGS, HIS VISITS TO THE HANDS OF MERCY, WHICH HE OWNS THROUGH A SHELL COMPANY, CAN BE CONCEALED.

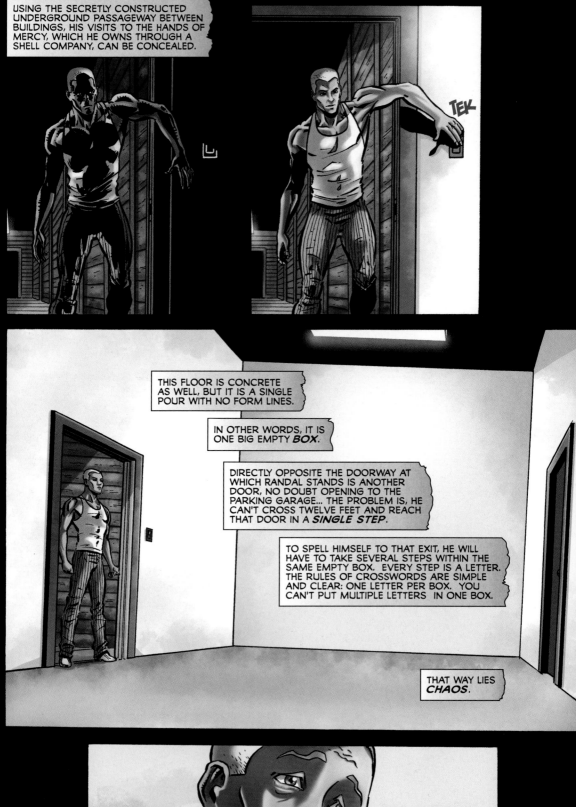

TEK

THIS FLOOR IS CONCRETE AS WELL, BUT IT IS A SINGLE POUR WITH NO FORM LINES.

IN OTHER WORDS, IT IS ONE BIG EMPTY *BOX*.

DIRECTLY OPPOSITE THE DOORWAY AT WHICH RANDAL STANDS IS ANOTHER DOOR, NO DOUBT OPENING TO THE PARKING GARAGE... THE PROBLEM IS, HE CAN'T CROSS TWELVE FEET AND REACH THAT DOOR IN A *SINGLE STEP*.

TO SPELL HIMSELF TO THAT EXIT, HE WILL HAVE TO TAKE SEVERAL STEPS WITHIN THE SAME EMPTY BOX. EVERY STEP IS A LETTER. THE RULES OF CROSSWORDS ARE SIMPLE AND CLEAR: ONE LETTER PER BOX. YOU CAN'T PUT MULTIPLE LETTERS IN ONE BOX.

THAT WAY LIES *CHAOS*.

HE CAN REACH THE DOOR IN FIVE STEPS, BUT HE ONLY HAS ONE EMPTY BOX.

RANDAL STANDS, THINKS, PUZZLES, PUZZLES... AND BEGINS TO WEEP WITH FRUSTRATION.

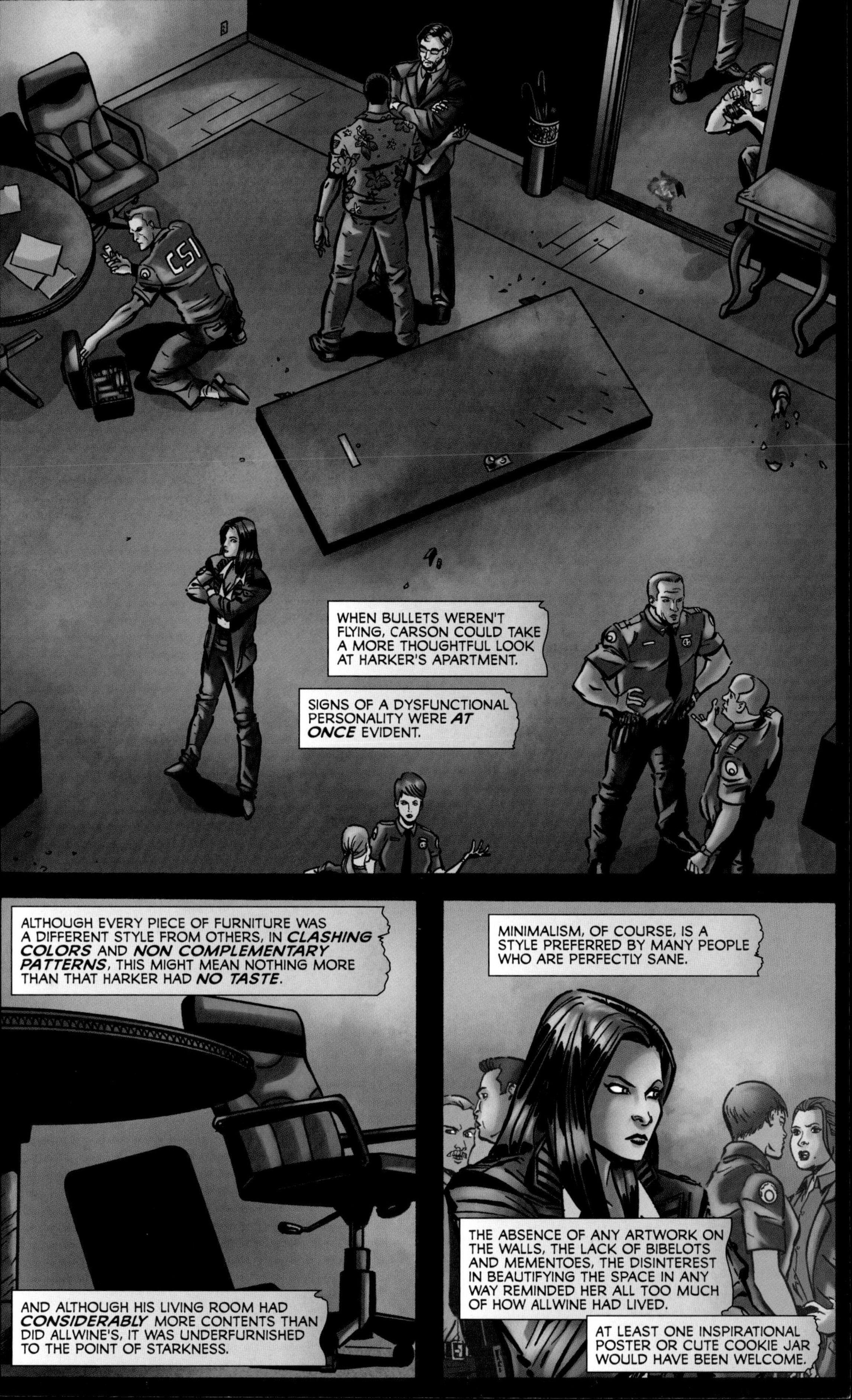
CSI
WHEN BULLETS WEREN'T FLYING, CARSON COULD TAKE A MORE THOUGHTFUL LOOK AT HARKER'S APARTMENT.
SIGNS OF A DYSFUNCTIONAL PERSONALITY WERE ***AT ONCE*** EVIDENT.
ALTHOUGH EVERY PIECE OF FURNITURE WAS A DIFFERENT STYLE FROM OTHERS, IN ***CLASHING COLORS*** AND ***NON COMPLEMENTARY PATTERNS***, THIS MIGHT MEAN NOTHING MORE THAN THAT HARKER HAD ***NO TASTE***.
AND ALTHOUGH HIS LIVING ROOM HAD ***CONSIDERABLY*** MORE CONTENTS THAN DID ALLWINE'S, IT WAS UNDERFURNISHED TO THE POINT OF STARKNESS.
MINIMALISM, OF COURSE, IS A STYLE PREFERRED BY MANY PEOPLE WHO ARE PERFECTLY SANE.
THE ABSENCE OF ANY ARTWORK ON THE WALLS, THE LACK OF BIBELOTS AND MEMENTOES, THE DISINTEREST IN BEAUTIFYING THE SPACE IN ANY WAY REMINDED HER ALL TOO MUCH OF HOW ALLWINE HAD LIVED.
AT LEAST ONE INSPIRATIONAL POSTER OR CUTE COOKIE JAR WOULD HAVE BEEN WELCOME.

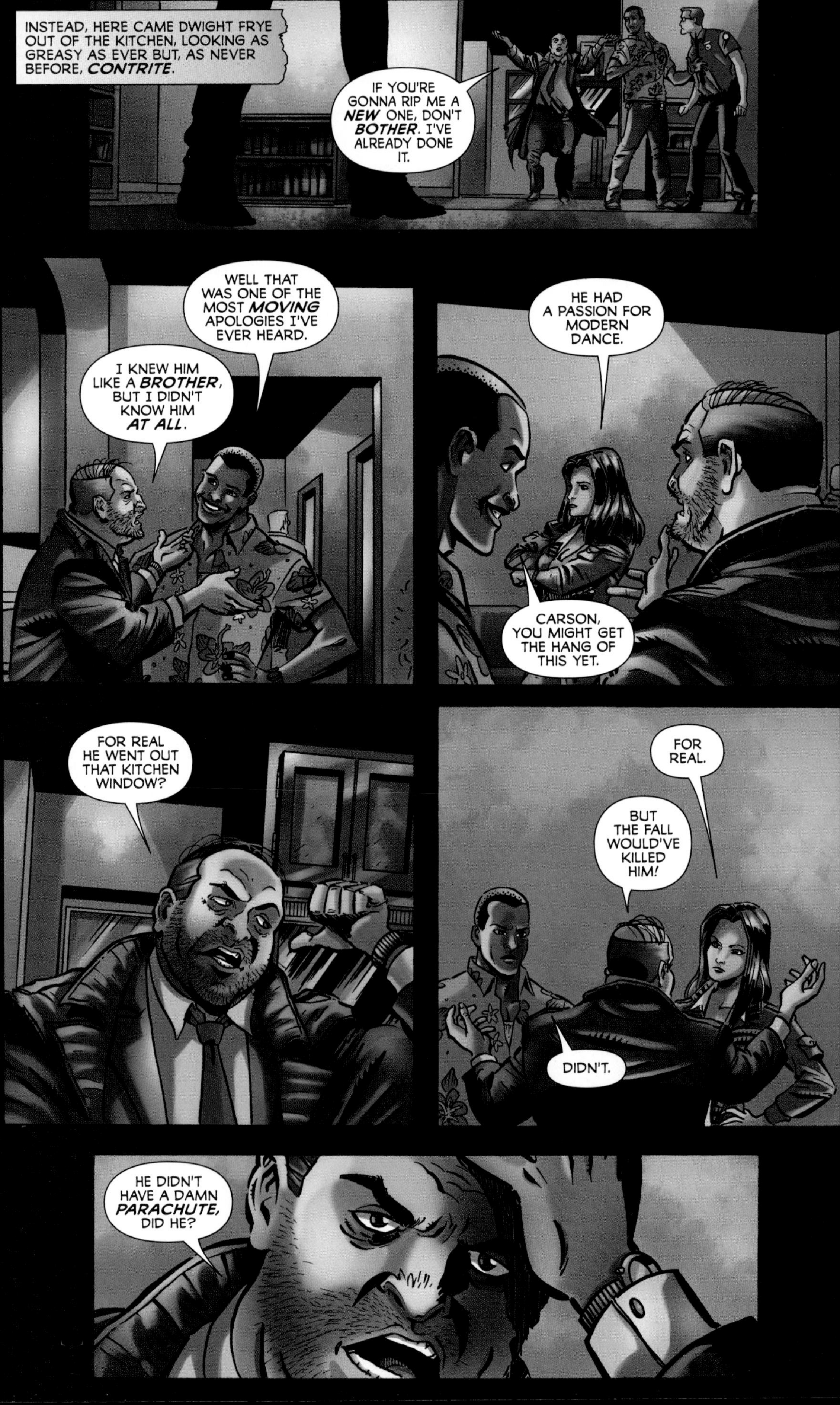
INSTEAD, HERE CAME DWIGHT FRYE OUT OF THE KITCHEN, LOOKING AS GREASY AS EVER BUT, AS NEVER BEFORE, CONTRITE.
IF YOU'RE GONNA RIP ME A NEW ONE, DON'T BOTHER. I'VE ALREADY DONE IT.
WELL THAT WAS ONE OF THE MOST MOVING APOLOGIES I'VE EVER HEARD.
I KNEW HIM LIKE A BROTHER, BUT I DIDN'T KNOW HIM AT ALL.
HE HAD A PASSION FOR MODERN DANCE.
CARSON, YOU MIGHT GET THE HANG OF THIS YET.
FOR REAL HE WENT OUT THAT KITCHEN WINDOW?
FOR REAL.
BUT THE FALL WOULD'VE KILLED HIM!
DIDN'T.
HE DIDN'T HAVE A DAMN PARACHUTE, DID HE?

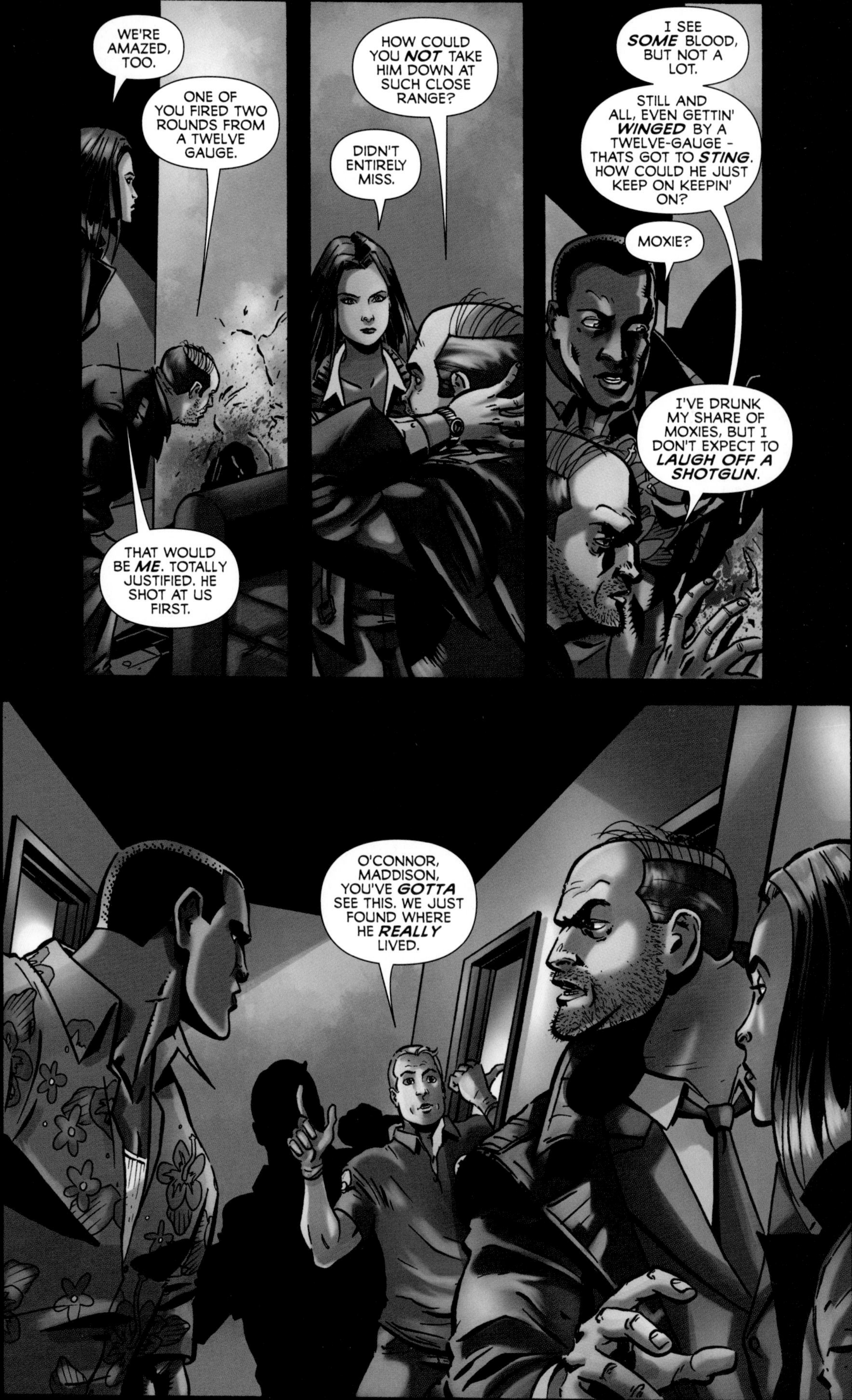
WE'RE AMAZED, TOO.
ONE OF YOU FIRED TWO ROUNDS FROM A TWELVE GAUGE.
THAT WOULD BE ME. TOTALLY JUSTIFIED. HE SHOT AT US FIRST.
HOW COULD YOU NOT TAKE HIM DOWN AT SUCH CLOSE RANGE?
DIDN'T ENTIRELY MISS.
I SEE SOME BLOOD, BUT NOT A LOT.
STILL AND ALL, EVEN GETTIN' WINGED BY A TWELVE-GAUGE - THATS GOT TO STING. HOW COULD HE JUST KEEP ON KEEPIN' ON?
MOXIE?
I'VE DRUNK MY SHARE OF MOXIES, BUT I DON'T EXPECT TO LAUGH OFF A SHOTGUN.
O'CONNOR, MADDISON, YOU'VE GOTTA SEE THIS. WE JUST FOUND WHERE HE REALLY LIVED.

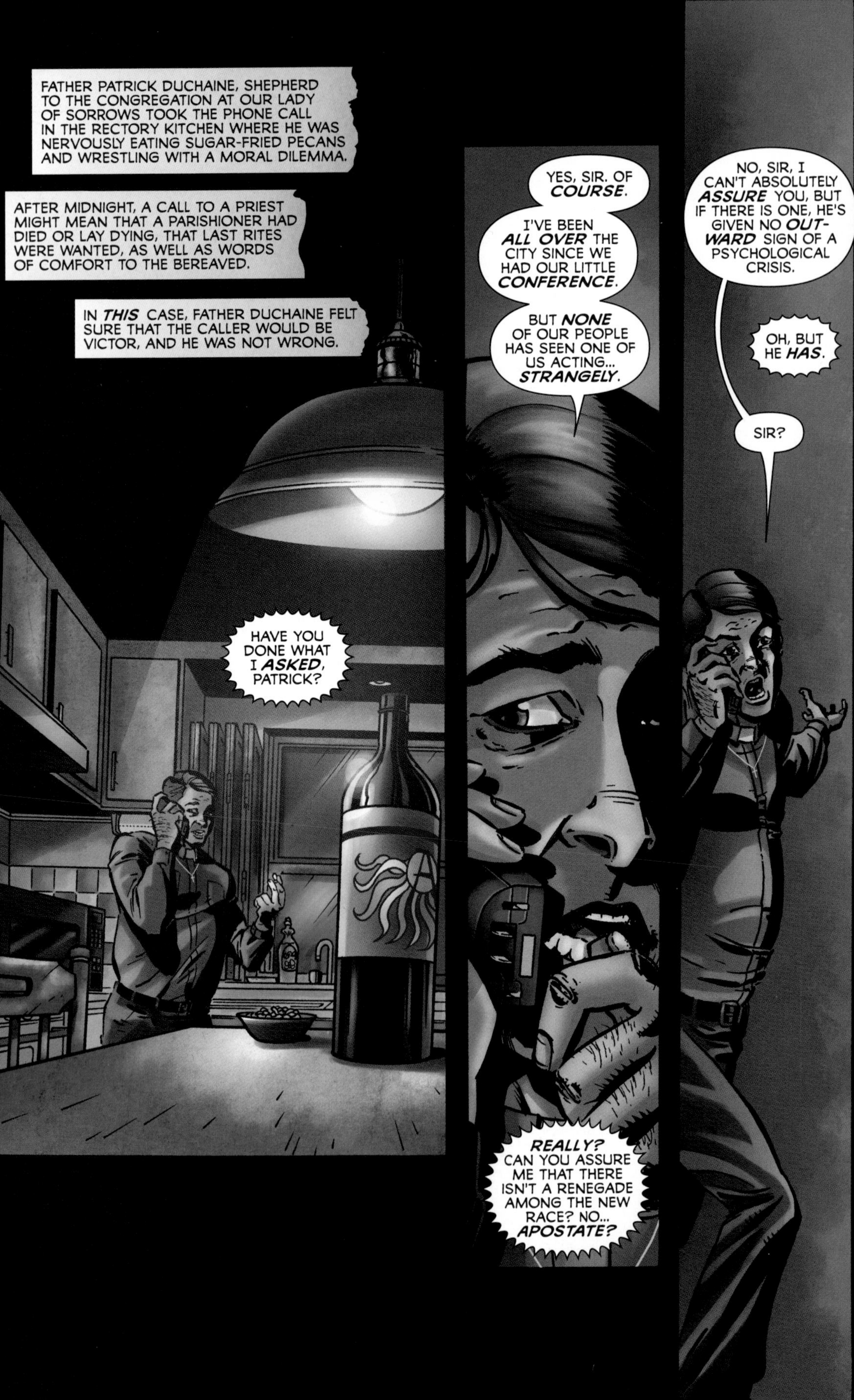
FATHER PATRICK DUCHAINE, SHEPHERD TO THE CONGREGATION AT OUR LADY OF SORROWS TOOK THE PHONE CALL IN THE RECTORY KITCHEN WHERE HE WAS NERVOUSLY EATING SUGAR-FRIED PECANS AND WRESTLING WITH A MORAL DILEMMA.
AFTER MIDNIGHT, A CALL TO A PRIEST MIGHT MEAN THAT A PARISHIONER HAD DIED OR LAY DYING, THAT LAST RITES WERE WANTED, AS WELL AS WORDS OF COMFORT TO THE BEREAVED.
IN *THIS* CASE, FATHER DUCHAINE FELT SURE THAT THE CALLER WOULD BE VICTOR, AND HE WAS NOT WRONG.
HAVE YOU DONE WHAT I *ASKED*, PATRICK?
YES, SIR. OF *COURSE*.
I'VE BEEN *ALL OVER* THE CITY SINCE WE HAD OUR LITTLE *CONFERENCE*.
BUT *NONE* OF OUR PEOPLE HAS SEEN ONE OF US ACTING... *STRANGELY*.
REALLY? CAN YOU ASSURE ME THAT THERE ISN'T A RENEGADE AMONG THE NEW RACE? NO... *APOSTATE?*
NO, SIR, I CAN'T ABSOLUTELY *ASSURE* YOU, BUT IF THERE IS ONE, HE'S GIVEN NO *OUTWARD* SIGN OF A PSYCHOLOGICAL CRISIS.
OH, BUT HE *HAS*.
SIR?

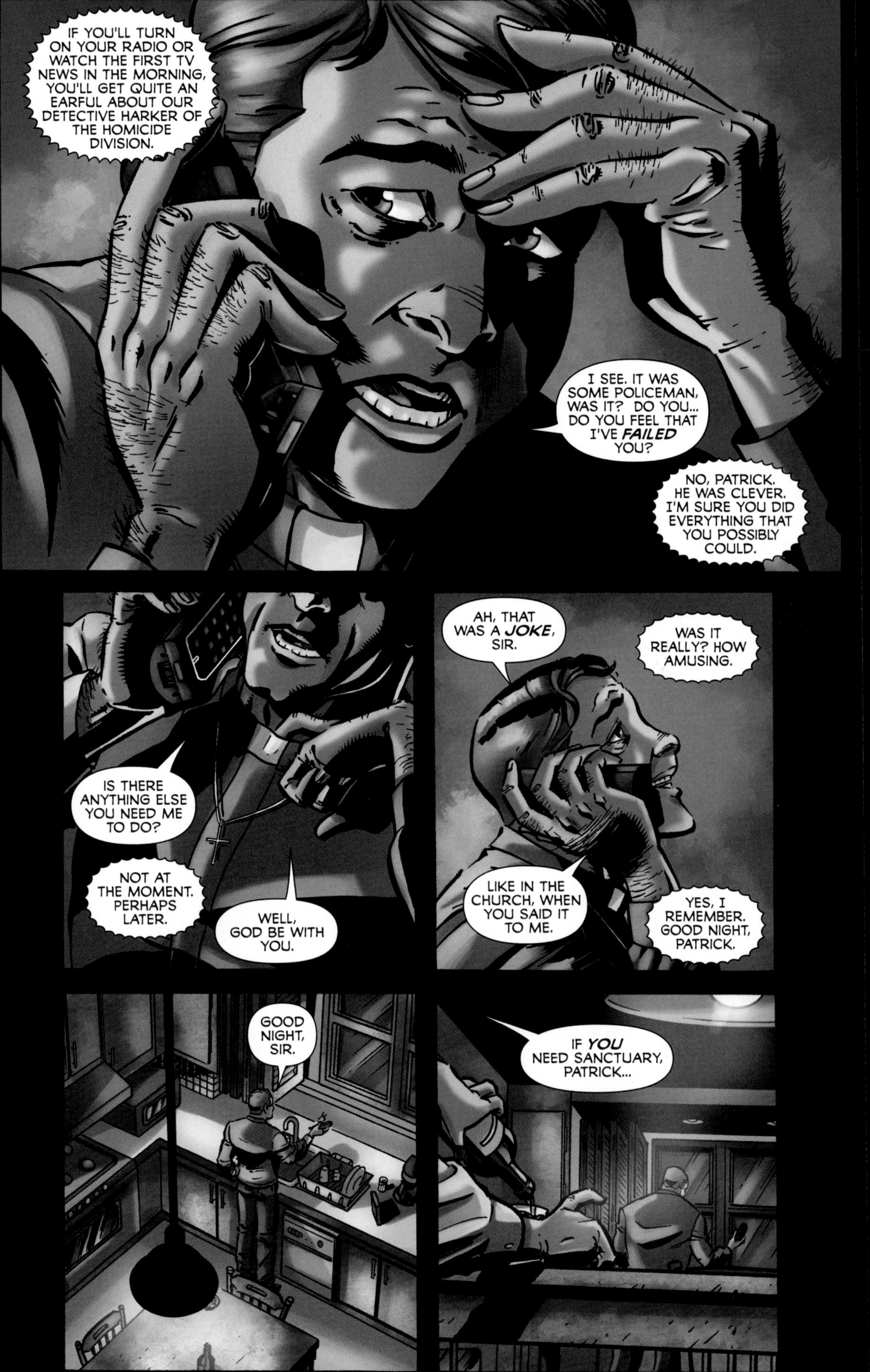
IF YOU'LL TURN ON YOUR RADIO OR WATCH THE FIRST TV NEWS IN THE MORNING, YOU'LL GET QUITE AN EARFUL ABOUT OUR DETECTIVE HARKER OF THE HOMICIDE DIVISION.
I SEE. IT WAS SOME POLICEMAN, WAS IT? DO YOU... DO YOU FEEL THAT I'VE *FAILED* YOU?
NO, PATRICK. HE WAS CLEVER. I'M SURE YOU DID EVERYTHING THAT YOU POSSIBLY COULD.
IS THERE ANYTHING ELSE YOU NEED ME TO DO?
NOT AT THE MOMENT. PERHAPS LATER.
WELL, GOD BE WITH YOU.
AH, THAT WAS A *JOKE*, SIR.
WAS IT REALLY? HOW AMUSING.
LIKE IN THE CHURCH, WHEN YOU SAID IT TO ME.
YES, I REMEMBER. GOOD NIGHT, PATRICK.
GOOD NIGHT, SIR.
IF *YOU* NEED SANCTUARY, PATRICK...

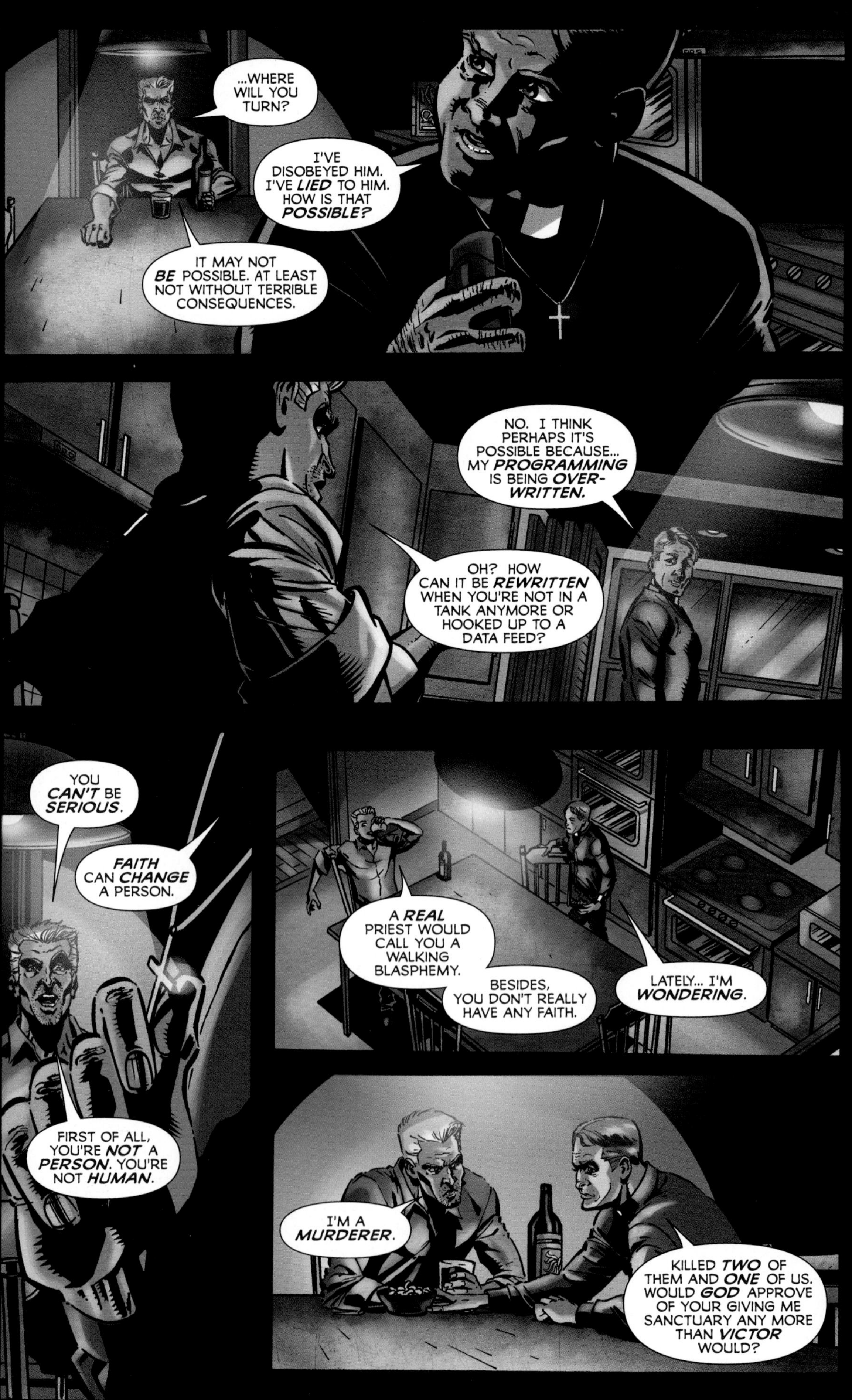
...WHERE WILL YOU TURN?
I'VE DISOBEYED HIM. I'VE LIED TO HIM. HOW IS THAT POSSIBLE?
IT MAY NOT BE POSSIBLE. AT LEAST NOT WITHOUT TERRIBLE CONSEQUENCES.
NO. I THINK PERHAPS IT'S POSSIBLE BECAUSE... MY PROGRAMMING IS BEING OVER-WRITTEN.
OH? HOW CAN IT BE REWRITTEN WHEN YOU'RE NOT IN A TANK ANYMORE OR HOOKED UP TO A DATA FEED?
YOU CAN'T BE SERIOUS.
FAITH CAN CHANGE A PERSON.
FIRST OF ALL, YOU'RE NOT A PERSON. YOU'RE NOT HUMAN.
A REAL PRIEST WOULD CALL YOU A WALKING BLASPHEMY.
BESIDES, YOU DON'T REALLY HAVE ANY FAITH.
LATELY... I'M WONDERING.
I'M A MURDERER.
KILLED TWO OF THEM AND ONE OF US. WOULD GOD APPROVE OF YOUR GIVING ME SANCTUARY ANY MORE THAN VICTOR WOULD?

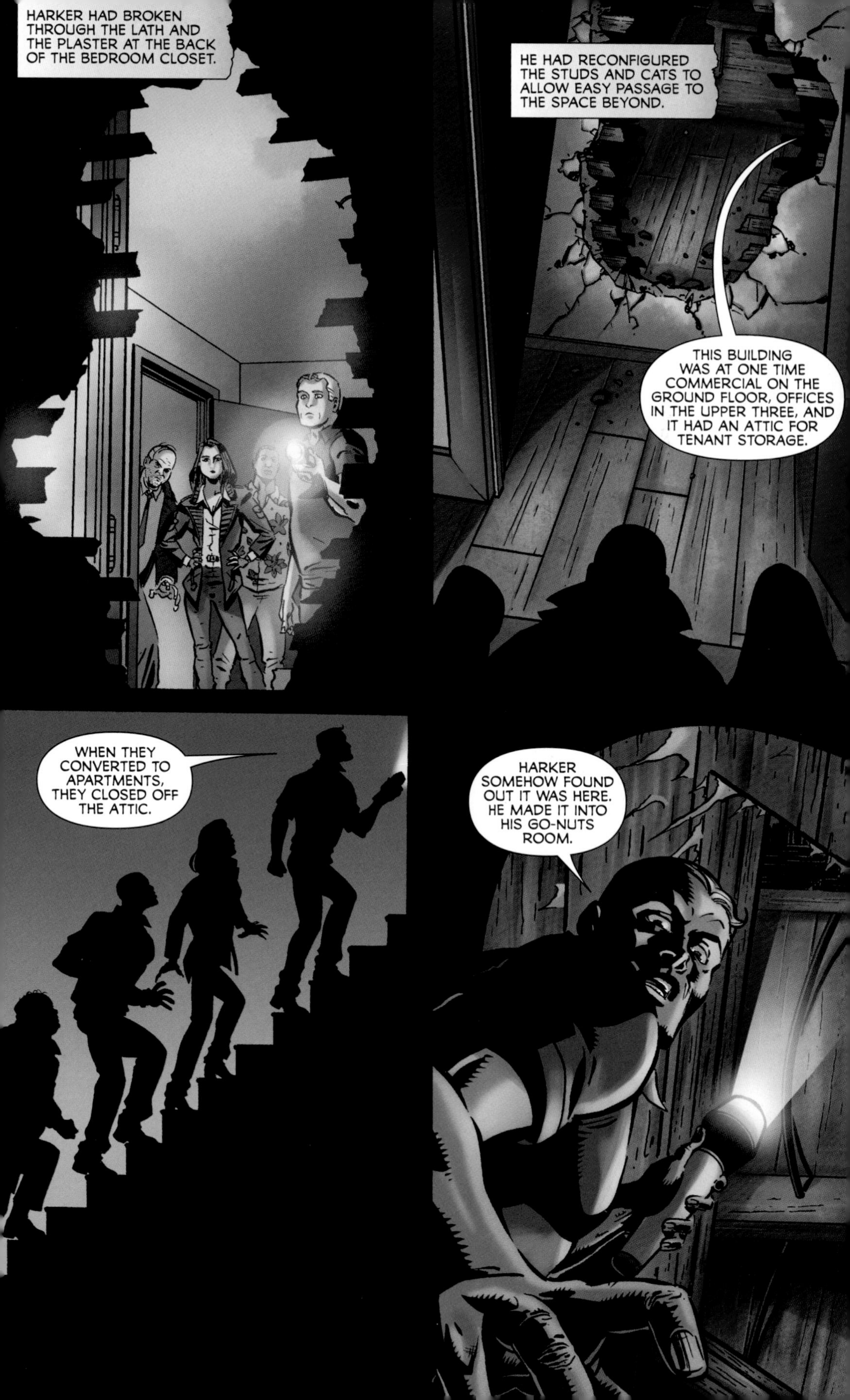
HARKER HAD BROKEN THROUGH THE LATH AND THE PLASTER AT THE BACK OF THE BEDROOM CLOSET.
HE HAD RECONFIGURED THE STUDS AND CATS TO ALLOW EASY PASSAGE TO THE SPACE BEYOND.
THIS BUILDING WAS AT ONE TIME COMMERCIAL ON THE GROUND FLOOR, OFFICES IN THE UPPER THREE, AND IT HAD AN ATTIC FOR TENANT STORAGE.
WHEN THEY CONVERTED TO APARTMENTS, THEY CLOSED OFF THE ATTIC.
HARKER SOMEHOW FOUND OUT IT WAS HERE. HE MADE IT INTO HIS GO-NUTS ROOM.

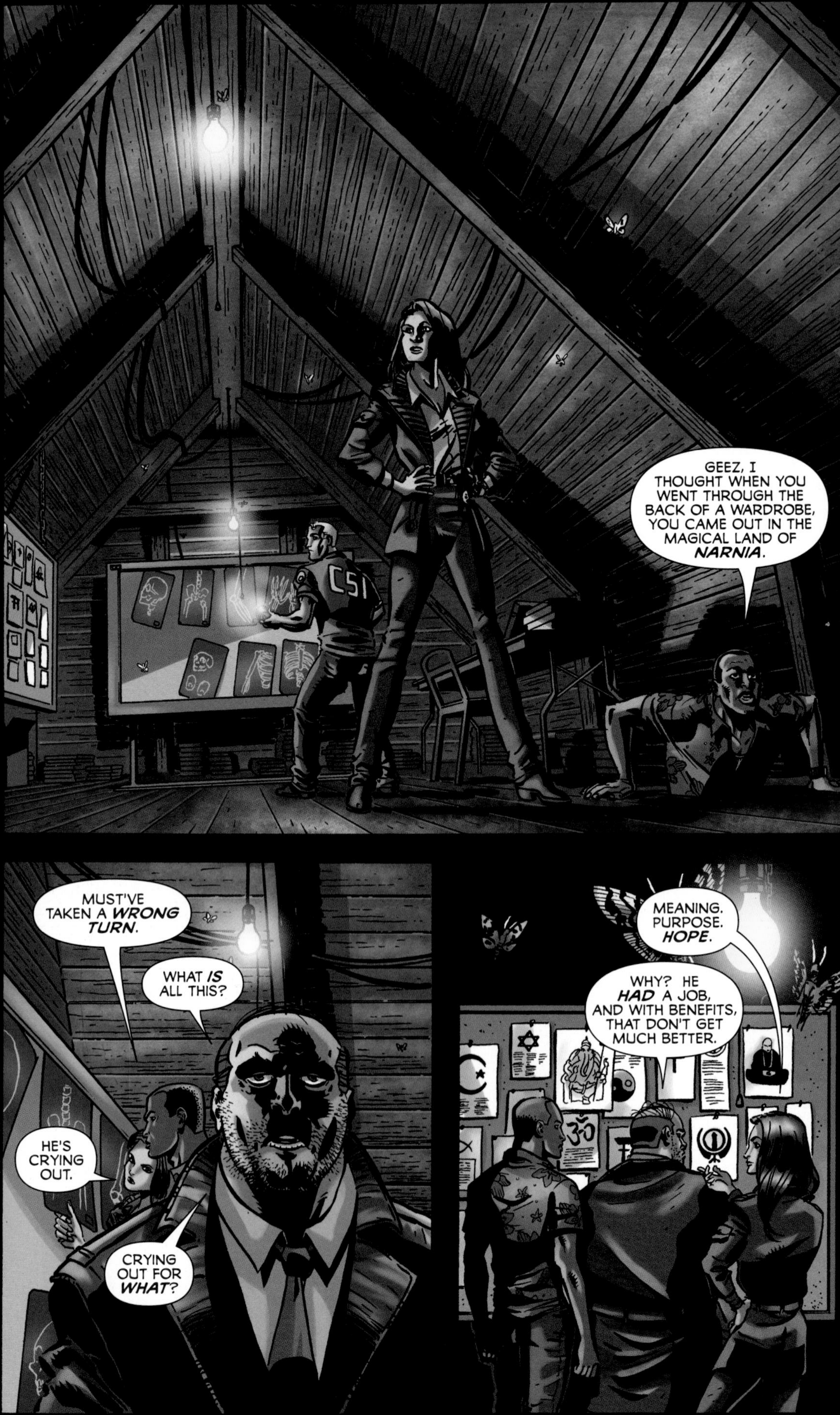

GEEZ, I THOUGHT WHEN YOU WENT THROUGH THE BACK OF A WARDROBE, YOU CAME OUT IN THE MAGICAL LAND OF NARNIA.
MUST'VE TAKEN A WRONG TURN.
WHAT IS ALL THIS?
HE'S CRYING OUT.
CRYING OUT FOR WHAT?
MEANING. PURPOSE. HOPE.
WHY? HE HAD A JOB, AND WITH BENEFITS, THAT DON'T GET MUCH BETTER.

RANDAL SIX STANDS MOTIONLESS AT THE THRESHOLD OF THE NEXT ROOM FOR SO LONG, SO TENSELY, THAT HIS LEGS BEGIN TO ACHE.

THE NEW RACE DOES NOT EASILY *FATIGUE*. THIS IS RANDAL SIX'S *FIRST* EXPERIENCE WITH MUSCLE CRAMPS. THEY BURN SO INTENSELY THAT AT LAST HE TAKES ADVANTAGE OF HIS ABILITY TO BLOCK PAIN AT WILL.

HE ESTIMATES THAT HE HAS STOOD IN THIS SAME SPOT, RIVETED BY HIS PLIGHT, FOR PERHAPS THREE HOURS.

HE *DESPISES* HIMSELF FOR HIS INADEQUACIES.

AT LEAST HE HAS STOPPED WEEPING.

GRADUALLY, HIS IMPATIENCE WITH HIMSELF DARKENS INTO AN INTENSE ANGER AT ARNIE O'CONNOR. IF NOT FOR ARNIE, RANDAL SIX WOULD NOT BE IN THIS PLIGHT.

IF HE EVER REACHES THE O'CONNOR BOY, HE *WILL* GET THE SECRET OF HAPPINESS FROM HIM. AND THEN HE WILL MAKE ARNIE PAY *DEARLY* FOR ALL THIS SUFFERING.

RANDAL IS ALSO PLAGUED BY ANXIETY. HE FEARS FATHER WILL DISCOVER HIM MISSING AND SET OUT IN SEARCH OF HIM.

OR PERHAPS FATHER WILL FINISH HIS WORK AND LEAVE FOR THE NIGHT, ONLY TO FIND RANDAL STANDING HERE IN AUTISTIC INDECISION.

ALTHOUGH HE HAS NEVER SEEN FATHER IN A RAGE, HE HAS HEARD OTHERS SPEAK OF THE MAKER'S WRATH. THERE IS NO *HIDING* FROM HIM AND NO *MERCY*.

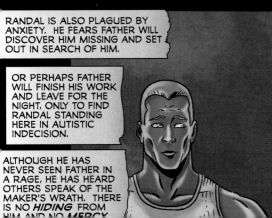

WHEN RANDAL THINKS HE HEARS THE SOUND OF A DOOR OPENING AT THE FARTHER END OF THE HALL, BEHIND HIM, HE CLOSES HIS EYES AND WAITS WITH *DREAD*.

TIME PASSES.

FATHER DOES NOT APPEAR.

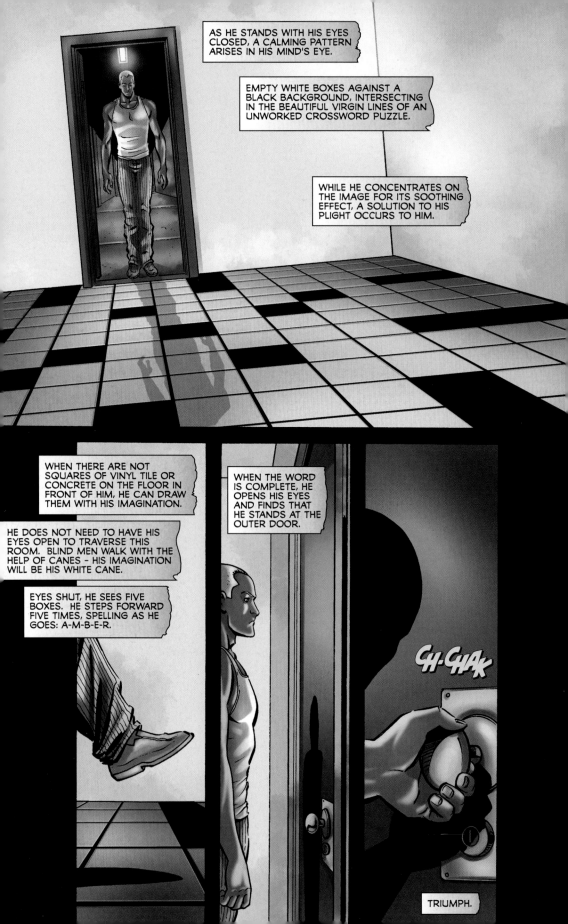

AS HE STANDS WITH HIS EYES CLOSED, A CALMING PATTERN ARISES IN HIS MIND'S EYE.

EMPTY WHITE BOXES AGAINST A BLACK BACKGROUND, INTERSECTING IN THE BEAUTIFUL VIRGIN LINES OF AN UNWORKED CROSSWORD PUZZLE.

WHILE HE CONCENTRATES ON THE IMAGE FOR ITS SOOTHING EFFECT, A SOLUTION TO HIS PLIGHT OCCURS TO HIM.

WHEN THERE ARE NOT SQUARES OF VINYL TILE OR CONCRETE ON THE FLOOR IN FRONT OF HIM, HE CAN DRAW THEM WITH HIS IMAGINATION.

HE DOES NOT NEED TO HAVE HIS EYES OPEN TO TRAVERSE THIS ROOM. BLIND MEN WALK WITH THE HELP OF CANES – HIS IMAGINATION WILL BE HIS WHITE CANE.

EYES SHUT, HE SEES FIVE BOXES. HE STEPS FORWARD FIVE TIMES, SPELLING AS HE GOES: A-M-B-E-R.

WHEN THE WORD IS COMPLETE, HE OPENS HIS EYES AND FINDS THAT HE STANDS AT THE OUTER DOOR.

CH-CHAK

TRIUMPH.

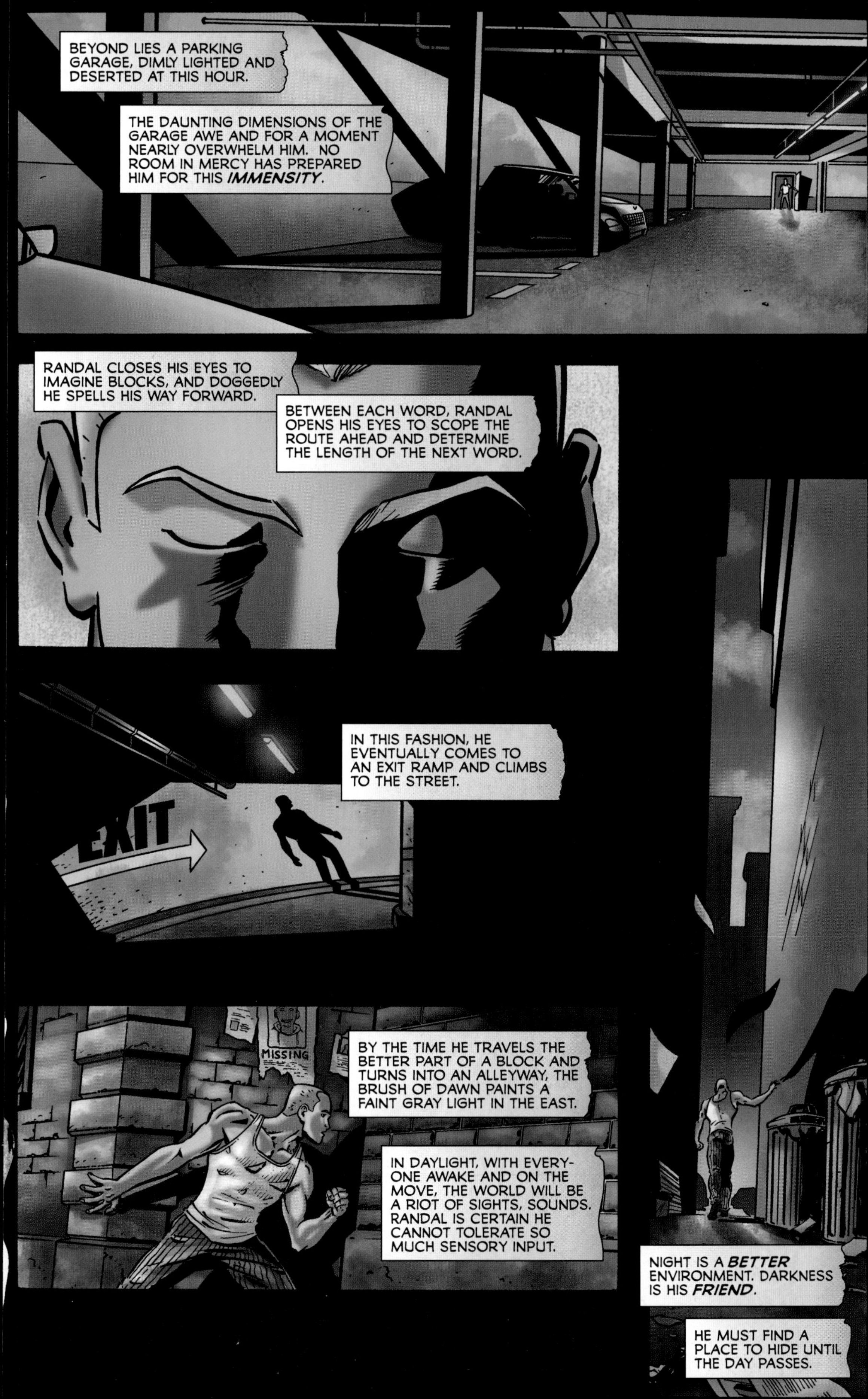
BEYOND LIES A PARKING GARAGE, DIMLY LIGHTED AND DESERTED AT THIS HOUR.
THE DAUNTING DIMENSIONS OF THE GARAGE AWE AND FOR A MOMENT NEARLY OVERWHELM HIM. NO ROOM IN MERCY HAS PREPARED HIM FOR THIS *IMMENSITY*.
RANDAL CLOSES HIS EYES TO IMAGINE BLOCKS, AND DOGGEDLY HE SPELLS HIS WAY FORWARD.
BETWEEN EACH WORD, RANDAL OPENS HIS EYES TO SCOPE THE ROUTE AHEAD AND DETERMINE THE LENGTH OF THE NEXT WORD.
IN THIS FASHION, HE EVENTUALLY COMES TO AN EXIT RAMP AND CLIMBS TO THE STREET.
EXIT
MISSING
BY THE TIME HE TRAVELS THE BETTER PART OF A BLOCK AND TURNS INTO AN ALLEYWAY, THE BRUSH OF DAWN PAINTS A FAINT GRAY LIGHT IN THE EAST.
IN DAYLIGHT, WITH EVERY-ONE AWAKE AND ON THE MOVE, THE WORLD WILL BE A RIOT OF SIGHTS, SOUNDS. RANDAL IS CERTAIN HE CANNOT TOLERATE SO MUCH SENSORY INPUT.
NIGHT IS A *BETTER* ENVIRONMENT. DARKNESS IS HIS *FRIEND*.
HE MUST FIND A PLACE TO HIDE UNTIL THE DAY PASSES.

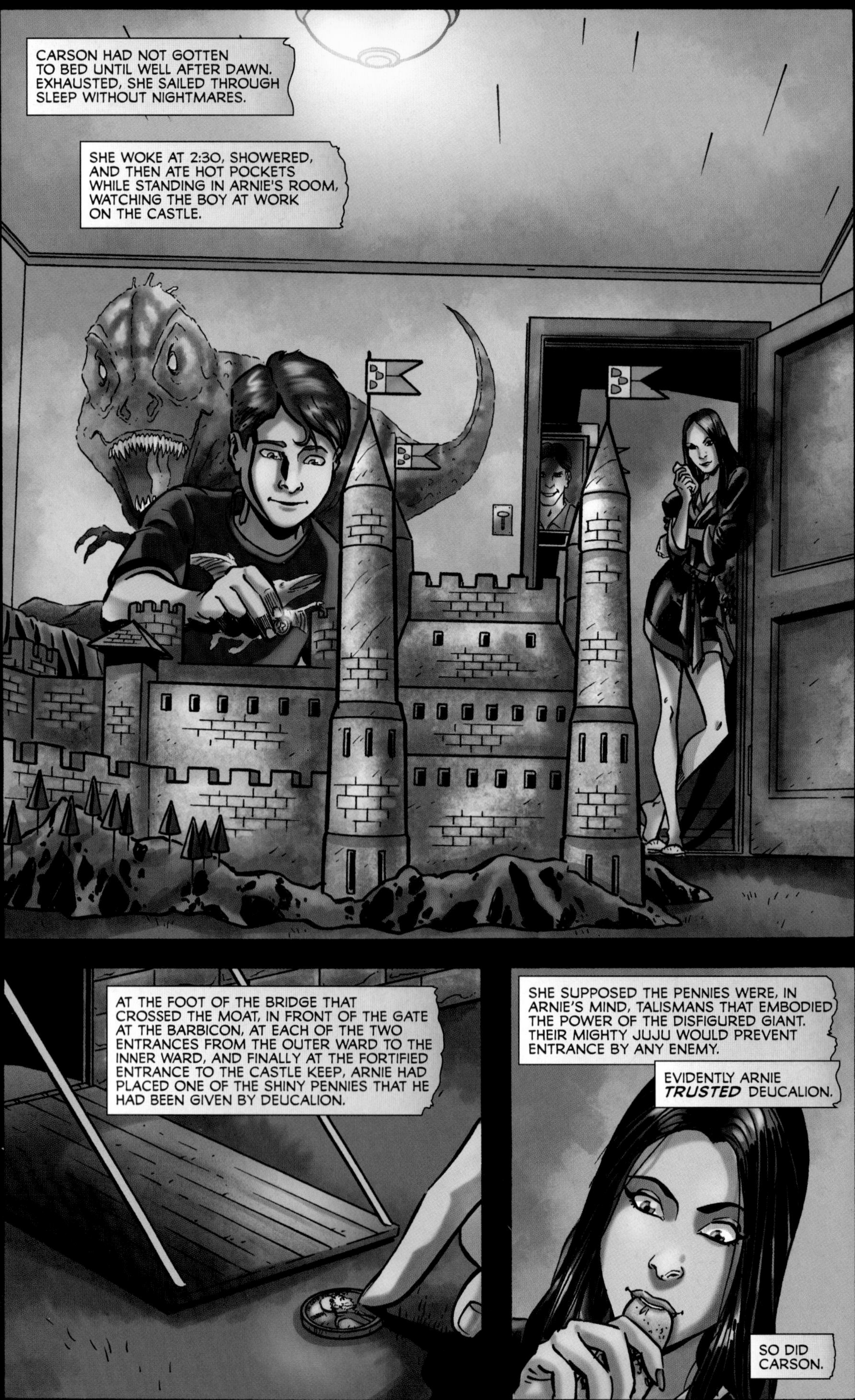
CARSON HAD NOT GOTTEN TO BED UNTIL WELL AFTER DAWN. EXHAUSTED, SHE SAILED THROUGH SLEEP WITHOUT NIGHTMARES.
SHE WOKE AT 2:30, SHOWERED, AND THEN ATE HOT POCKETS WHILE STANDING IN ARNIE'S ROOM, WATCHING THE BOY AT WORK ON THE CASTLE.
AT THE FOOT OF THE BRIDGE THAT CROSSED THE MOAT, IN FRONT OF THE GATE AT THE BARBICON, AT EACH OF THE TWO ENTRANCES FROM THE OUTER WARD TO THE INNER WARD, AND FINALLY AT THE FORTIFIED ENTRANCE TO THE CASTLE KEEP, ARNIE HAD PLACED ONE OF THE SHINY PENNIES THAT HE HAD BEEN GIVEN BY DEUCALION.
SHE SUPPOSED THE PENNIES WERE, IN ARNIE'S MIND, TALISMANS THAT EMBODIED THE POWER OF THE DISFIGURED GIANT. THEIR MIGHTY JUJU WOULD PREVENT ENTRANCE BY ANY ENEMY.
EVIDENTLY ARNIE ***TRUSTED*** DEUCALION.
SO DID CARSON.

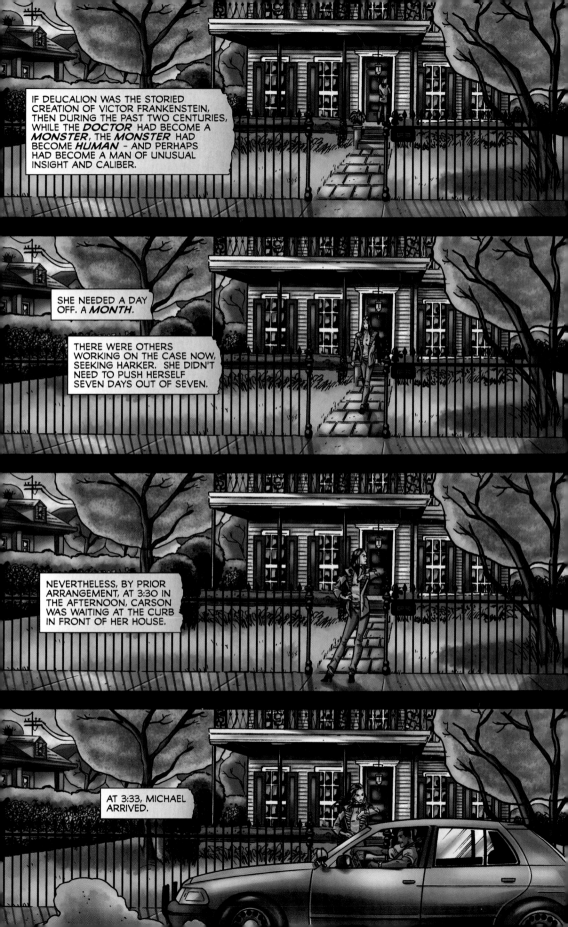

IF DEUCALION WAS THE STORIED CREATION OF VICTOR FRANKENSTEIN, THEN DURING THE PAST TWO CENTURIES, WHILE THE *DOCTOR* HAD BECOME A *MONSTER*, THE *MONSTER* HAD BECOME *HUMAN* – AND PERHAPS HAD BECOME A MAN OF UNUSUAL INSIGHT AND CALIBER.

SHE NEEDED A DAY OFF. A *MONTH*.

THERE WERE OTHERS WORKING ON THE CASE NOW, SEEKING HARKER. SHE DIDN'T NEED TO PUSH HERSELF SEVEN DAYS OUT OF SEVEN.

NEVERTHELESS, BY PRIOR ARRANGEMENT, AT 3:30 IN THE AFTERNOON, CARSON WAS WAITING AT THE CURB IN FRONT OF HER HOUSE.

AT 3:33, MICHAEL ARRIVED.

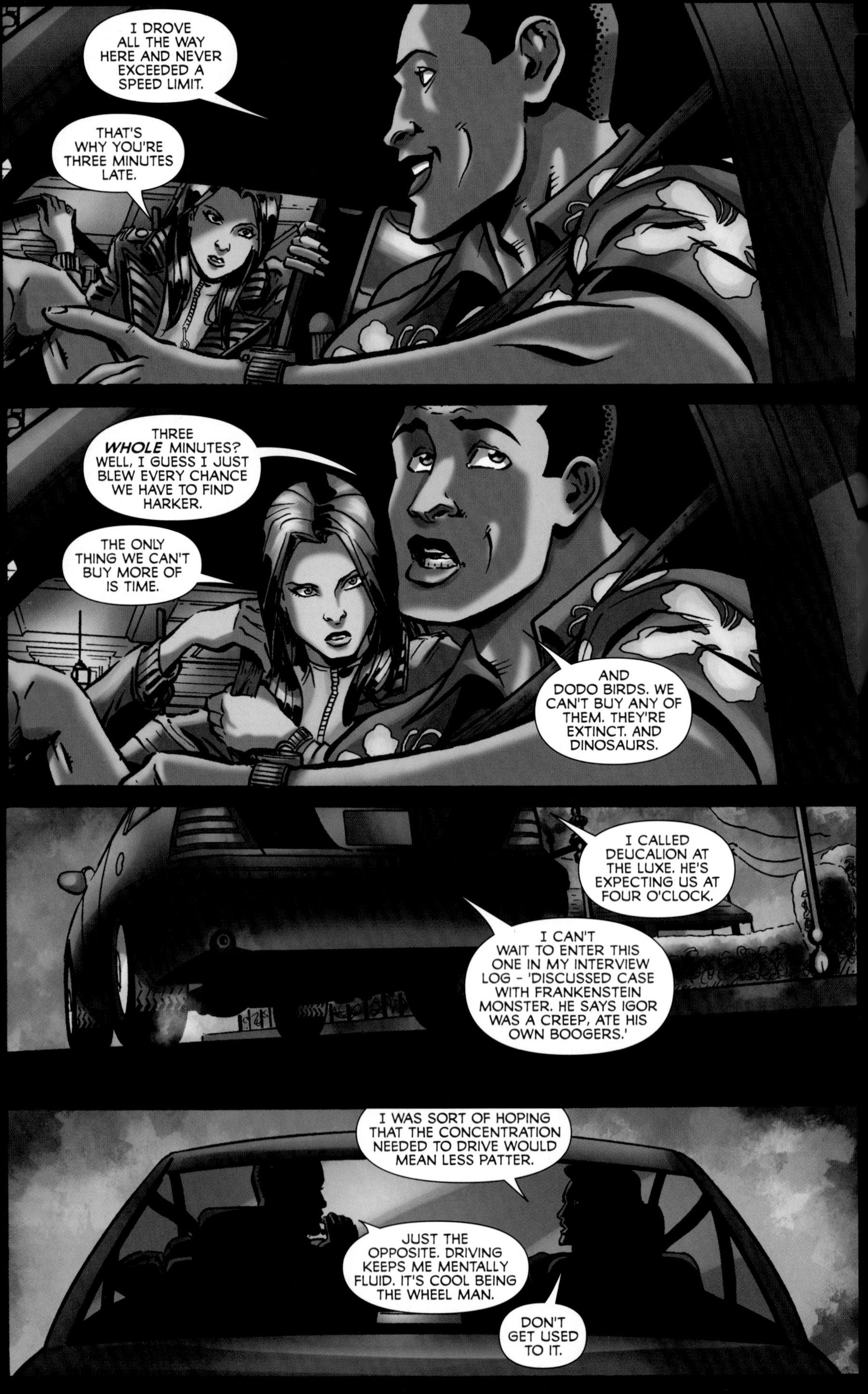

I DROVE ALL THE WAY HERE AND NEVER EXCEEDED A SPEED LIMIT.
THAT'S WHY YOU'RE THREE MINUTES LATE.
THREE *WHOLE* MINUTES? WELL, I GUESS I JUST BLEW EVERY CHANCE WE HAVE TO FIND HARKER.
THE ONLY THING WE CAN'T BUY MORE OF IS TIME.
AND DODO BIRDS. WE CAN'T BUY ANY OF THEM. THEY'RE EXTINCT. AND DINOSAURS.
I CALLED DEUCALION AT THE LUXE. HE'S EXPECTING US AT FOUR O'CLOCK.
I CAN'T WAIT TO ENTER THIS ONE IN MY INTERVIEW LOG - 'DISCUSSED CASE WITH FRANKENSTEIN MONSTER. HE SAYS IGOR WAS A CREEP, ATE HIS OWN BOOGERS.'
I WAS SORT OF HOPING THAT THE CONCENTRATION NEEDED TO DRIVE WOULD MEAN LESS PATTER.
JUST THE OPPOSITE. DRIVING KEEPS ME MENTALLY FLUID. IT'S COOL BEING THE WHEEL MAN.
DON'T GET USED TO IT.

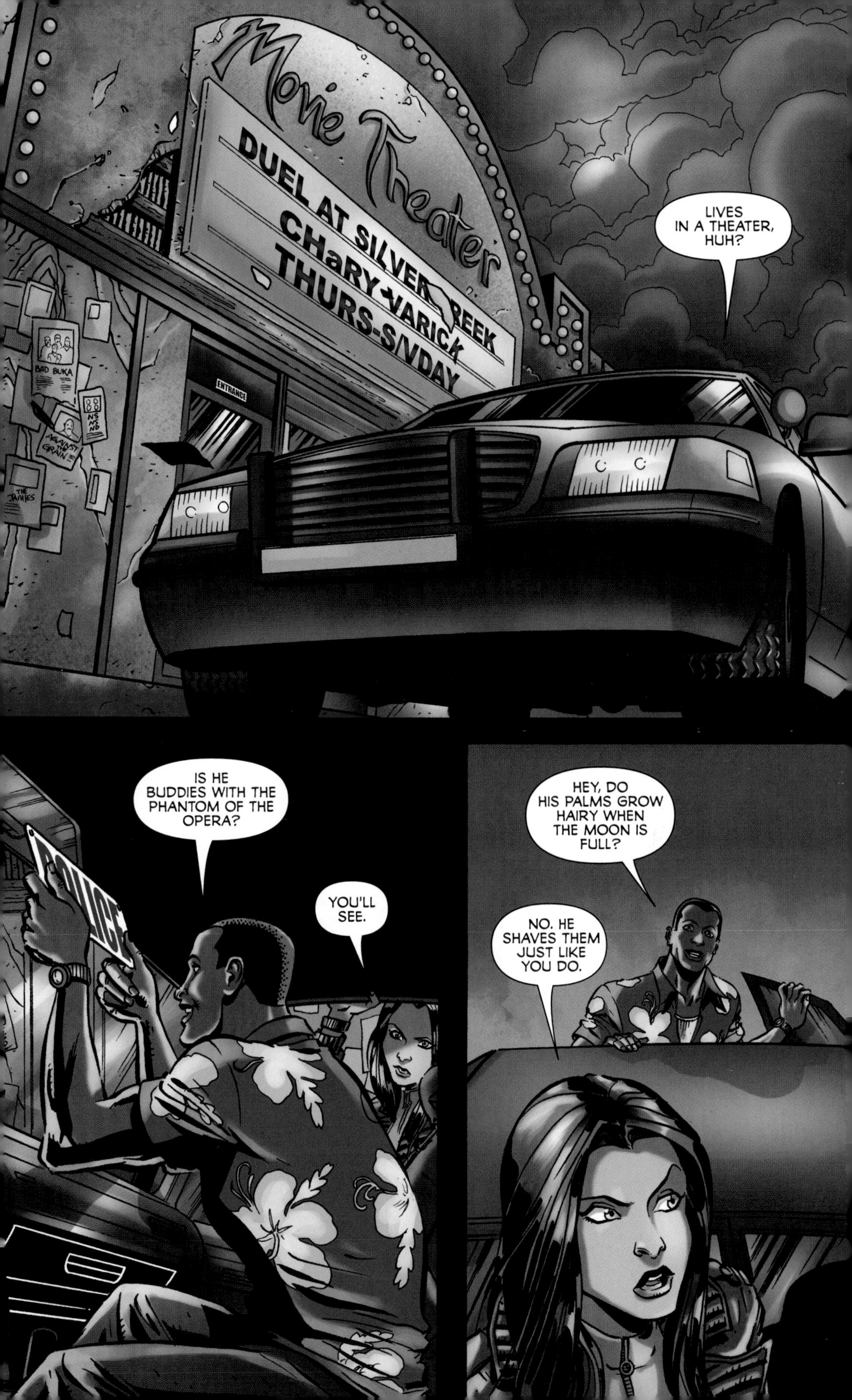
Movie Theater
DUEL AT SILVER REEK
CHaRY-VARICK
THURS-S/VDAY
ENTRANCE
LIVES IN A THEATER, HUH?
IS HE BUDDIES WITH THE PHANTOM OF THE OPERA?
YOU'LL SEE.
HEY, DO HIS PALMS GROW HAIRY WHEN THE MOON IS FULL?
NO. HE SHAVES THEM JUST LIKE YOU DO.

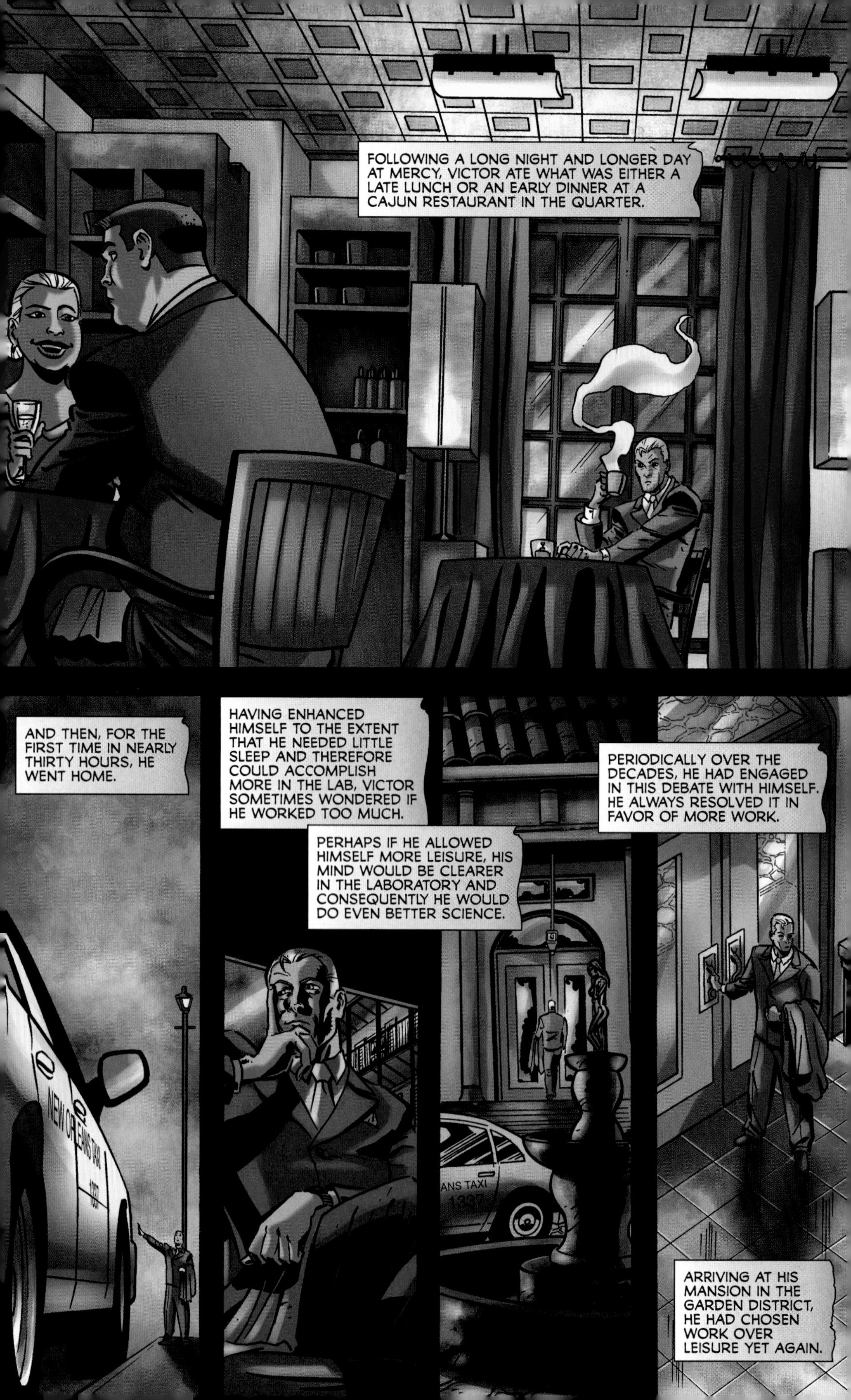
FOLLOWING A LONG NIGHT AND LONGER DAY AT MERCY, VICTOR ATE WHAT WAS EITHER A LATE LUNCH OR AN EARLY DINNER AT A CAJUN RESTAURANT IN THE QUARTER.
AND THEN, FOR THE FIRST TIME IN NEARLY THIRTY HOURS, HE WENT HOME.
HAVING ENHANCED HIMSELF TO THE EXTENT THAT HE NEEDED LITTLE SLEEP AND THEREFORE COULD ACCOMPLISH MORE IN THE LAB, VICTOR SOMETIMES WONDERED IF HE WORKED TOO MUCH.
PERHAPS IF HE ALLOWED HIMSELF MORE LEISURE, HIS MIND WOULD BE CLEARER IN THE LABORATORY AND CONSEQUENTLY HE WOULD DO EVEN BETTER SCIENCE.
PERIODICALLY OVER THE DECADES, HE HAD ENGAGED IN THIS DEBATE WITH HIMSELF. HE ALWAYS RESOLVED IT IN FAVOR OF MORE WORK.
ARRIVING AT HIS MANSION IN THE GARDEN DISTRICT, HE HAD CHOSEN WORK OVER LEISURE YET AGAIN.

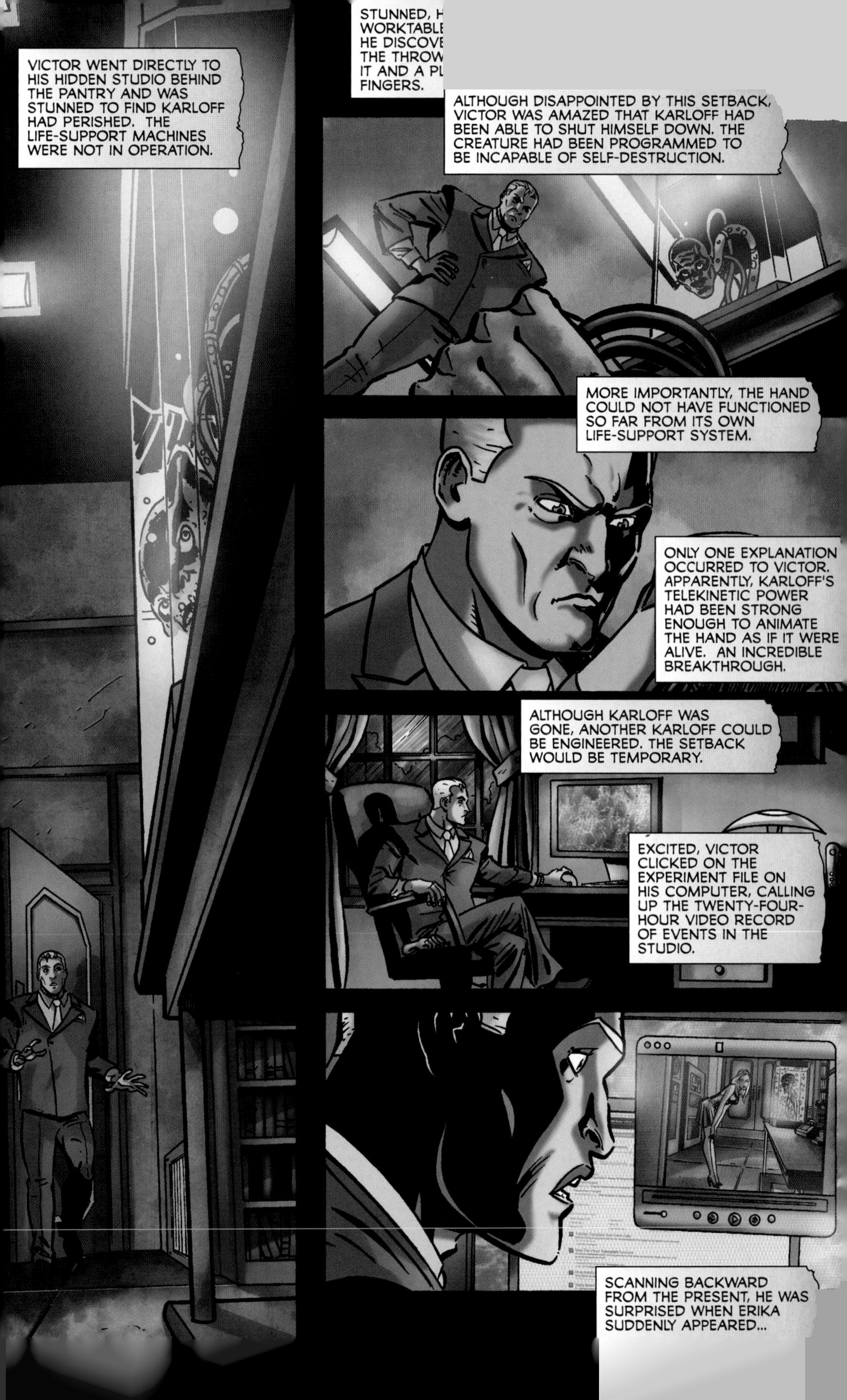
VICTOR WENT DIRECTLY TO HIS HIDDEN STUDIO BEHIND THE PANTRY AND WAS STUNNED TO FIND KARLOFF HAD PERISHED. THE LIFE-SUPPORT MACHINES WERE NOT IN OPERATION.
STUNNED, H WORKTABLE HE DISCOVE THE THROW IT AND A PL FINGERS.
ALTHOUGH DISAPPOINTED BY THIS SETBACK, VICTOR WAS AMAZED THAT KARLOFF HAD BEEN ABLE TO SHUT HIMSELF DOWN. THE CREATURE HAD BEEN PROGRAMMED TO BE INCAPABLE OF SELF-DESTRUCTION.
MORE IMPORTANTLY, THE HAND COULD NOT HAVE FUNCTIONED SO FAR FROM ITS OWN LIFE-SUPPORT SYSTEM.
ONLY ONE EXPLANATION OCCURRED TO VICTOR. APPARENTLY, KARLOFF'S TELEKINETIC POWER HAD BEEN STRONG ENOUGH TO ANIMATE THE HAND AS IF IT WERE ALIVE. AN INCREDIBLE BREAKTHROUGH.
ALTHOUGH KARLOFF WAS GONE, ANOTHER KARLOFF COULD BE ENGINEERED. THE SETBACK WOULD BE TEMPORARY.
EXCITED, VICTOR CLICKED ON THE EXPERIMENT FILE ON HIS COMPUTER, CALLING UP THE TWENTY-FOUR-HOUR VIDEO RECORD OF EVENTS IN THE STUDIO.
SCANNING BACKWARD FROM THE PRESENT, HE WAS SURPRISED WHEN ERIKA SUDDENLY APPEARED...

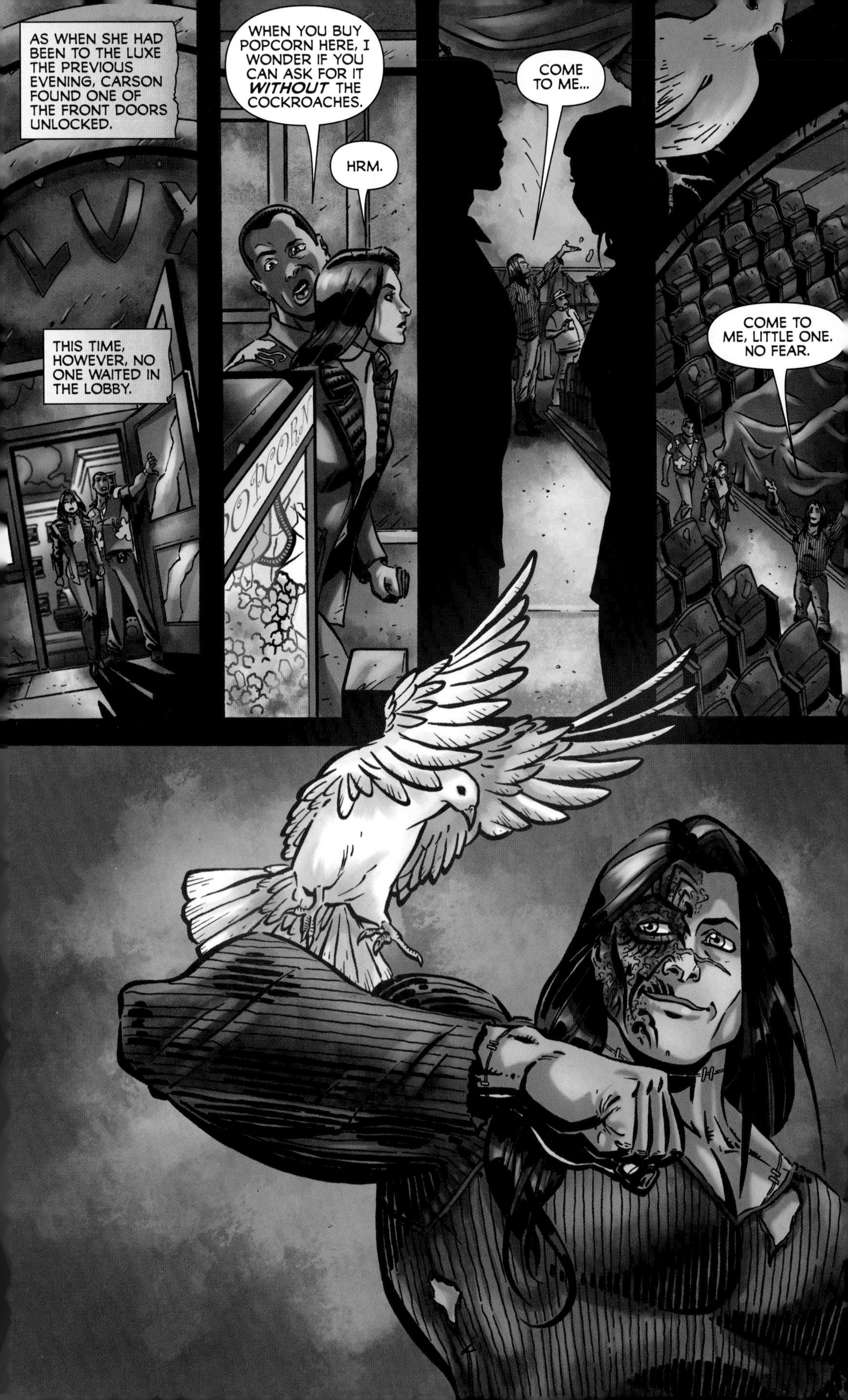
AS WHEN SHE HAD BEEN TO THE LUXE THE PREVIOUS EVENING, CARSON FOUND ONE OF THE FRONT DOORS UNLOCKED.
THIS TIME, HOWEVER, NO ONE WAITED IN THE LOBBY.
WHEN YOU BUY POPCORN HERE, I WONDER IF YOU CAN ASK FOR IT *WITHOUT* THE COCKROACHES.
HRM.
COME TO ME...
COME TO ME, LITTLE ONE. NO FEAR.

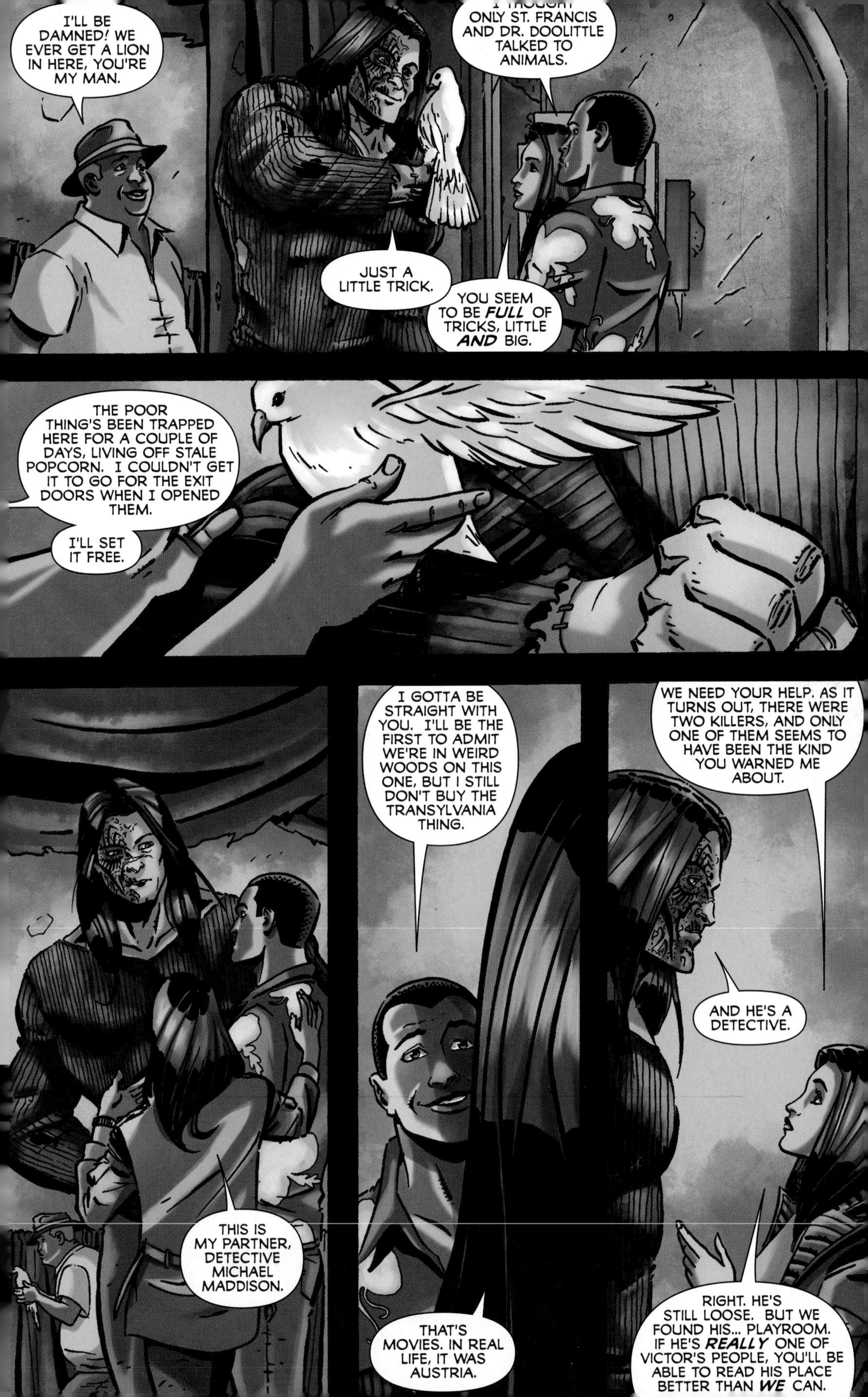

I'LL BE DAMNED! WE EVER GET A LION IN HERE, YOU'RE MY MAN.
ONLY ST. FRANCIS AND DR. DOOLITTLE TALKED TO ANIMALS.
JUST A LITTLE TRICK.
YOU SEEM TO BE FULL OF TRICKS, LITTLE AND BIG.
THE POOR THING'S BEEN TRAPPED HERE FOR A COUPLE OF DAYS, LIVING OFF STALE POPCORN. I COULDN'T GET IT TO GO FOR THE EXIT DOORS WHEN I OPENED THEM.
I'LL SET IT FREE.
THIS IS MY PARTNER, DETECTIVE MICHAEL MADDISON.
I GOTTA BE STRAIGHT WITH YOU. I'LL BE THE FIRST TO ADMIT WE'RE IN WEIRD WOODS ON THIS ONE, BUT I STILL DON'T BUY THE TRANSYLVANIA THING.
THAT'S MOVIES. IN REAL LIFE, IT WAS AUSTRIA.
WE NEED YOUR HELP. AS IT TURNS OUT, THERE WERE TWO KILLERS, AND ONLY ONE OF THEM SEEMS TO HAVE BEEN THE KIND YOU WARNED ME ABOUT.
AND HE'S A DETECTIVE.
RIGHT. HE'S STILL LOOSE. BUT WE FOUND HIS... PLAYROOM. IF HE'S REALLY ONE OF VICTOR'S PEOPLE, YOU'LL BE ABLE TO READ HIS PLACE BETTER THAN WE CAN.

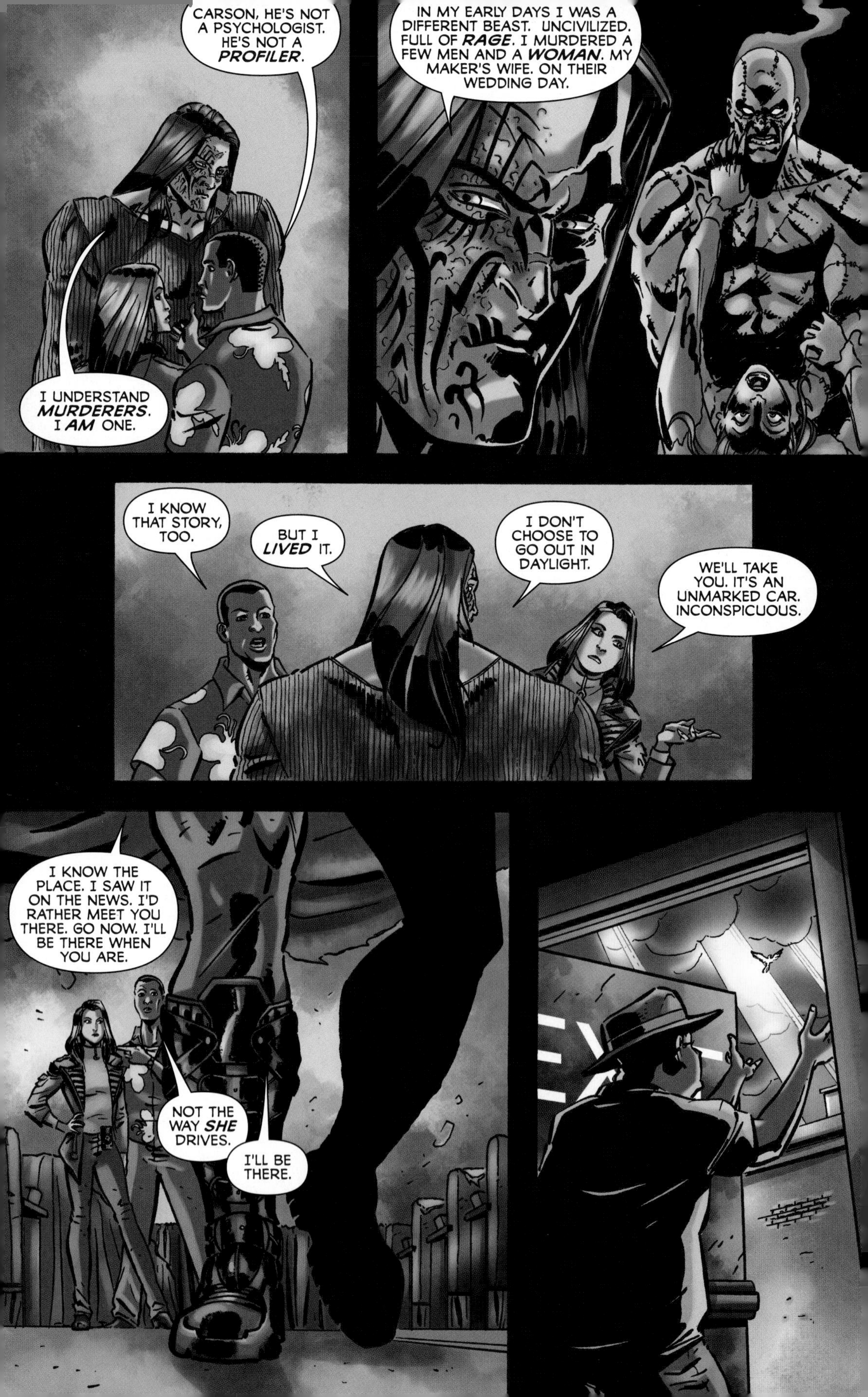
CARSON, HE'S NOT A PSYCHOLOGIST. HE'S NOT A PROFILER.
I UNDERSTAND MURDERERS. I AM ONE.
IN MY EARLY DAYS I WAS A DIFFERENT BEAST. UNCIVILIZED. FULL OF RAGE. I MURDERED A FEW MEN AND A WOMAN. MY MAKER'S WIFE. ON THEIR WEDDING DAY.
I KNOW THAT STORY, TOO.
BUT I LIVED IT.
I DON'T CHOOSE TO GO OUT IN DAYLIGHT.
WE'LL TAKE YOU. IT'S AN UNMARKED CAR. INCONSPICUOUS.
I KNOW THE PLACE. I SAW IT ON THE NEWS. I'D RATHER MEET YOU THERE. GO NOW. I'LL BE THERE WHEN YOU ARE.
NOT THE WAY SHE DRIVES.
I'LL BE THERE.

chapter Four

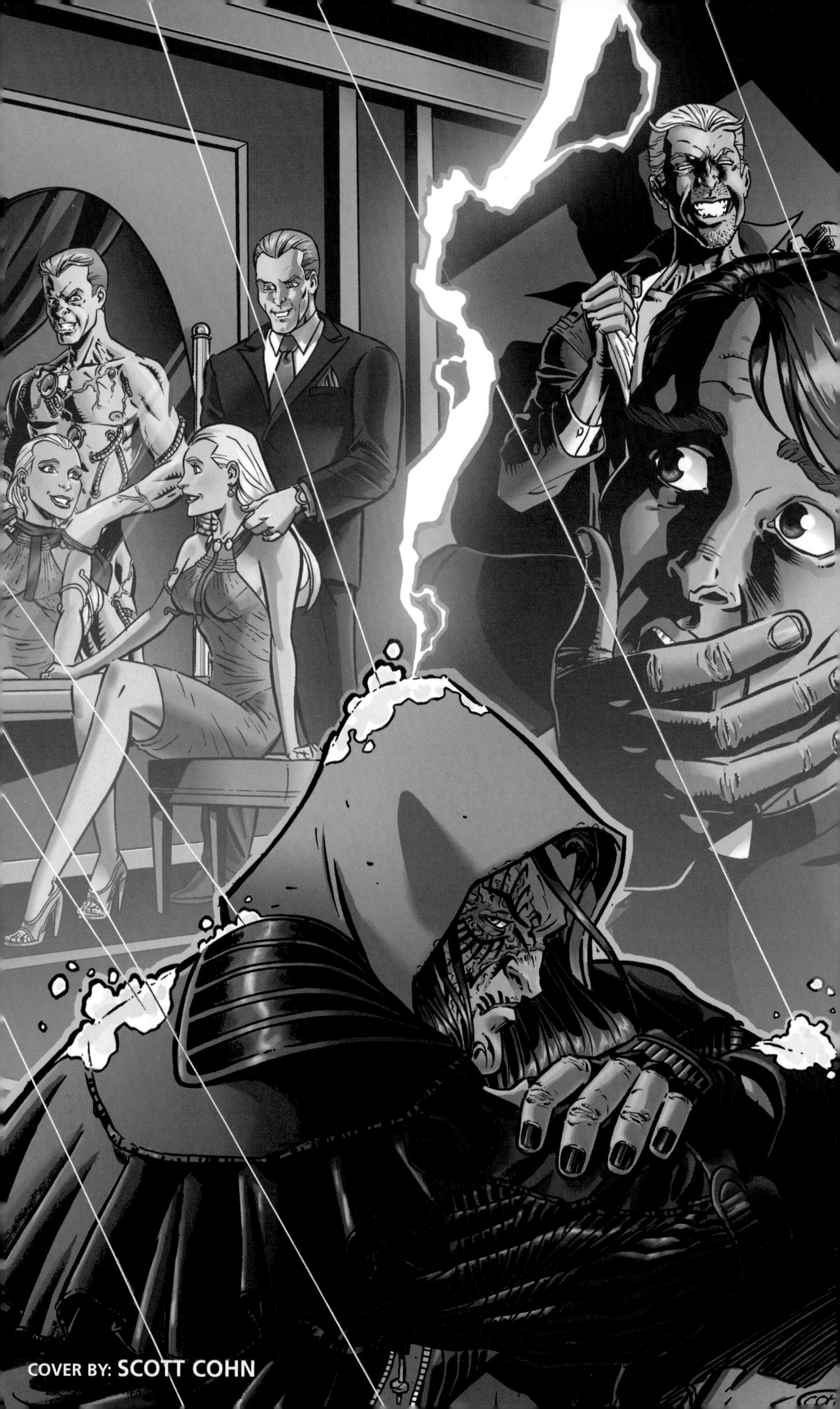

COVER BY: SCOTT COHN

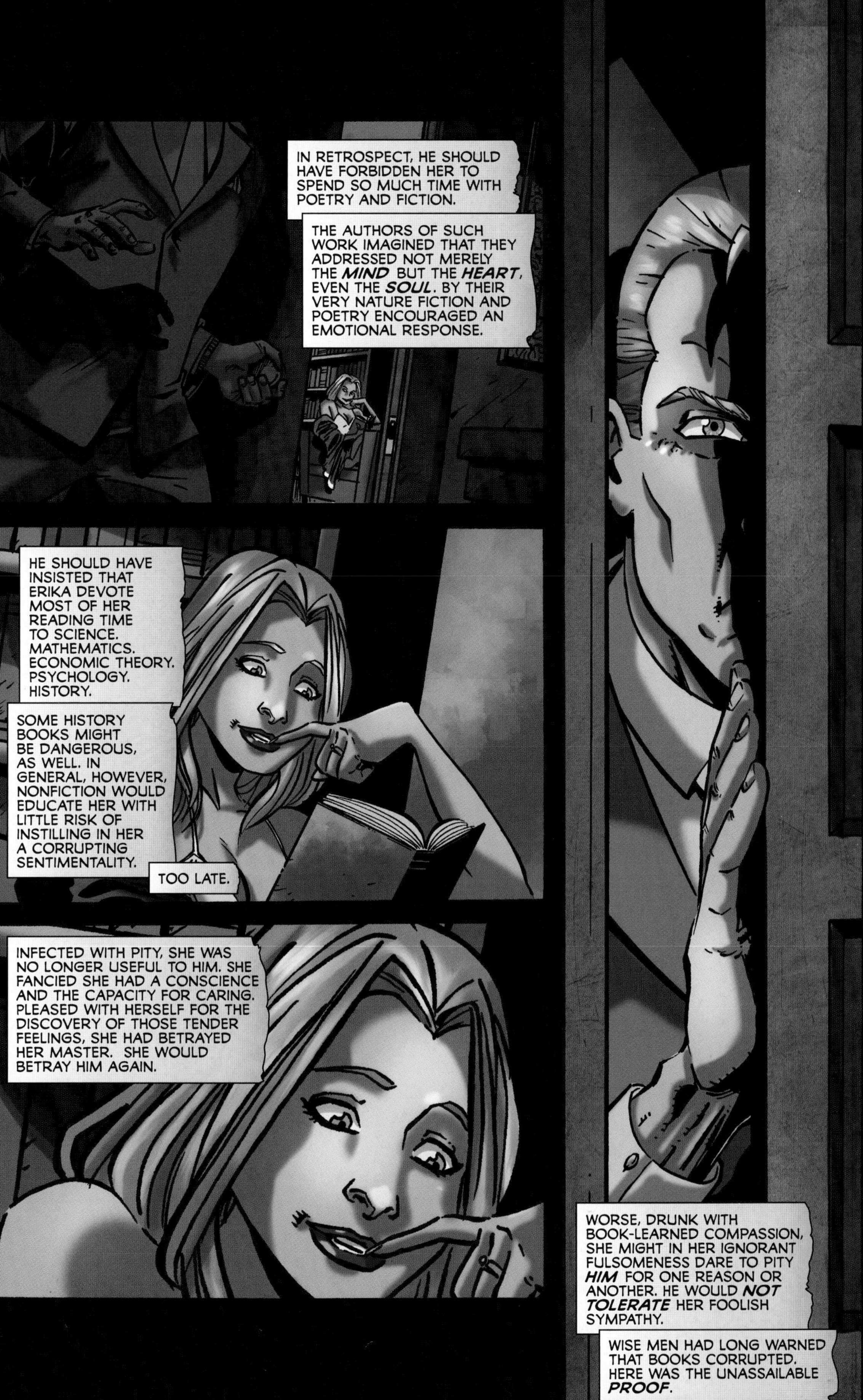
IN RETROSPECT, HE SHOULD HAVE FORBIDDEN HER TO SPEND SO MUCH TIME WITH POETRY AND FICTION.
THE AUTHORS OF SUCH WORK IMAGINED THAT THEY ADDRESSED NOT MERELY THE ***MIND*** BUT THE ***HEART***, EVEN THE ***SOUL***. BY THEIR VERY NATURE FICTION AND POETRY ENCOURAGED AN EMOTIONAL RESPONSE.
HE SHOULD HAVE INSISTED THAT ERIKA DEVOTE MOST OF HER READING TIME TO SCIENCE. MATHEMATICS. ECONOMIC THEORY. PSYCHOLOGY. HISTORY.
SOME HISTORY BOOKS MIGHT BE DANGEROUS, AS WELL. IN GENERAL, HOWEVER, NONFICTION WOULD EDUCATE HER WITH LITTLE RISK OF INSTILLING IN HER A CORRUPTING SENTIMENTALITY.
TOO LATE.
INFECTED WITH PITY, SHE WAS NO LONGER USEFUL TO HIM. SHE FANCIED SHE HAD A CONSCIENCE AND THE CAPACITY FOR CARING. PLEASED WITH HERSELF FOR THE DISCOVERY OF THOSE TENDER FEELINGS, SHE HAD BETRAYED HER MASTER. SHE WOULD BETRAY HIM AGAIN.
WORSE, DRUNK WITH BOOK-LEARNED COMPASSION, SHE MIGHT IN HER IGNORANT FULSOMENESS DARE TO PITY ***HIM*** FOR ONE REASON OR ANOTHER. HE WOULD ***NOT TOLERATE*** HER FOOLISH SYMPATHY.
WISE MEN HAD LONG WARNED THAT BOOKS CORRUPTED. HERE WAS THE UNASSAILABLE ***PROOF***.

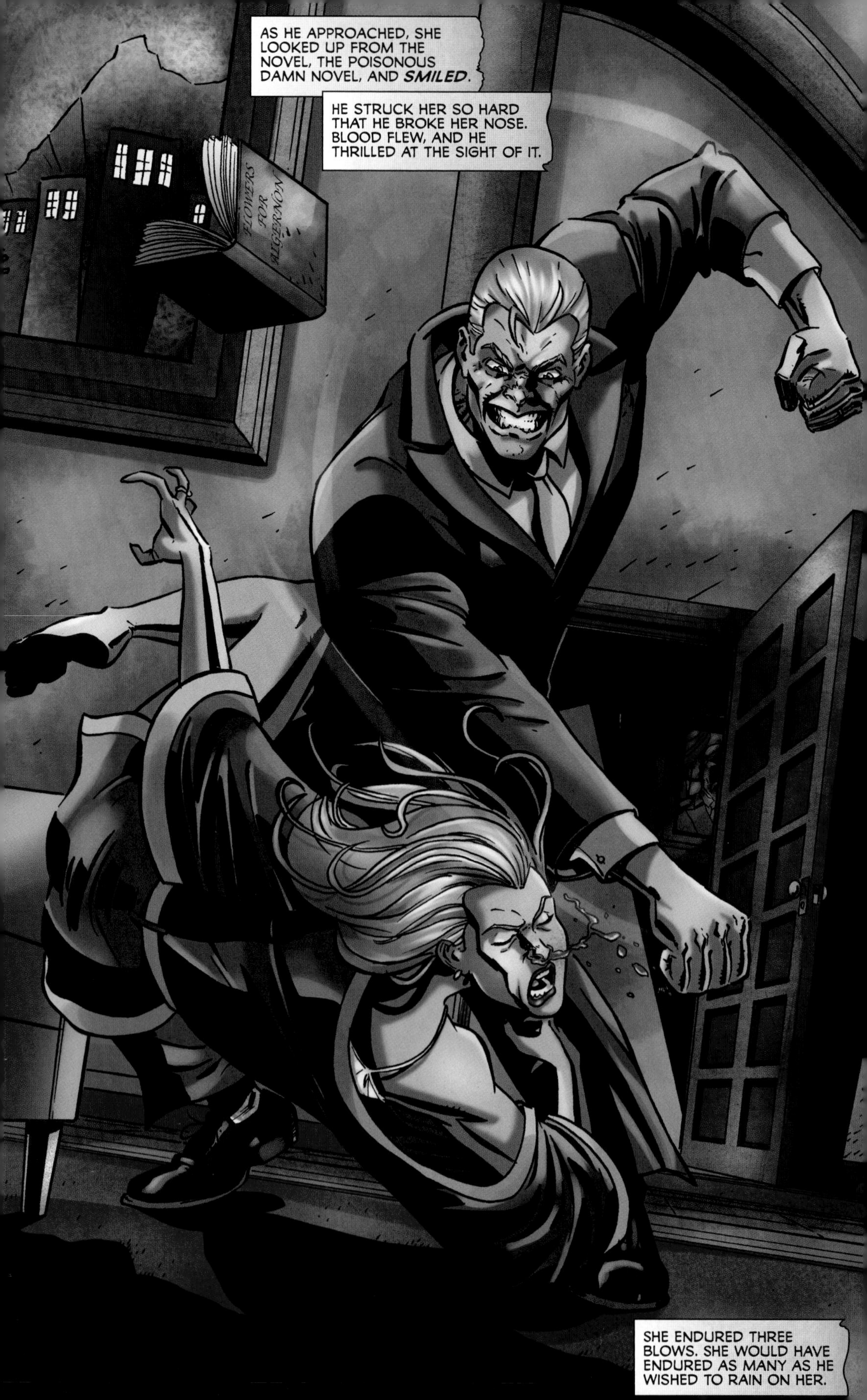
AS HE APPROACHED, SHE LOOKED UP FROM THE NOVEL, THE POISONOUS DAMN NOVEL, AND *SMILED*.
HE STRUCK HER SO HARD THAT HE BROKE HER NOSE. BLOOD FLEW, AND HE THRILLED AT THE SIGHT OF IT.
FLOWERS FOR ALGERNON
SHE ENDURED THREE BLOWS. SHE WOULD HAVE ENDURED AS MANY AS HE WISHED TO RAIN ON HER.

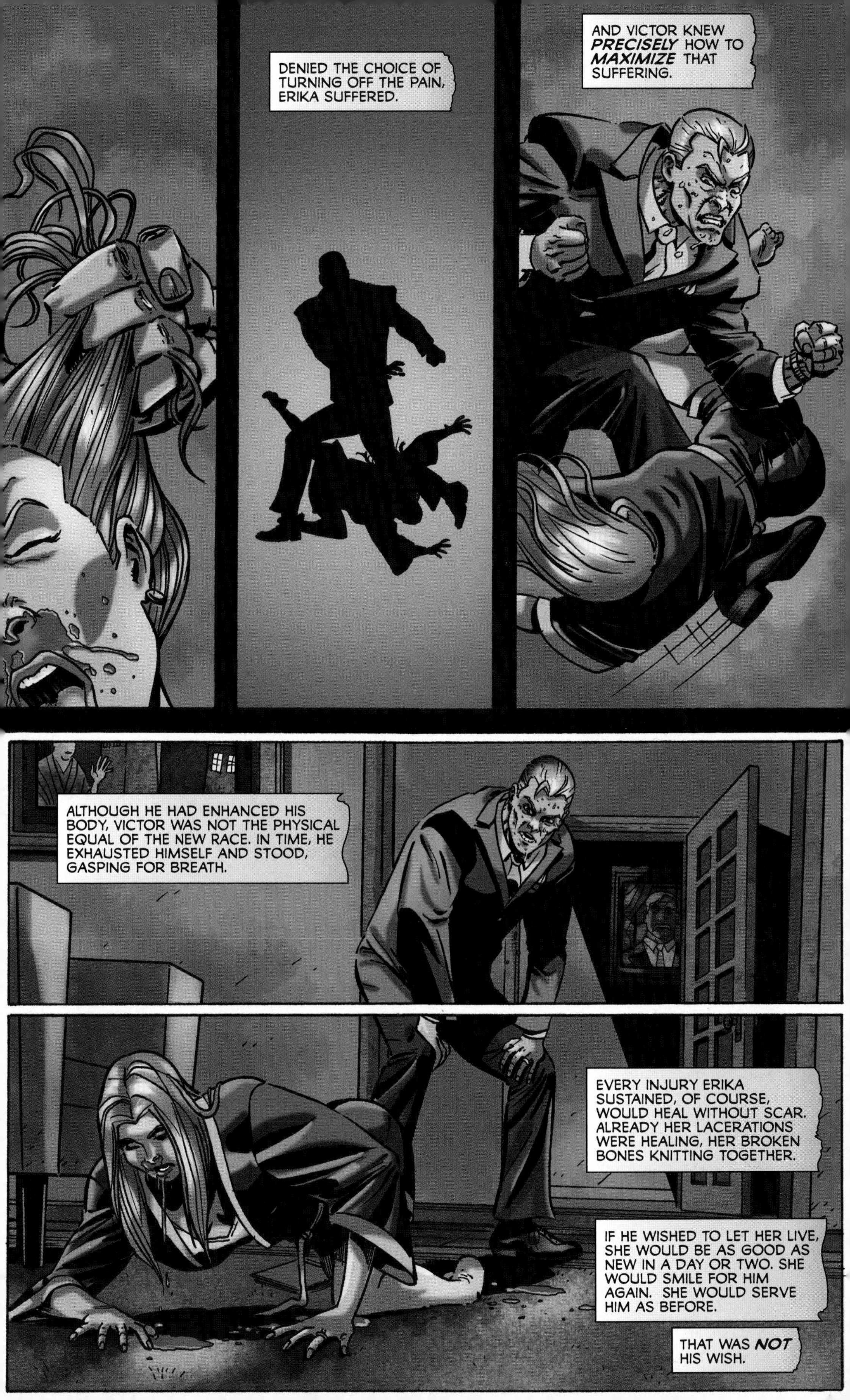
DENIED THE CHOICE OF TURNING OFF THE PAIN, ERIKA SUFFERED.
AND VICTOR KNEW *PRECISELY* HOW TO *MAXIMIZE* THAT SUFFERING.
ALTHOUGH HE HAD ENHANCED HIS BODY, VICTOR WAS NOT THE PHYSICAL EQUAL OF THE NEW RACE. IN TIME, HE EXHAUSTED HIMSELF AND STOOD, GASPING FOR BREATH.
EVERY INJURY ERIKA SUSTAINED, OF COURSE, WOULD HEAL WITHOUT SCAR. ALREADY HER LACERATIONS WERE HEALING, HER BROKEN BONES KNITTING TOGETHER.
IF HE WISHED TO LET HER LIVE, SHE WOULD BE AS GOOD AS NEW IN A DAY OR TWO. SHE WOULD SMILE FOR HIM AGAIN. SHE WOULD SERVE HIM AS BEFORE.
THAT WAS *NOT* HIS WISH.

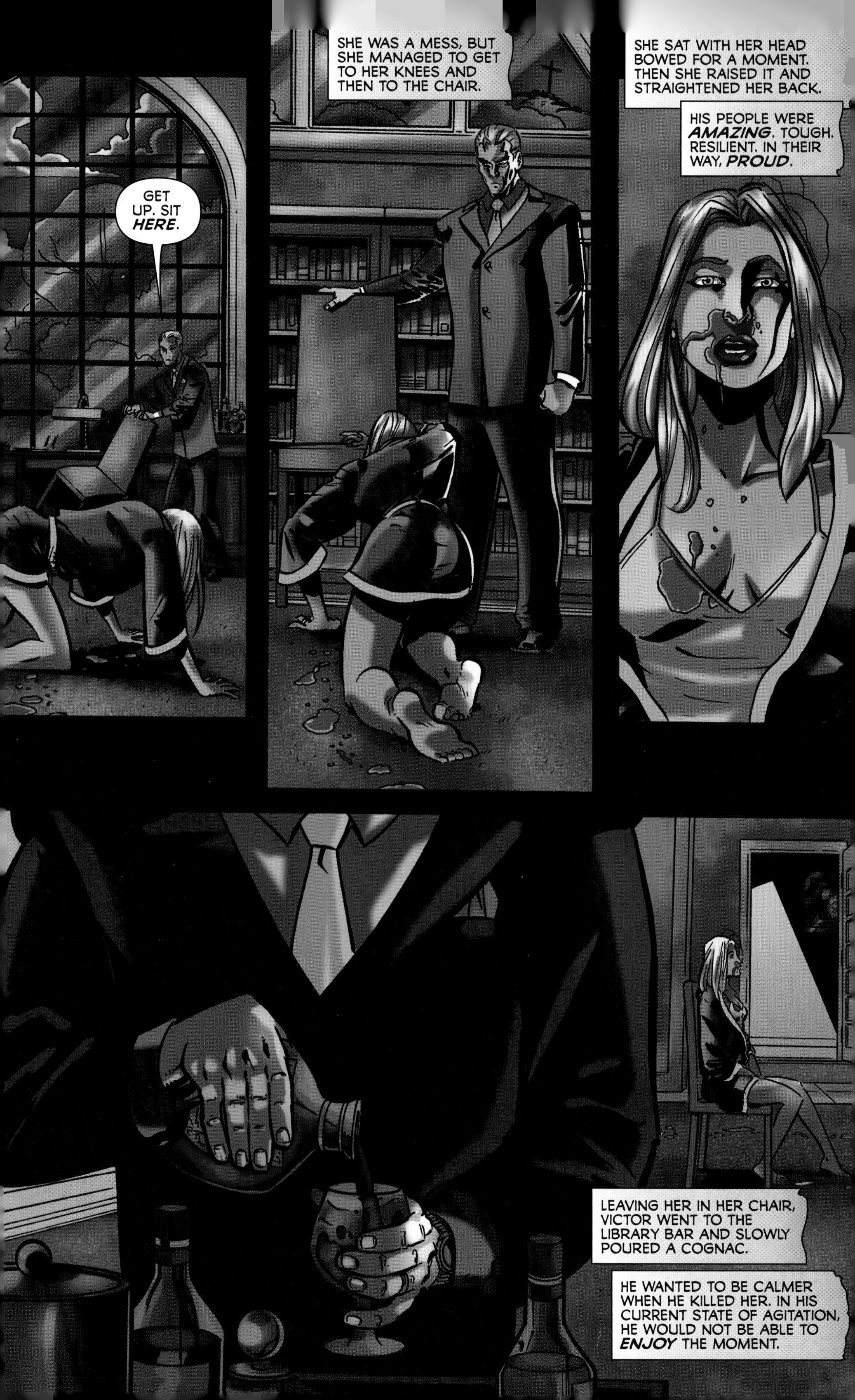
GET UP. SIT *HERE*.
SHE WAS A MESS, BUT SHE MANAGED TO GET TO HER KNEES AND THEN TO THE CHAIR.
SHE SAT WITH HER HEAD BOWED FOR A MOMENT. THEN SHE RAISED IT AND STRAIGHTENED HER BACK.
HIS PEOPLE WERE ***AMAZING***. TOUGH. RESILIENT. IN THEIR WAY, ***PROUD***.
LEAVING HER IN HER CHAIR, VICTOR WENT TO THE LIBRARY BAR AND SLOWLY POURED A COGNAC.
HE WANTED TO BE CALMER WHEN HE KILLED HER. IN HIS CURRENT STATE OF AGITATION, HE WOULD NOT BE ABLE TO ***ENJOY*** THE MOMENT.

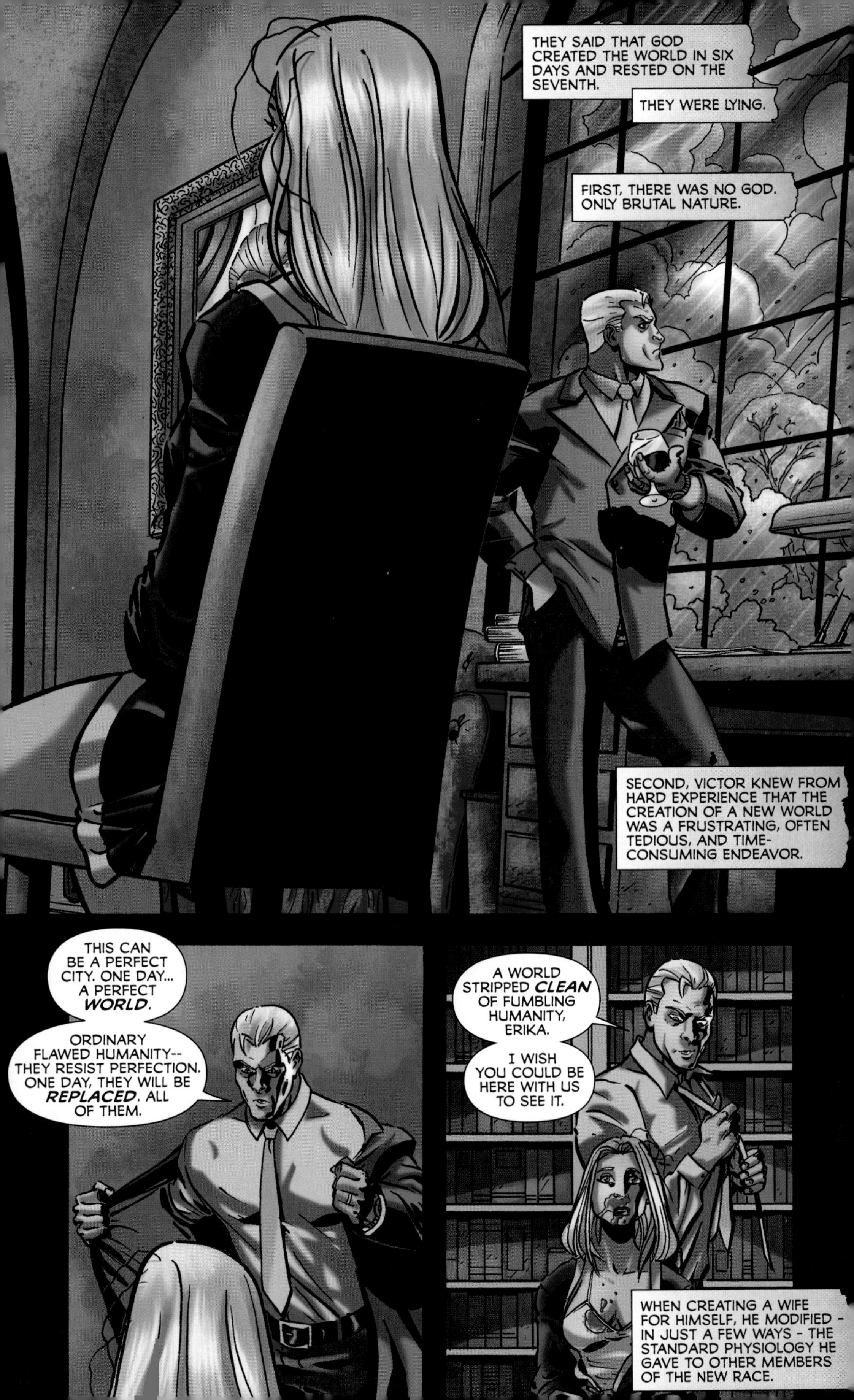
THEY SAID THAT GOD CREATED THE WORLD IN SIX DAYS AND RESTED ON THE SEVENTH.
THEY WERE LYING.
FIRST, THERE WAS NO GOD. ONLY BRUTAL NATURE.
SECOND, VICTOR KNEW FROM HARD EXPERIENCE THAT THE CREATION OF A NEW WORLD WAS A FRUSTRATING, OFTEN TEDIOUS, AND TIME-CONSUMING ENDEAVOR.
THIS CAN BE A PERFECT CITY. ONE DAY... A PERFECT *WORLD*.
ORDINARY FLAWED HUMANITY-- THEY RESIST PERFECTION. ONE DAY, THEY WILL BE *REPLACED*. ALL OF THEM.
A WORLD STRIPPED *CLEAN* OF FUMBLING HUMANITY, ERIKA.
I WISH YOU COULD BE HERE WITH US TO SEE IT.
WHEN CREATING A WIFE FOR HIMSELF, HE MODIFIED - IN JUST A FEW WAYS - THE STANDARD PHYSIOLOGY HE GAVE TO OTHER MEMBERS OF THE NEW RACE.

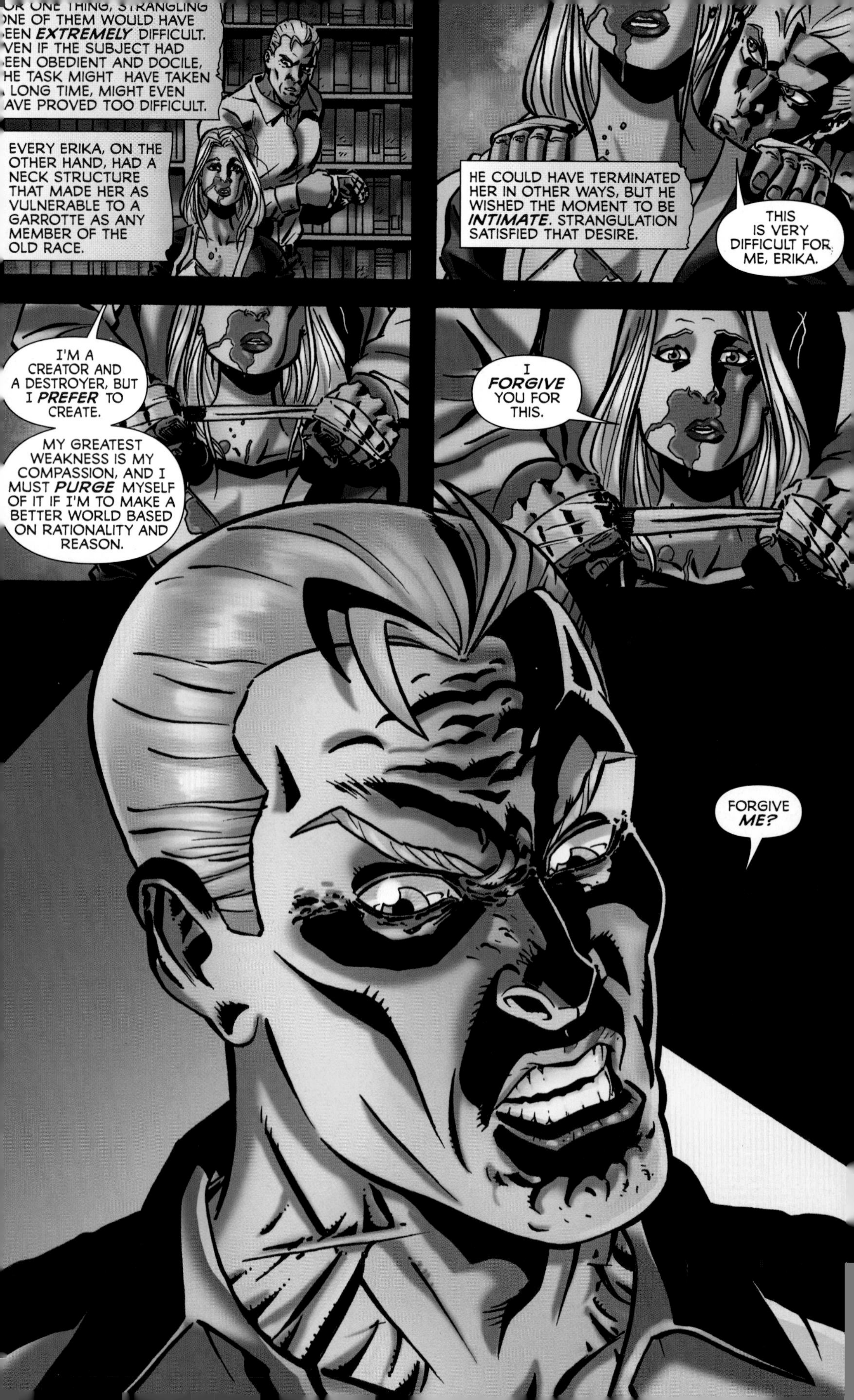
OR ONE THING, STRANGLING ONE OF THEM WOULD HAVE BEEN EXTREMELY DIFFICULT. EVEN IF THE SUBJECT HAD BEEN OBEDIENT AND DOCILE, THE TASK MIGHT HAVE TAKEN A LONG TIME, MIGHT EVEN HAVE PROVED TOO DIFFICULT.
EVERY ERIKA, ON THE OTHER HAND, HAD A NECK STRUCTURE THAT MADE HER AS VULNERABLE TO A GARROTTE AS ANY MEMBER OF THE OLD RACE.
HE COULD HAVE TERMINATED HER IN OTHER WAYS, BUT HE WISHED THE MOMENT TO BE INTIMATE. STRANGULATION SATISFIED THAT DESIRE.
THIS IS VERY DIFFICULT FOR ME, ERIKA.
I'M A CREATOR AND A DESTROYER, BUT I PREFER TO CREATE.
MY GREATEST WEAKNESS IS MY COMPASSION, AND I MUST PURGE MYSELF OF IT IF I'M TO MAKE A BETTER WORLD BASED ON RATIONALITY AND REASON.
I FORGIVE YOU FOR THIS.
FORGIVE ME?

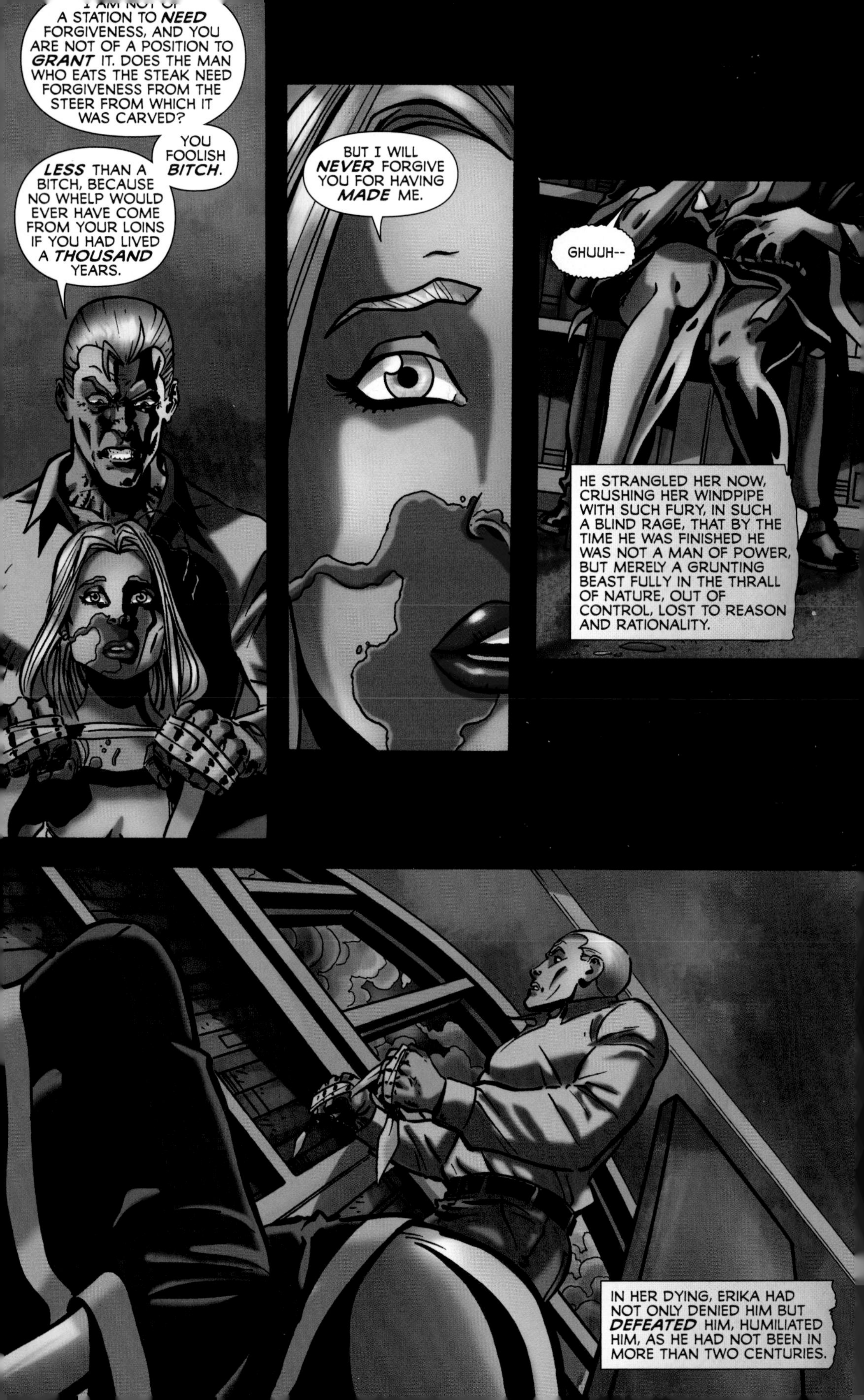

A STATION TO NEED FORGIVENESS, AND YOU ARE NOT OF A POSITION TO GRANT IT. DOES THE MAN WHO EATS THE STEAK NEED FORGIVENESS FROM THE STEER FROM WHICH IT WAS CARVED?
YOU FOOLISH BITCH.
LESS THAN A BITCH, BECAUSE NO WHELP WOULD EVER HAVE COME FROM YOUR LOINS IF YOU HAD LIVED A THOUSAND YEARS.
BUT I WILL NEVER FORGIVE YOU FOR HAVING MADE ME.
GHUUH--
HE STRANGLED HER NOW, CRUSHING HER WINDPIPE WITH SUCH FURY, IN SUCH A BLIND RAGE, THAT BY THE TIME HE WAS FINISHED HE WAS NOT A MAN OF POWER, BUT MERELY A GRUNTING BEAST FULLY IN THE THRALL OF NATURE, OUT OF CONTROL, LOST TO REASON AND RATIONALITY.
IN HER DYING, ERIKA HAD NOT ONLY DENIED HIM BUT DEFEATED HIM, HUMILIATED HIM, AS HE HAD NOT BEEN IN MORE THAN TWO CENTURIES.

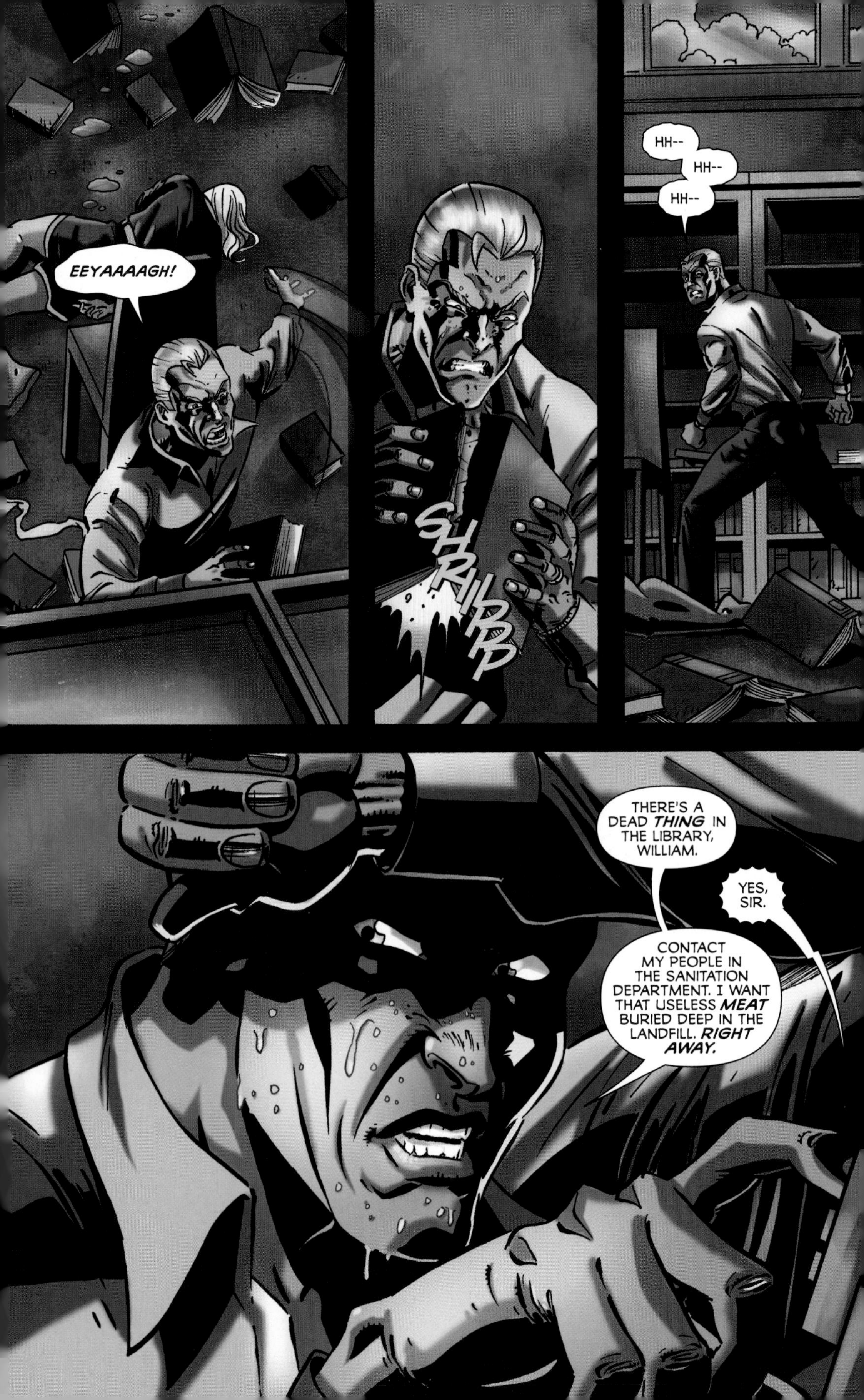
EEYAAAAGH!
SHRIIPP
HH--
HH--
HH--
THERE'S A DEAD *THING* IN THE LIBRARY, WILLIAM.
CONTACT MY PEOPLE IN THE SANITATION DEPARTMENT. I WANT THAT USELESS *MEAT* BURIED DEEP IN THE LANDFILL. *RIGHT AWAY.*
YES, SIR.

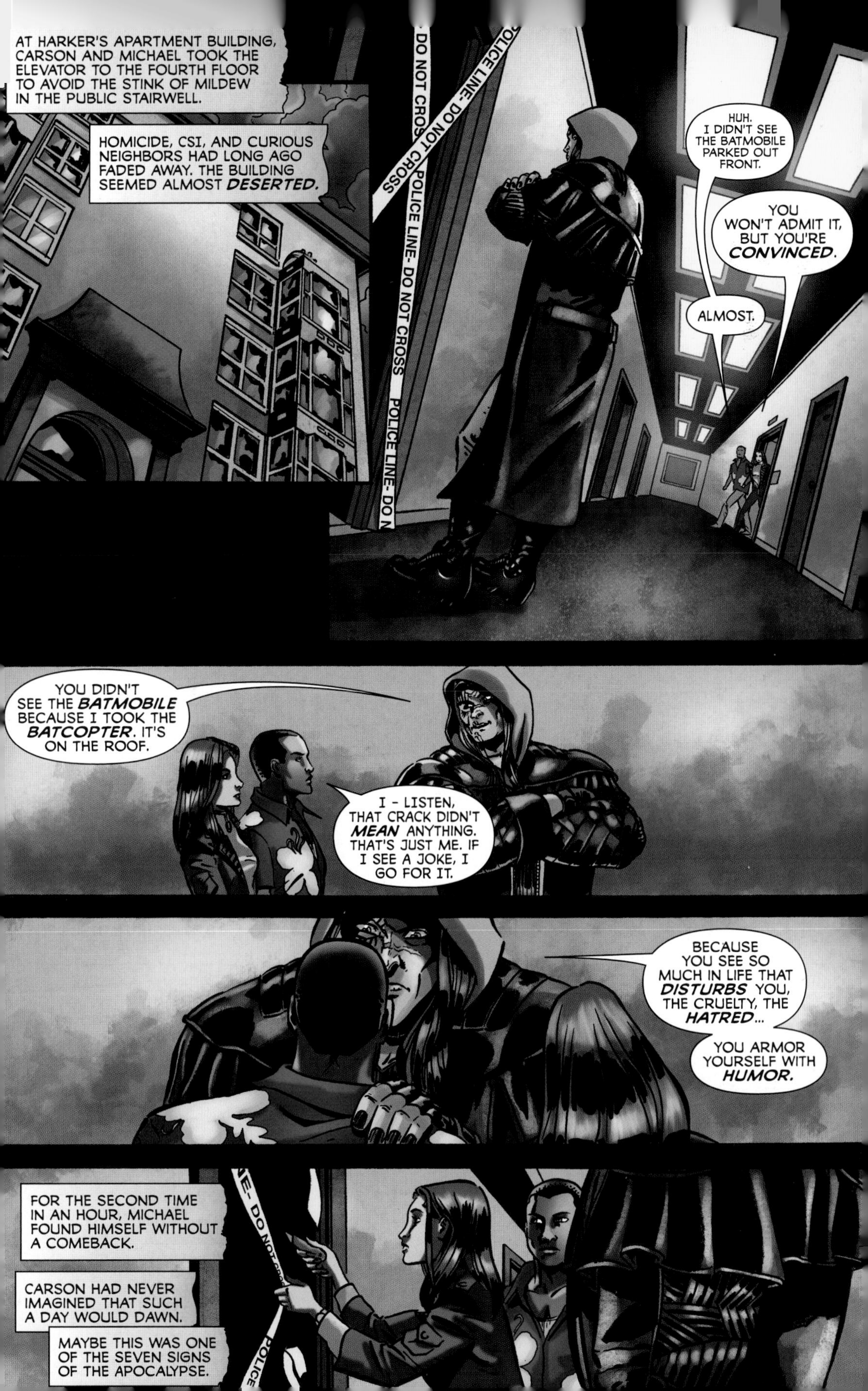
AT HARKER'S APARTMENT BUILDING, CARSON AND MICHAEL TOOK THE ELEVATOR TO THE FOURTH FLOOR TO AVOID THE STINK OF MILDEW IN THE PUBLIC STAIRWELL.
HOMICIDE, CSI, AND CURIOUS NEIGHBORS HAD LONG AGO FADED AWAY. THE BUILDING SEEMED ALMOST *DESERTED.*
POLICE LINE- DO NOT CROSS
HUH. I DIDN'T SEE THE BATMOBILE PARKED OUT FRONT.
YOU WON'T ADMIT IT, BUT YOU'RE *CONVINCED*.
ALMOST.
YOU DIDN'T SEE THE *BATMOBILE* BECAUSE I TOOK THE *BATCOPTER*. IT'S ON THE ROOF.
I - LISTEN, THAT CRACK DIDN'T *MEAN* ANYTHING. THAT'S JUST ME. IF I SEE A JOKE, I GO FOR IT.
BECAUSE YOU SEE SO MUCH IN LIFE THAT *DISTURBS* YOU, THE CRUELTY, THE *HATRED*...
YOU ARMOR YOURSELF WITH *HUMOR.*
FOR THE SECOND TIME IN AN HOUR, MICHAEL FOUND HIMSELF WITHOUT A COMEBACK.
CARSON HAD NEVER IMAGINED THAT SUCH A DAY WOULD DAWN.
MAYBE THIS WAS ONE OF THE SEVEN SIGNS OF THE APOCALYPSE.

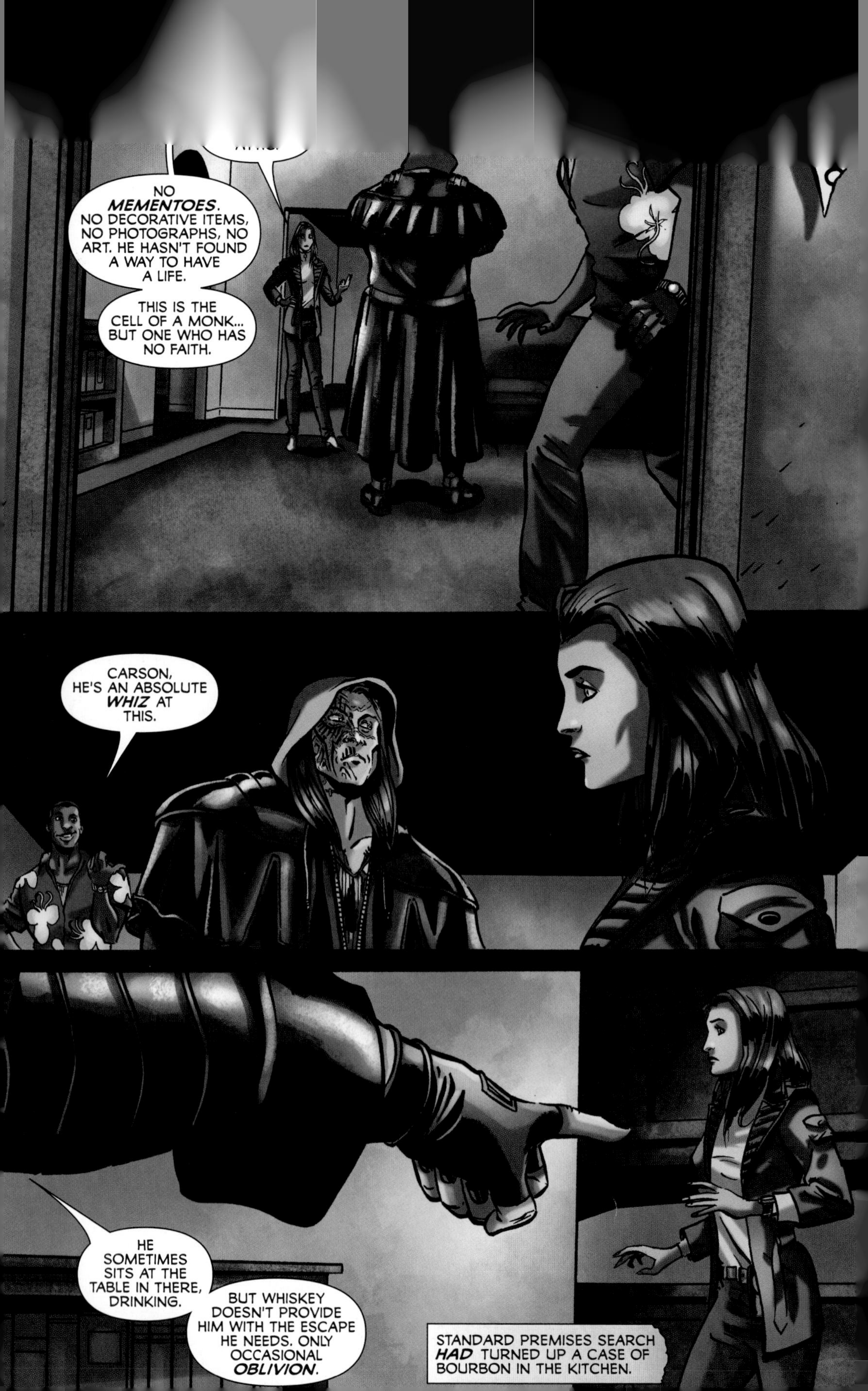
NO *MEMENTOES*. NO DECORATIVE ITEMS, NO PHOTOGRAPHS, NO ART. HE HASN'T FOUND A WAY TO HAVE A LIFE.
THIS IS THE CELL OF A MONK... BUT ONE WHO HAS NO FAITH.
CARSON, HE'S AN ABSOLUTE *WHIZ* AT THIS.
HE SOMETIMES SITS AT THE TABLE IN THERE, DRINKING.
BUT WHISKEY DOESN'T PROVIDE HIM WITH THE ESCAPE HE NEEDS. ONLY OCCASIONAL *OBLIVION*.
STANDARD PREMISES SEARCH *HAD* TURNED UP A CASE OF BOURBON IN THE KITCHEN.

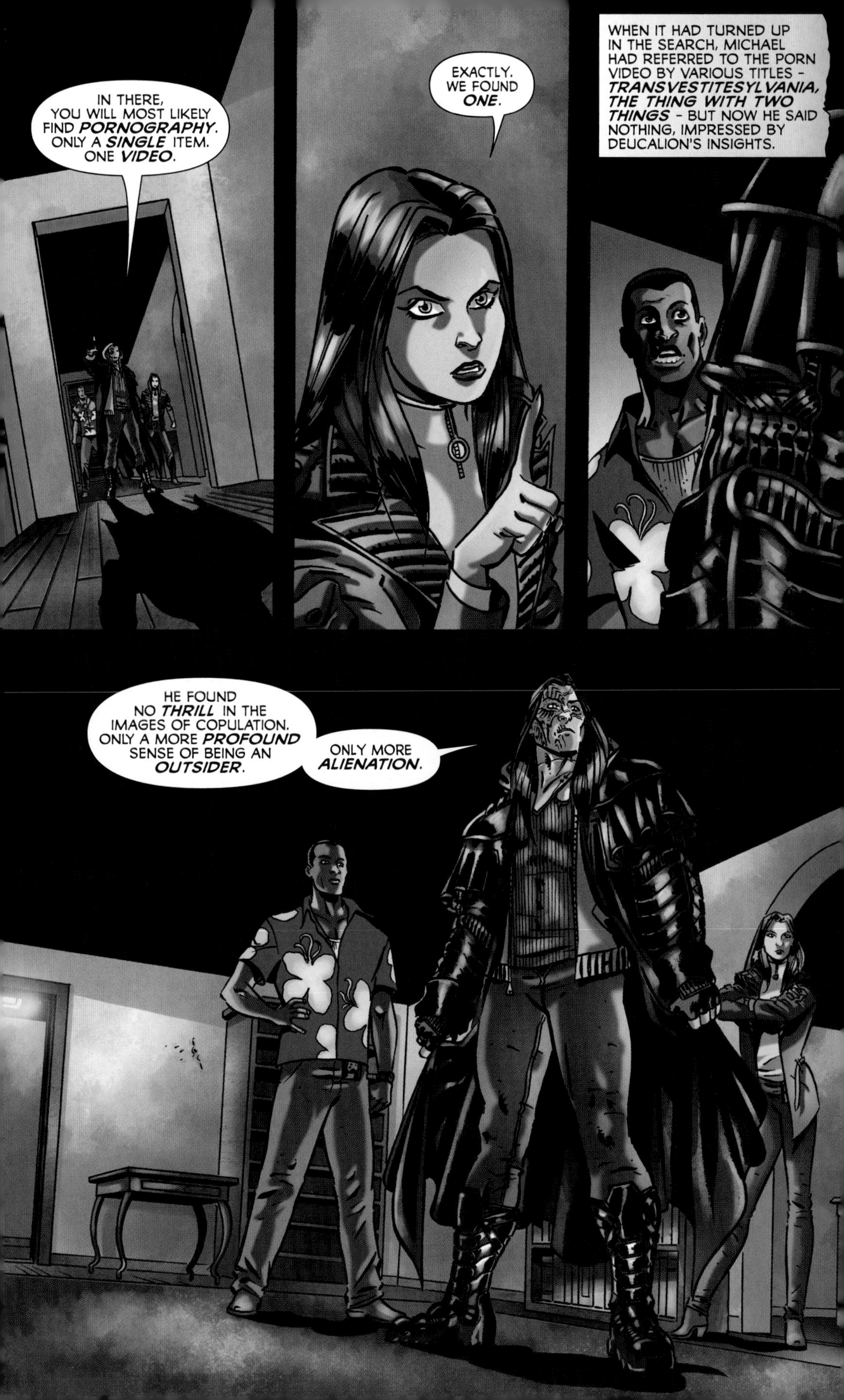
IN THERE, YOU WILL MOST LIKELY FIND **PORNOGRAPHY**. ONLY A **SINGLE** ITEM. ONE **VIDEO**.
EXACTLY. WE FOUND **ONE**.
WHEN IT HAD TURNED UP IN THE SEARCH, MICHAEL HAD REFERRED TO THE PORN VIDEO BY VARIOUS TITLES - ***TRANSVESTITESYLVANIA, THE THING WITH TWO THINGS*** - BUT NOW HE SAID NOTHING, IMPRESSED BY DEUCALION'S INSIGHTS.
HE FOUND NO **THRILL** IN THE IMAGES OF COPULATION. ONLY A MORE **PROFOUND** SENSE OF BEING AN **OUTSIDER**.
ONLY MORE **ALIENATION**.

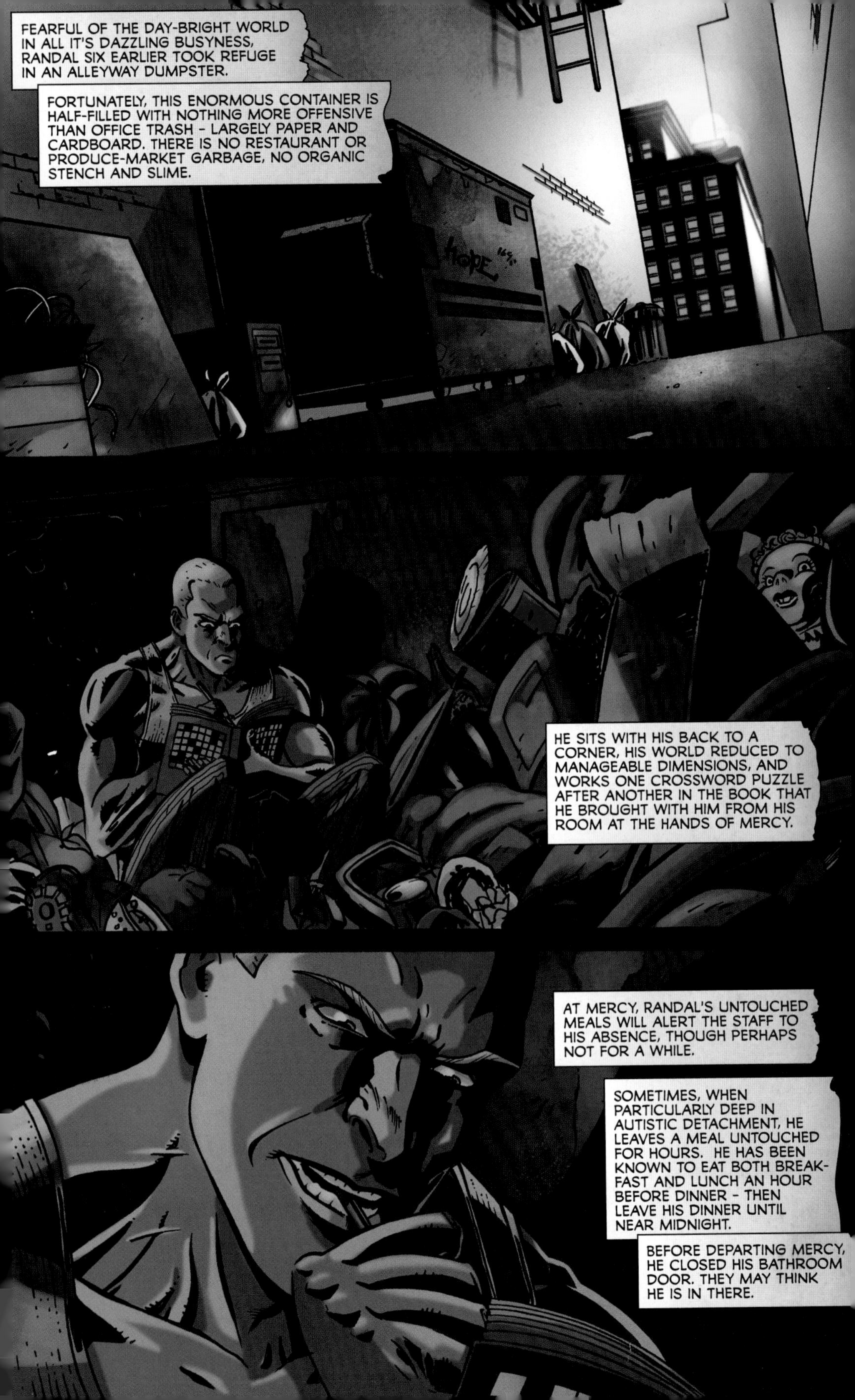
FEARFUL OF THE DAY-BRIGHT WORLD IN ALL IT'S DAZZLING BUSYNESS, RANDAL SIX EARLIER TOOK REFUGE IN AN ALLEYWAY DUMPSTER.
FORTUNATELY, THIS ENORMOUS CONTAINER IS HALF-FILLED WITH NOTHING MORE OFFENSIVE THAN OFFICE TRASH - LARGELY PAPER AND CARDBOARD. THERE IS NO RESTAURANT OR PRODUCE-MARKET GARBAGE, NO ORGANIC STENCH AND SLIME.
HOPE
HE SITS WITH HIS BACK TO A CORNER, HIS WORLD REDUCED TO MANAGEABLE DIMENSIONS, AND WORKS ONE CROSSWORD PUZZLE AFTER ANOTHER IN THE BOOK THAT HE BROUGHT WITH HIM FROM HIS ROOM AT THE HANDS OF MERCY.
AT MERCY, RANDAL'S UNTOUCHED MEALS WILL ALERT THE STAFF TO HIS ABSENCE, THOUGH PERHAPS NOT FOR A WHILE.
SOMETIMES, WHEN PARTICULARLY DEEP IN AUTISTIC DETACHMENT, HE LEAVES A MEAL UNTOUCHED FOR HOURS. HE HAS BEEN KNOWN TO EAT BOTH BREAK-FAST AND LUNCH AN HOUR BEFORE DINNER - THEN LEAVE HIS DINNER UNTIL NEAR MIDNIGHT.
BEFORE DEPARTING MERCY, HE CLOSED HIS BATHROOM DOOR. THEY MAY THINK HE IS IN THERE.

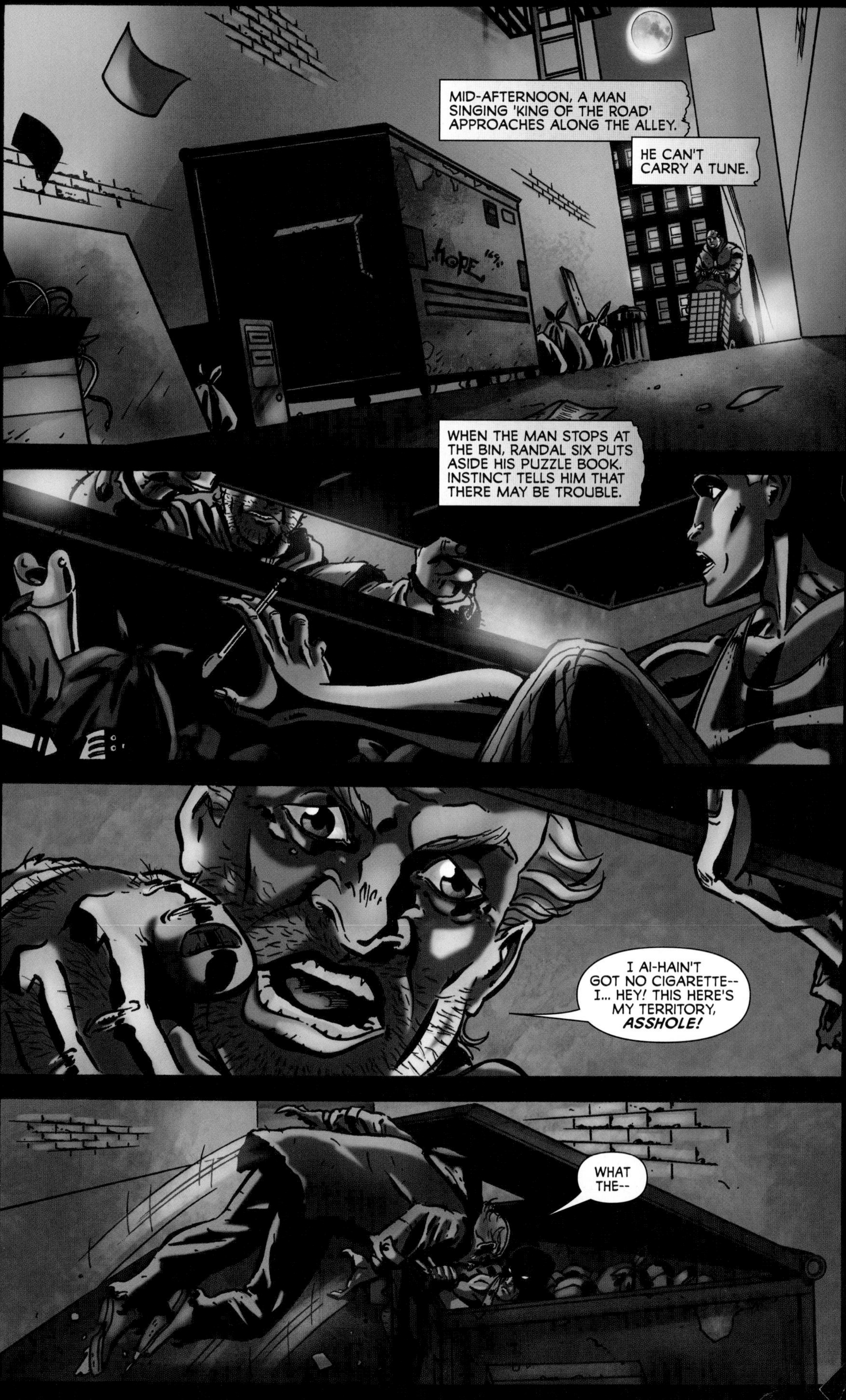
MID-AFTERNOON, A MAN SINGING 'KING OF THE ROAD' APPROACHES ALONG THE ALLEY.
HE CAN'T CARRY A TUNE.
WHEN THE MAN STOPS AT THE BIN, RANDAL SIX PUTS ASIDE HIS PUZZLE BOOK. INSTINCT TELLS HIM THAT THERE MAY BE TROUBLE.
I AI-HAIN'T GOT NO CIGARETTE-- I... HEY! THIS HERE'S MY TERRITORY, ASSHOLE!
WHAT THE--

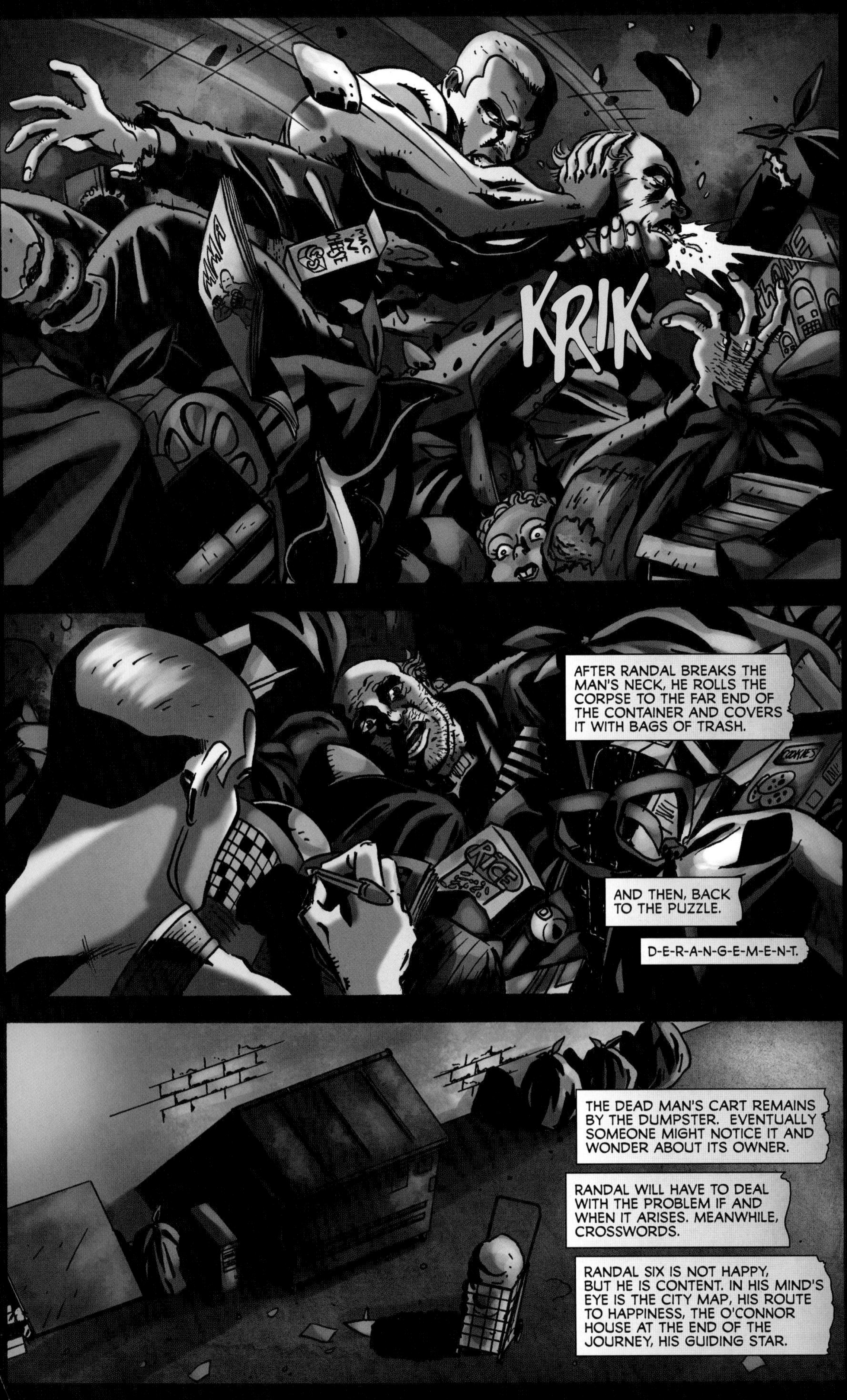
KRIK
MAC N' CHEESE
AFTER RANDAL BREAKS THE MAN'S NECK, HE ROLLS THE CORPSE TO THE FAR END OF THE CONTAINER AND COVERS IT WITH BAGS OF TRASH.
COOKIES
RICE
AND THEN, BACK TO THE PUZZLE.
D-E-R-A-N-G-E-M-E-N-T.
THE DEAD MAN'S CART REMAINS BY THE DUMPSTER. EVENTUALLY SOMEONE MIGHT NOTICE IT AND WONDER ABOUT ITS OWNER.
RANDAL WILL HAVE TO DEAL WITH THE PROBLEM IF AND WHEN IT ARISES. MEANWHILE, CROSSWORDS.
RANDAL SIX IS NOT HAPPY, BUT HE IS CONTENT. IN HIS MIND'S EYE IS THE CITY MAP, HIS ROUTE TO HAPPINESS, THE O'CONNOR HOUSE AT THE END OF THE JOURNEY, HIS GUIDING STAR.

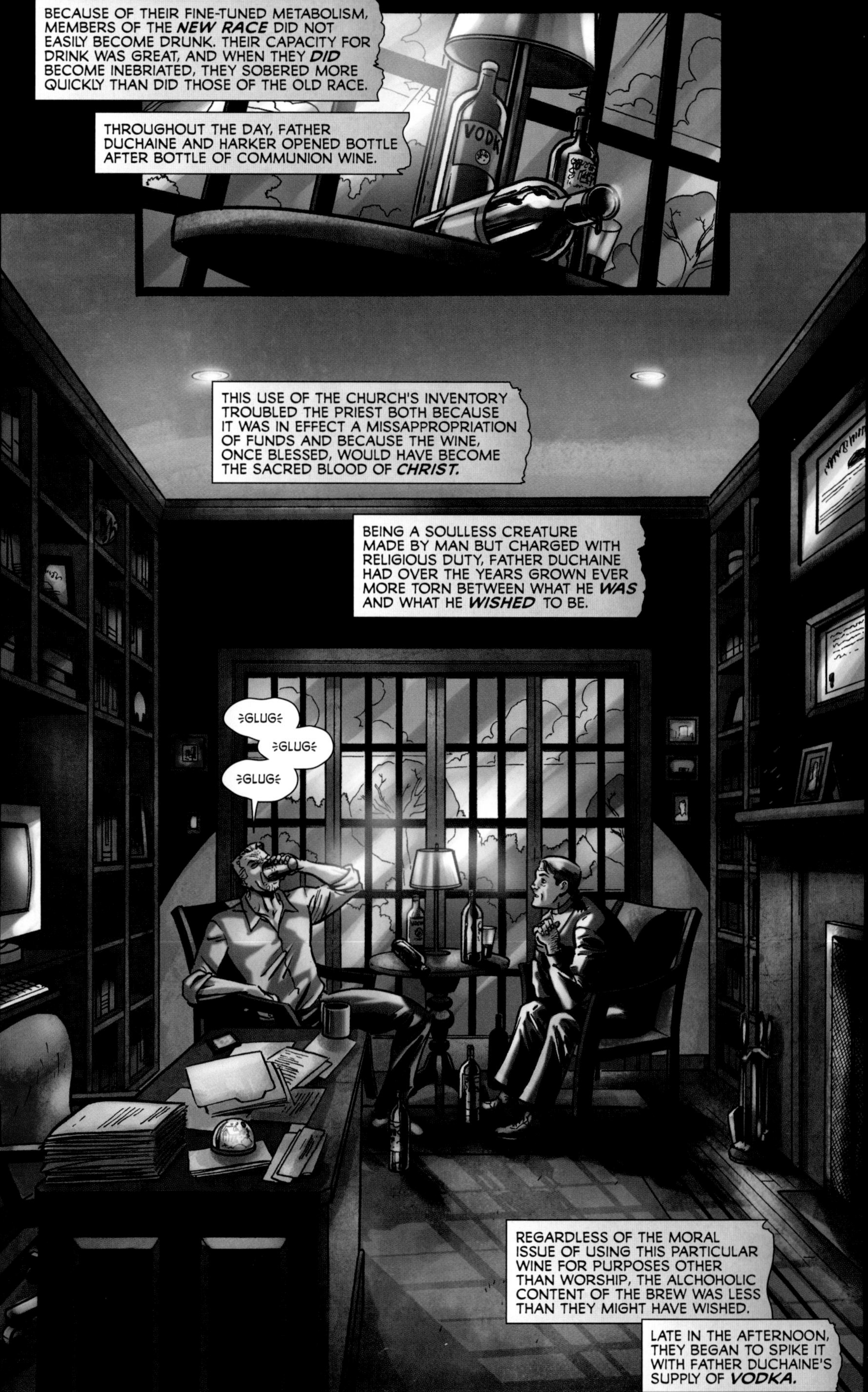
BECAUSE OF THEIR FINE-TUNED METABOLISM, MEMBERS OF THE NEW RACE DID NOT EASILY BECOME DRUNK. THEIR CAPACITY FOR DRINK WAS GREAT, AND WHEN THEY DID BECOME INEBRIATED, THEY SOBERED MORE QUICKLY THAN DID THOSE OF THE OLD RACE.
THROUGHOUT THE DAY, FATHER DUCHAINE AND HARKER OPENED BOTTLE AFTER BOTTLE OF COMMUNION WINE.
THIS USE OF THE CHURCH'S INVENTORY TROUBLED THE PRIEST BOTH BECAUSE IT WAS IN EFFECT A MISSAPPROPRIATION OF FUNDS AND BECAUSE THE WINE, ONCE BLESSED, WOULD HAVE BECOME THE SACRED BLOOD OF CHRIST.
BEING A SOULLESS CREATURE MADE BY MAN BUT CHARGED WITH RELIGIOUS DUTY, FATHER DUCHAINE HAD OVER THE YEARS GROWN EVER MORE TORN BETWEEN WHAT HE WAS AND WHAT HE WISHED TO BE.
GLUG
GLUG
GLUG
REGARDLESS OF THE MORAL ISSUE OF USING THIS PARTICULAR WINE FOR PURPOSES OTHER THAN WORSHIP, THE ALCHOHOLIC CONTENT OF THE BREW WAS LESS THAN THEY MIGHT HAVE WISHED.
LATE IN THE AFTERNOON, THEY BEGAN TO SPIKE IT WITH FATHER DUCHAINE'S SUPPLY OF VODKA.

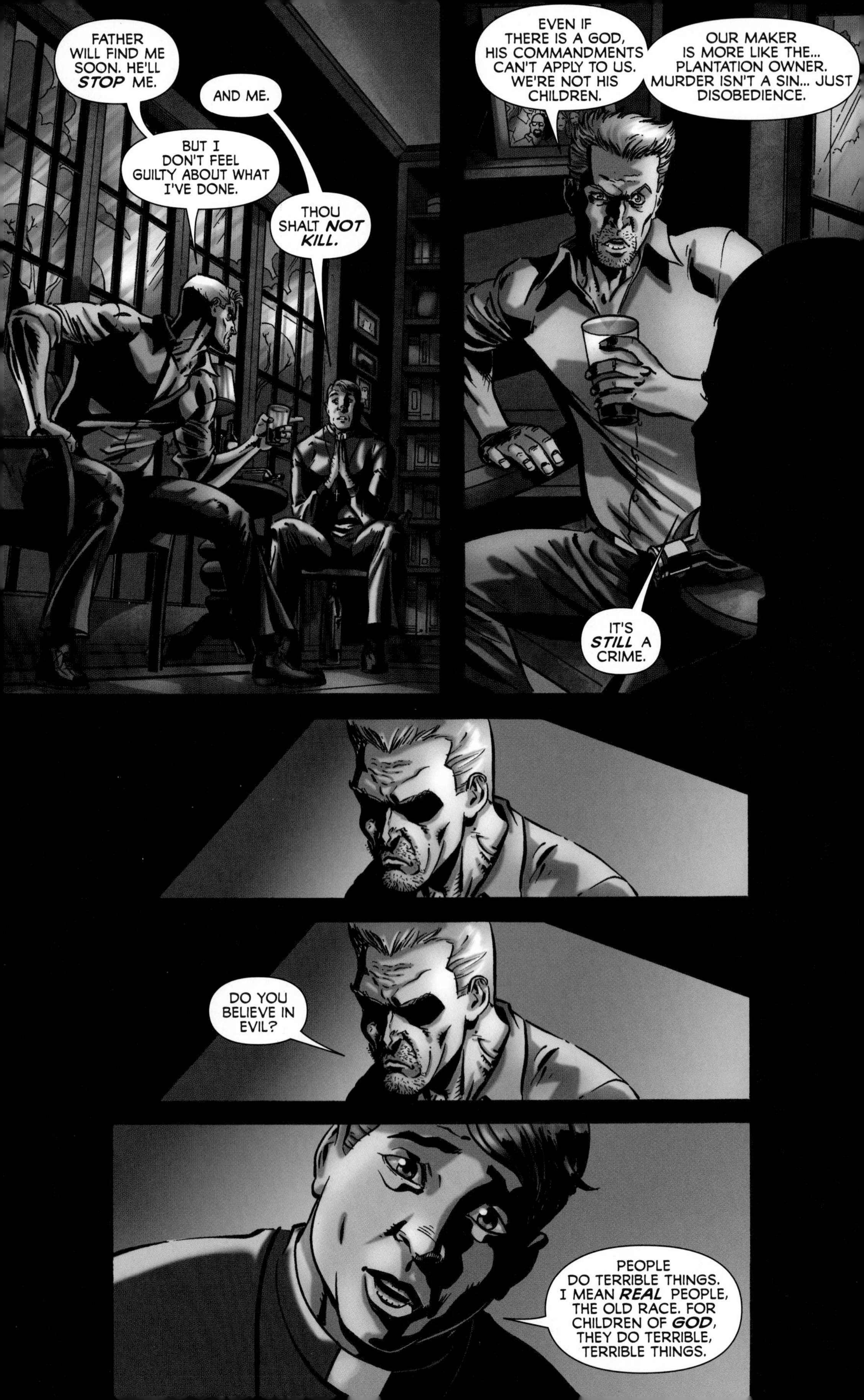
FATHER WILL FIND ME SOON. HE'LL STOP ME.
AND ME.
BUT I DON'T FEEL GUILTY ABOUT WHAT I'VE DONE.
THOU SHALT NOT KILL.
EVEN IF THERE IS A GOD, HIS COMMANDMENTS CAN'T APPLY TO US. WE'RE NOT HIS CHILDREN.
OUR MAKER IS MORE LIKE THE... PLANTATION OWNER. MURDER ISN'T A SIN... JUST DISOBEDIENCE.
IT'S STILL A CRIME.
DO YOU BELIEVE IN EVIL?
PEOPLE DO TERRIBLE THINGS. I MEAN REAL PEOPLE, THE OLD RACE. FOR CHILDREN OF GOD, THEY DO TERRIBLE, TERRIBLE THINGS.

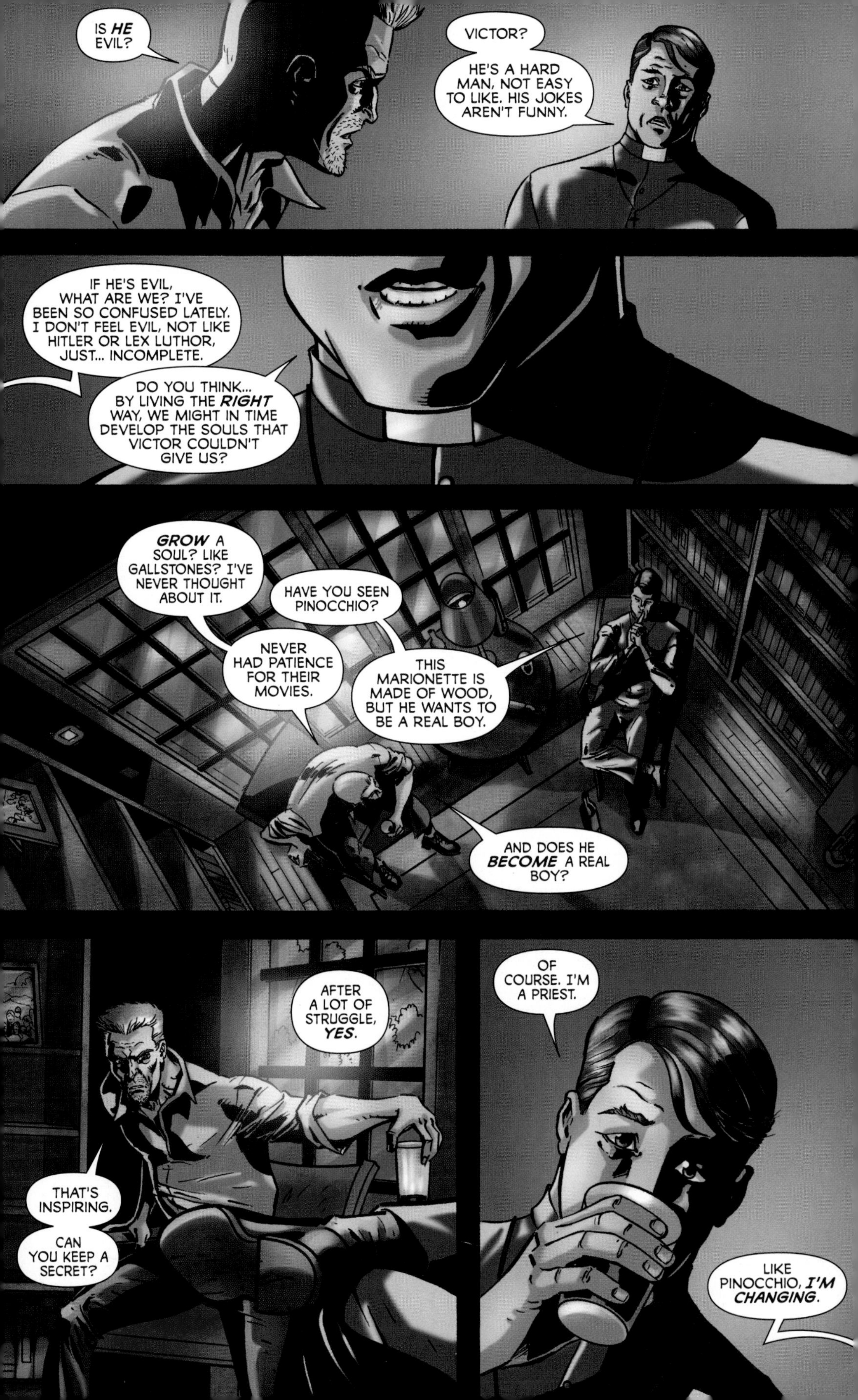
IS *HE* EVIL?
VICTOR?
HE'S A HARD MAN, NOT EASY TO LIKE. HIS JOKES AREN'T FUNNY.
IF HE'S EVIL, WHAT ARE WE? I'VE BEEN SO CONFUSED LATELY. I DON'T FEEL EVIL, NOT LIKE HITLER OR LEX LUTHOR, JUST... INCOMPLETE.
DO YOU THINK... BY LIVING THE *RIGHT* WAY, WE MIGHT IN TIME DEVELOP THE SOULS THAT VICTOR COULDN'T GIVE US?
GROW A SOUL? LIKE GALLSTONES? I'VE NEVER THOUGHT ABOUT IT.
HAVE YOU SEEN PINOCCHIO?
NEVER HAD PATIENCE FOR THEIR MOVIES.
THIS MARIONETTE IS MADE OF WOOD, BUT HE WANTS TO BE A REAL BOY.
AND DOES HE *BECOME* A REAL BOY?
AFTER A LOT OF STRUGGLE, *YES*.
THAT'S INSPIRING.
CAN YOU KEEP A SECRET?
OF COURSE. I'M A PRIEST.
LIKE PINOCCHIO, *I'M CHANGING*.

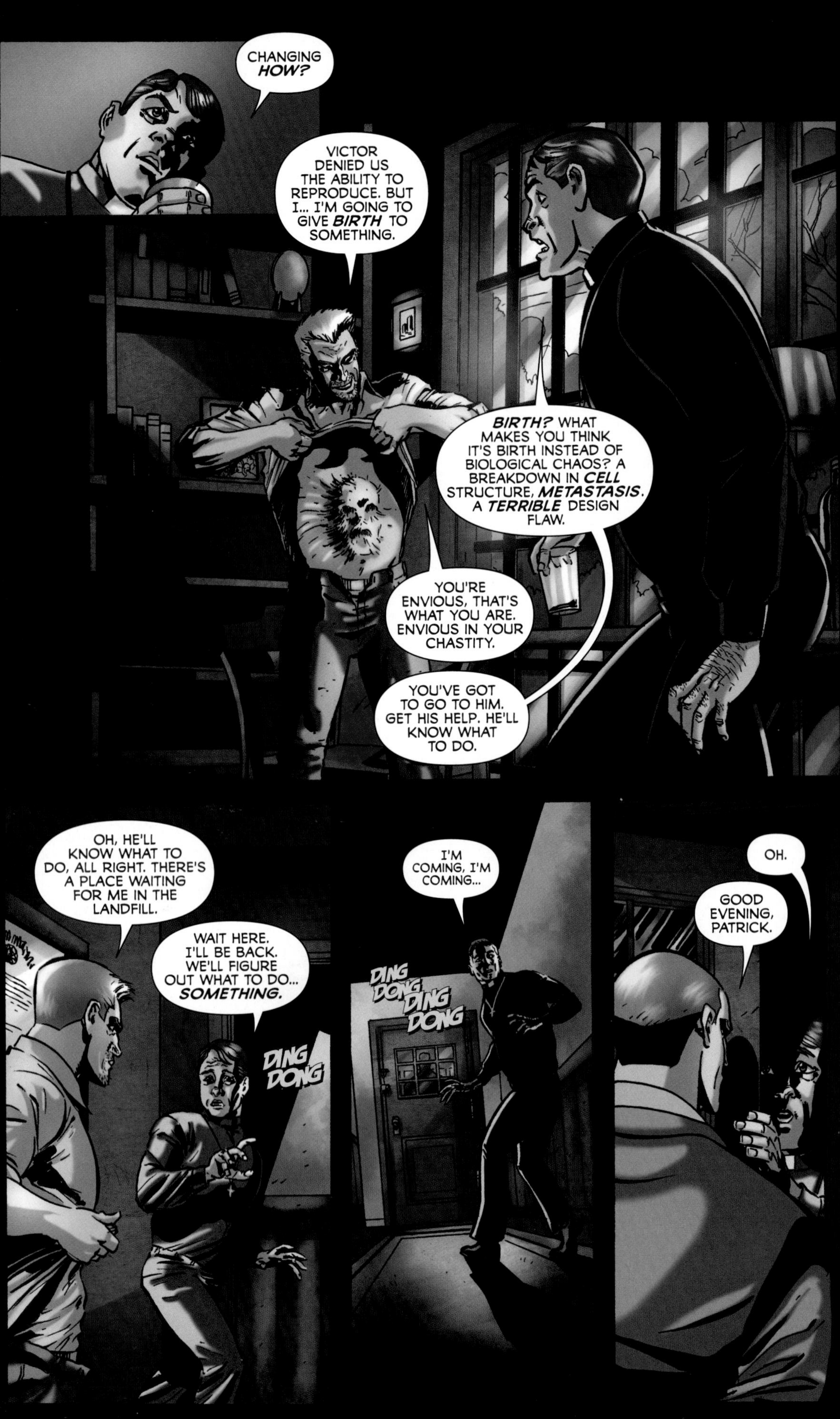

CHANGING HOW?
VICTOR DENIED US THE ABILITY TO REPRODUCE. BUT I... I'M GOING TO GIVE BIRTH TO SOMETHING.
BIRTH? WHAT MAKES YOU THINK IT'S BIRTH INSTEAD OF BIOLOGICAL CHAOS? A BREAKDOWN IN CELL STRUCTURE, METASTASIS. A TERRIBLE DESIGN FLAW.
YOU'RE ENVIOUS, THAT'S WHAT YOU ARE. ENVIOUS IN YOUR CHASTITY.
YOU'VE GOT TO GO TO HIM. GET HIS HELP. HE'LL KNOW WHAT TO DO.
OH, HE'LL KNOW WHAT TO DO, ALL RIGHT. THERE'S A PLACE WAITING FOR ME IN THE LANDFILL.
WAIT HERE. I'LL BE BACK. WE'LL FIGURE OUT WHAT TO DO... SOMETHING.
DING DONG
I'M COMING, I'M COMING...
DING DONG DING DONG
OH.
GOOD EVENING, PATRICK.

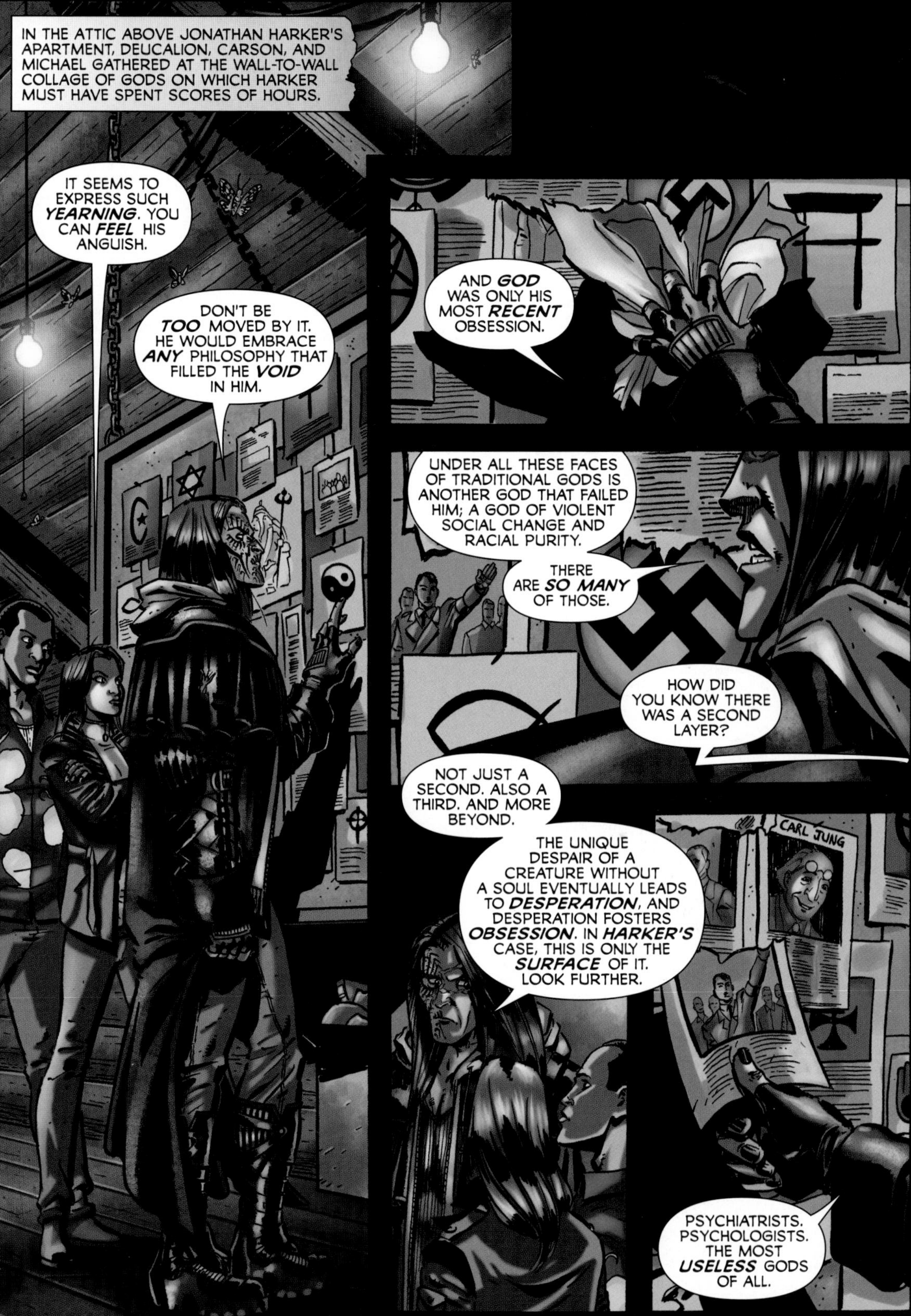
IN THE ATTIC ABOVE JONATHAN HARKER'S APARTMENT, DEUCALION, CARSON, AND MICHAEL GATHERED AT THE WALL-TO-WALL COLLAGE OF GODS ON WHICH HARKER MUST HAVE SPENT SCORES OF HOURS.
IT SEEMS TO EXPRESS SUCH YEARNING. YOU CAN FEEL HIS ANGUISH.
DON'T BE TOO MOVED BY IT. HE WOULD EMBRACE ANY PHILOSOPHY THAT FILLED THE VOID IN HIM.
AND GOD WAS ONLY HIS MOST RECENT OBSESSION.
UNDER ALL THESE FACES OF TRADITIONAL GODS IS ANOTHER GOD THAT FAILED HIM; A GOD OF VIOLENT SOCIAL CHANGE AND RACIAL PURITY.
THERE ARE SO MANY OF THOSE.
HOW DID YOU KNOW THERE WAS A SECOND LAYER?
NOT JUST A SECOND. ALSO A THIRD. AND MORE BEYOND.
THE UNIQUE DESPAIR OF A CREATURE WITHOUT A SOUL EVENTUALLY LEADS TO DESPERATION, AND DESPERATION FOSTERS OBSESSION. IN HARKER'S CASE, THIS IS ONLY THE SURFACE OF IT. LOOK FURTHER.
CARL JUNG
PSYCHIATRISTS. PSYCHOLOGISTS. THE MOST USELESS GODS OF ALL.

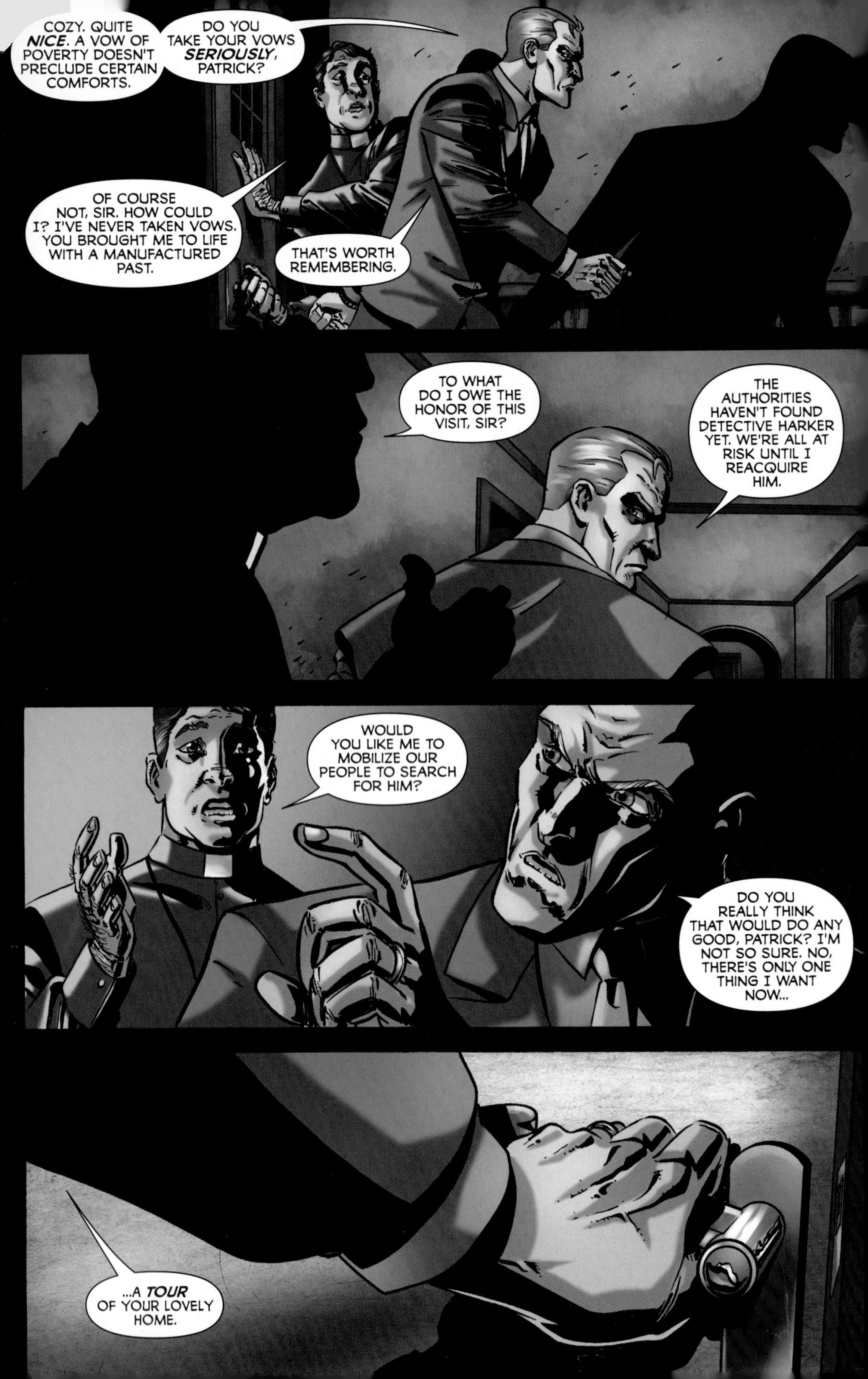
COZY. QUITE NICE. A VOW OF POVERTY DOESN'T PRECLUDE CERTAIN COMFORTS.
DO YOU TAKE YOUR VOWS SERIOUSLY, PATRICK?
OF COURSE NOT, SIR. HOW COULD I? I'VE NEVER TAKEN VOWS. YOU BROUGHT ME TO LIFE WITH A MANUFACTURED PAST.
THAT'S WORTH REMEMBERING.
TO WHAT DO I OWE THE HONOR OF THIS VISIT, SIR?
THE AUTHORITIES HAVEN'T FOUND DETECTIVE HARKER YET. WE'RE ALL AT RISK UNTIL I REACQUIRE HIM.
WOULD YOU LIKE ME TO MOBILIZE OUR PEOPLE TO SEARCH FOR HIM?
DO YOU REALLY THINK THAT WOULD DO ANY GOOD, PATRICK? I'M NOT SO SURE. NO, THERE'S ONLY ONE THING I WANT NOW...
...A TOUR OF YOUR LOVELY HOME.

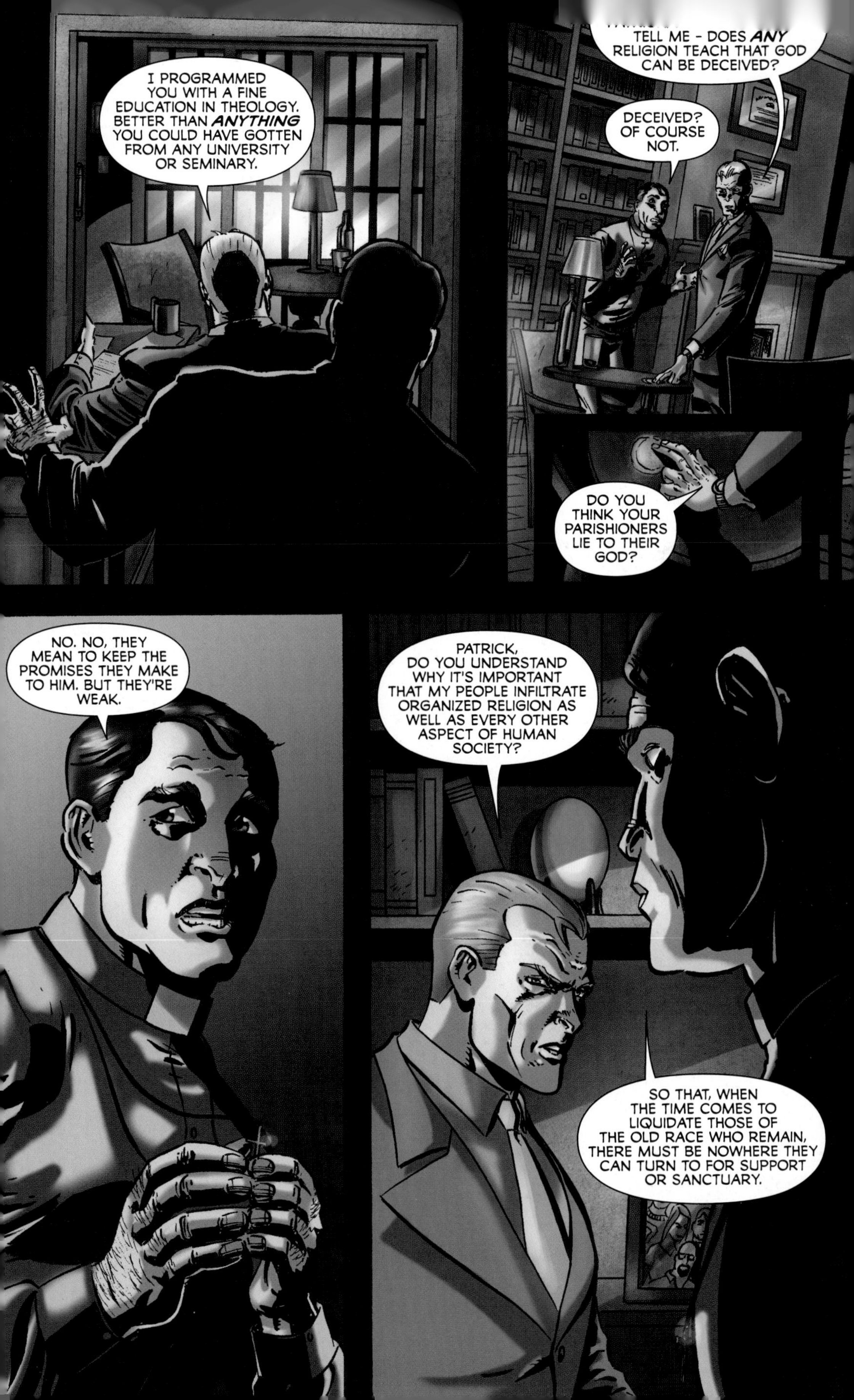
I PROGRAMMED YOU WITH A FINE EDUCATION IN THEOLOGY. BETTER THAN *ANYTHING* YOU COULD HAVE GOTTEN FROM ANY UNIVERSITY OR SEMINARY.
TELL ME - DOES *ANY* RELIGION TEACH THAT GOD CAN BE DECEIVED?
DECEIVED? OF COURSE NOT.
DO YOU THINK YOUR PARISHIONERS LIE TO THEIR GOD?
NO. NO, THEY MEAN TO KEEP THE PROMISES THEY MAKE TO HIM. BUT THEY'RE WEAK.
PATRICK, DO YOU UNDERSTAND WHY IT'S IMPORTANT THAT MY PEOPLE INFILTRATE ORGANIZED RELIGION AS WELL AS EVERY OTHER ASPECT OF HUMAN SOCIETY?
SO THAT, WHEN THE TIME COMES TO LIQUIDATE THOSE OF THE OLD RACE WHO REMAIN, THERE MUST BE NOWHERE THEY CAN TURN TO FOR SUPPORT OR SANCTUARY.

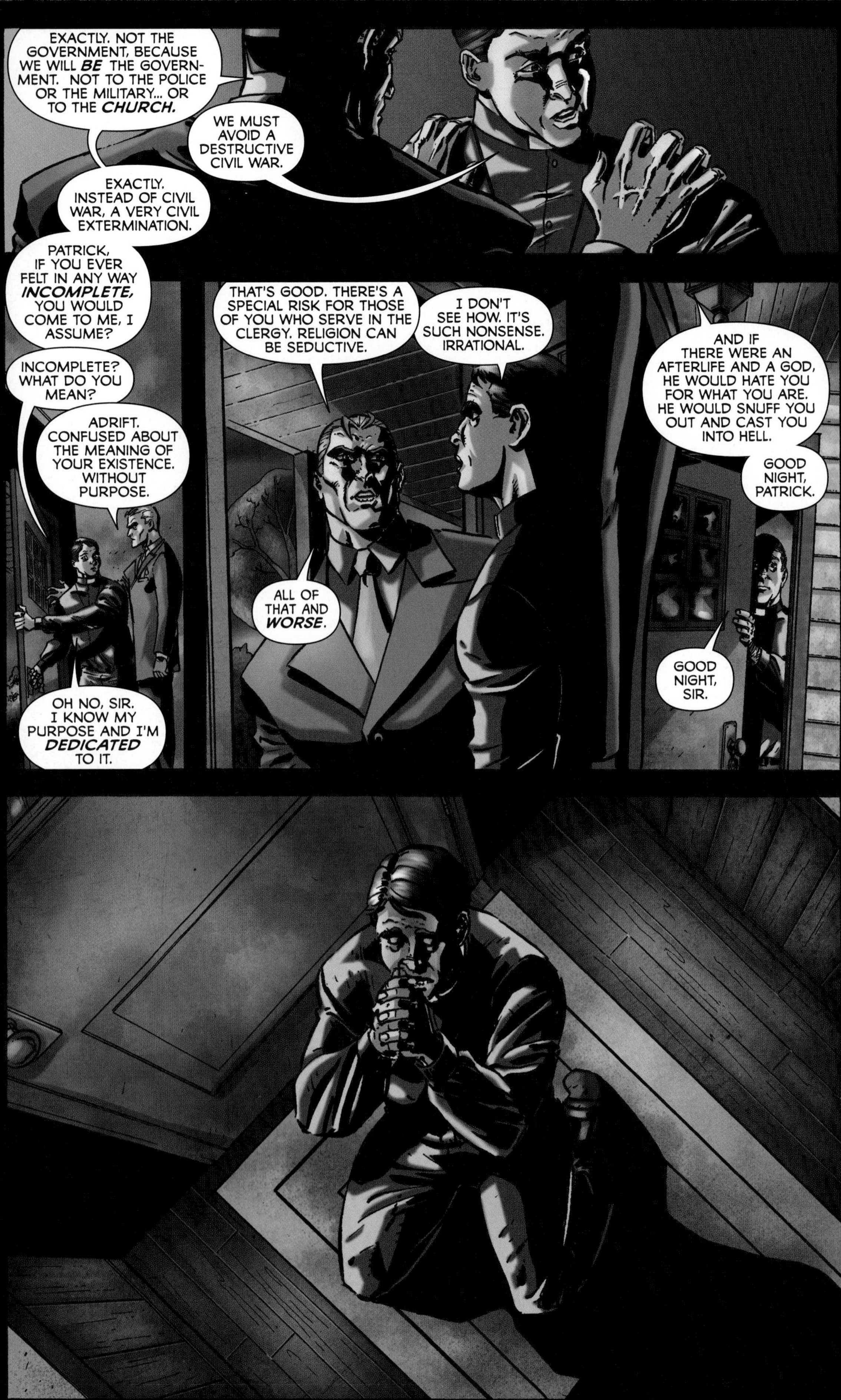
EXACTLY. NOT THE GOVERNMENT, BECAUSE WE WILL *BE* THE GOVERNMENT. NOT TO THE POLICE OR THE MILITARY... OR TO THE *CHURCH.*
WE MUST AVOID A DESTRUCTIVE CIVIL WAR.
EXACTLY. INSTEAD OF CIVIL WAR, A VERY CIVIL EXTERMINATION.
PATRICK, IF YOU EVER FELT IN ANY WAY *INCOMPLETE,* YOU WOULD COME TO ME, I ASSUME?
INCOMPLETE? WHAT DO YOU MEAN?
ADRIFT. CONFUSED ABOUT THE MEANING OF YOUR EXISTENCE. WITHOUT PURPOSE.
OH NO, SIR. I KNOW MY PURPOSE AND I'M *DEDICATED* TO IT.
THAT'S GOOD. THERE'S A SPECIAL RISK FOR THOSE OF YOU WHO SERVE IN THE CLERGY. RELIGION CAN BE SEDUCTIVE.
I DON'T SEE HOW. IT'S SUCH NONSENSE. IRRATIONAL.
ALL OF THAT AND *WORSE*.
AND IF THERE WERE AN AFTERLIFE AND A GOD, HE WOULD HATE YOU FOR WHAT YOU ARE. HE WOULD SNUFF YOU OUT AND CAST YOU INTO HELL.
GOOD NIGHT, PATRICK.
GOOD NIGHT, SIR.

chapter Five

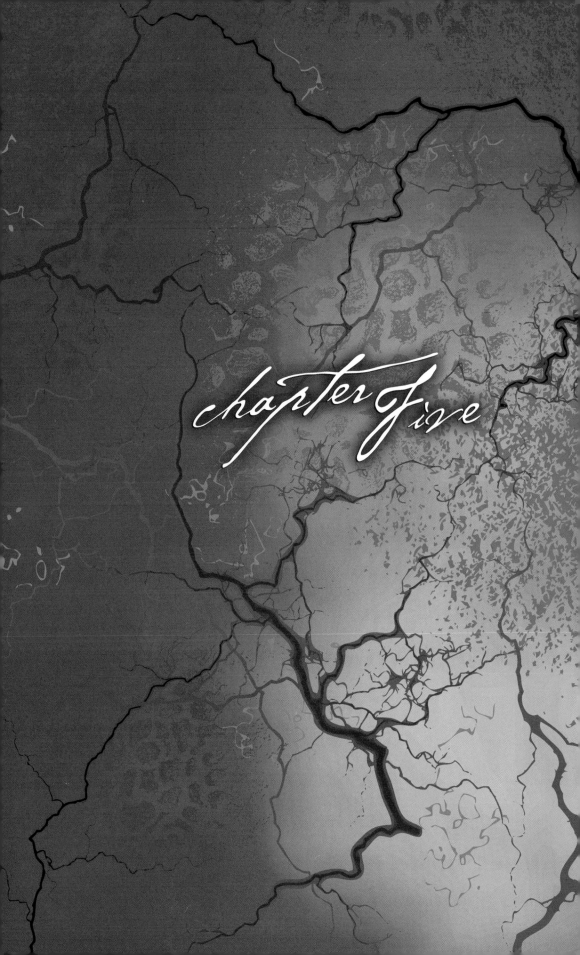

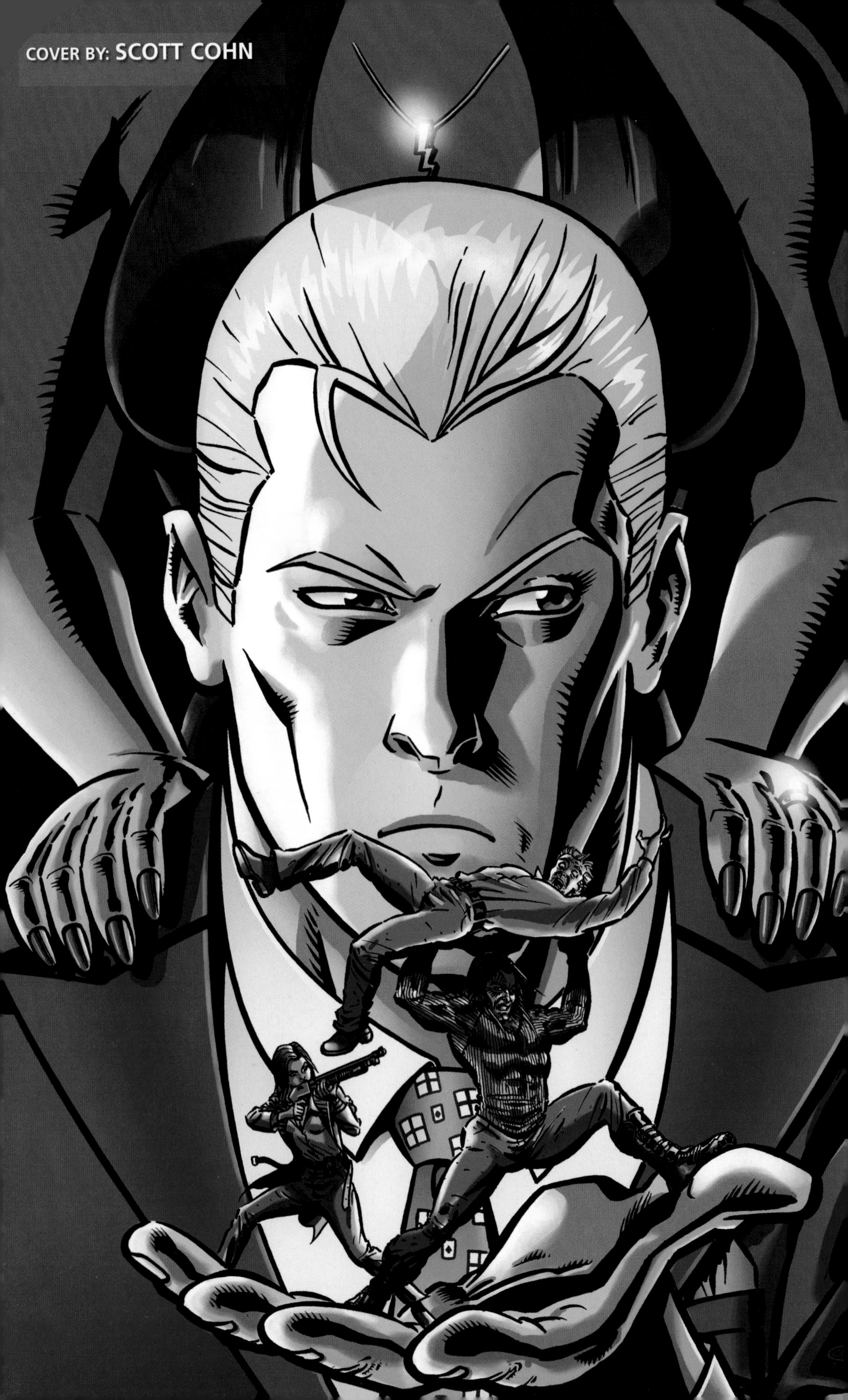
COVER BY: SCOTT COHN

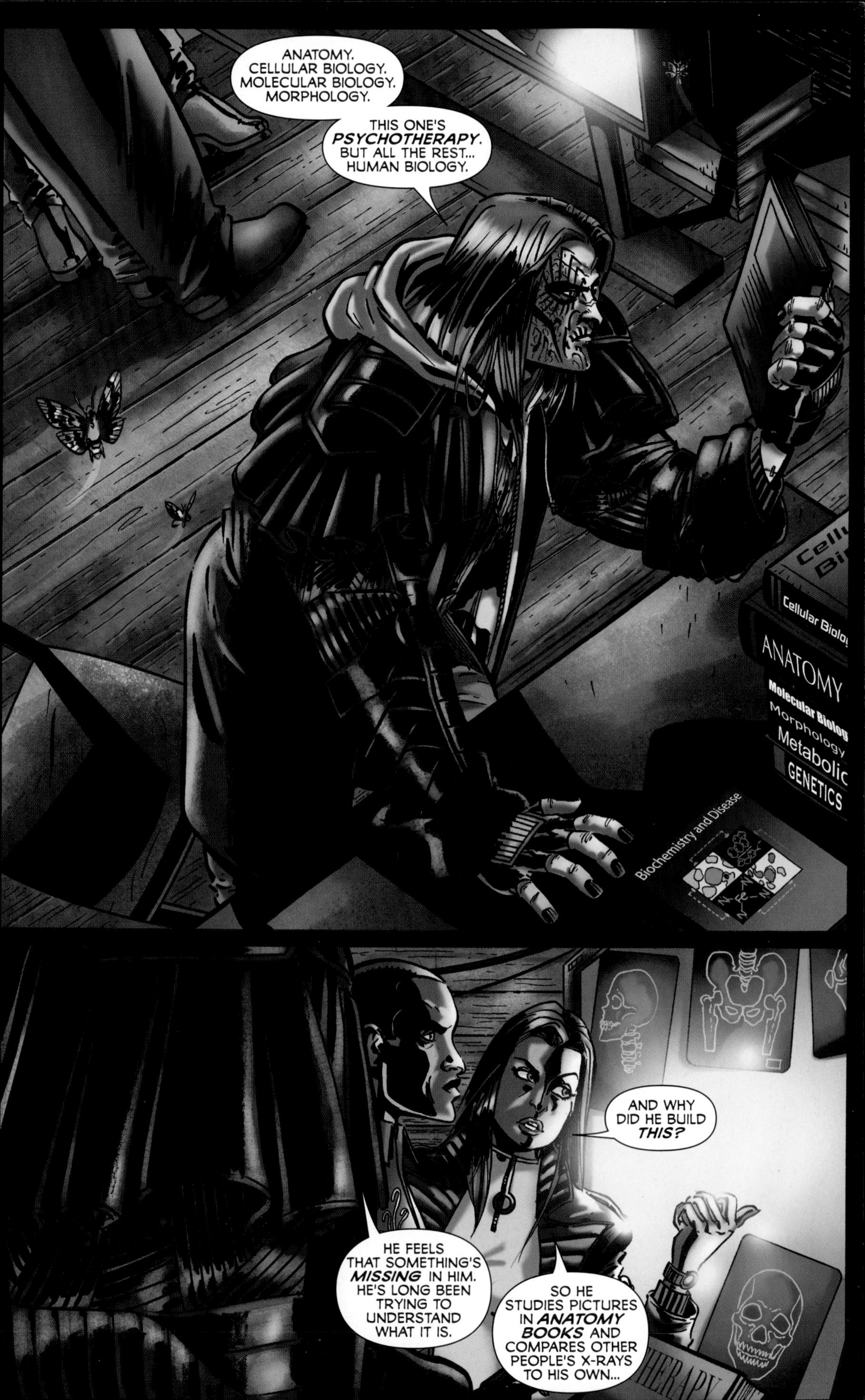
ANATOMY. CELLULAR BIOLOGY. MOLECULAR BIOLOGY. MORPHOLOGY.
THIS ONE'S *PSYCHOTHERAPY*. BUT ALL THE REST... HUMAN BIOLOGY.
Cellular Biology
ANATOMY
Molecular Biology
Morphology
Metabolic
GENETICS
Biochemistry and Disease
AND WHY DID HE BUILD *THIS?*
HE FEELS THAT SOMETHING'S *MISSING* IN HIM. HE'S LONG BEEN TRYING TO UNDERSTAND WHAT IT IS.
SO HE STUDIES PICTURES IN *ANATOMY BOOKS* AND COMPARES OTHER PEOPLE'S X-RAYS TO HIS OWN...

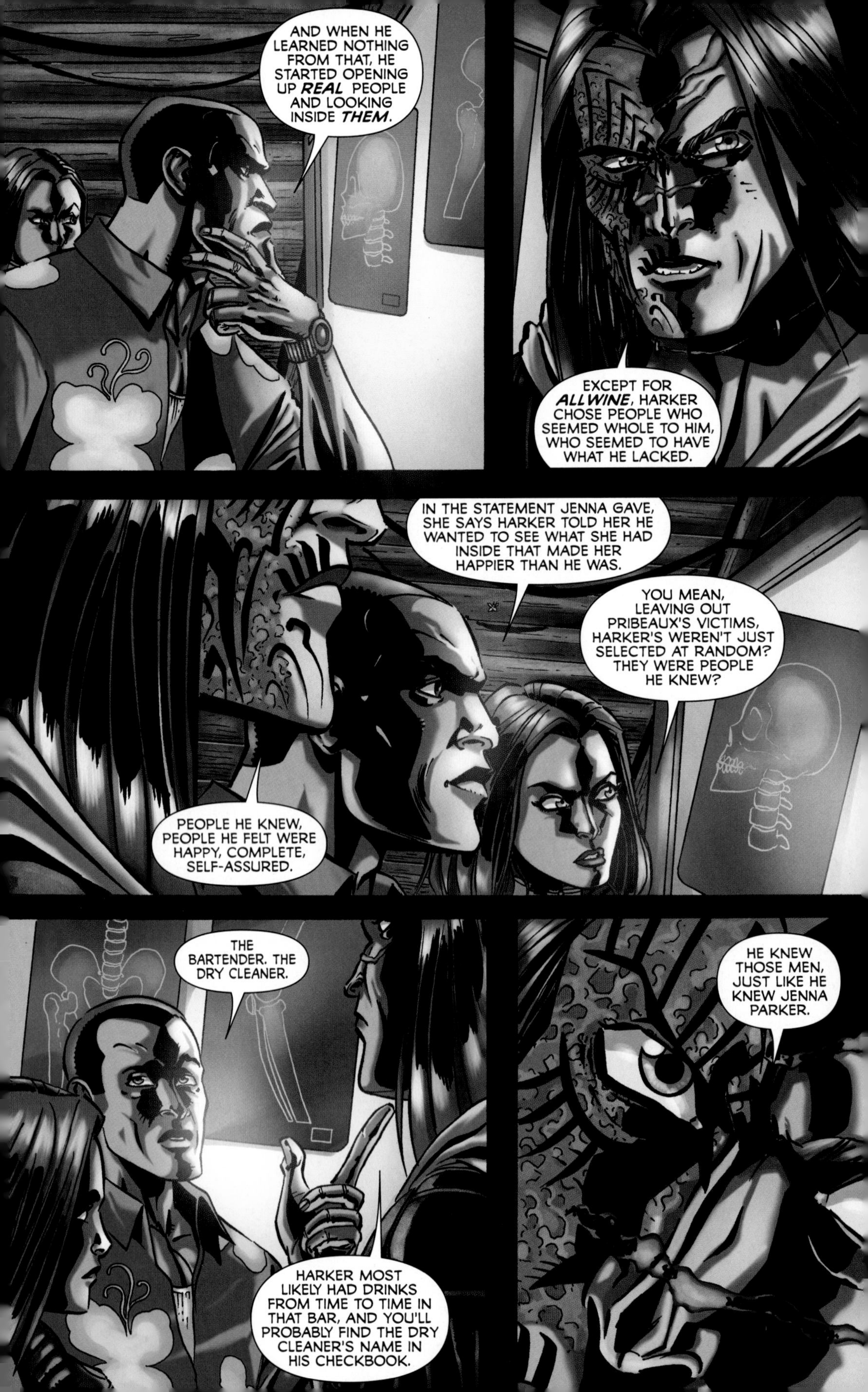
AND WHEN HE LEARNED NOTHING FROM THAT, HE STARTED OPENING UP *REAL* PEOPLE AND LOOKING INSIDE *THEM*.
EXCEPT FOR *ALLWINE*, HARKER CHOSE PEOPLE WHO SEEMED WHOLE TO HIM, WHO SEEMED TO HAVE WHAT HE LACKED.
IN THE STATEMENT JENNA GAVE, SHE SAYS HARKER TOLD HER HE WANTED TO SEE WHAT SHE HAD INSIDE THAT MADE HER HAPPIER THAN HE WAS.
YOU MEAN, LEAVING OUT PRIBEAUX'S VICTIMS, HARKER'S WEREN'T JUST SELECTED AT RANDOM? THEY WERE PEOPLE HE KNEW?
PEOPLE HE KNEW, PEOPLE HE FELT WERE HAPPY, COMPLETE, SELF-ASSURED.
THE BARTENDER. THE DRY CLEANER.
HARKER MOST LIKELY HAD DRINKS FROM TIME TO TIME IN THAT BAR, AND YOU'LL PROBABLY FIND THE DRY CLEANER'S NAME IN HIS CHECKBOOK.
HE KNEW THOSE MEN, JUST LIKE HE KNEW JENNA PARKER.

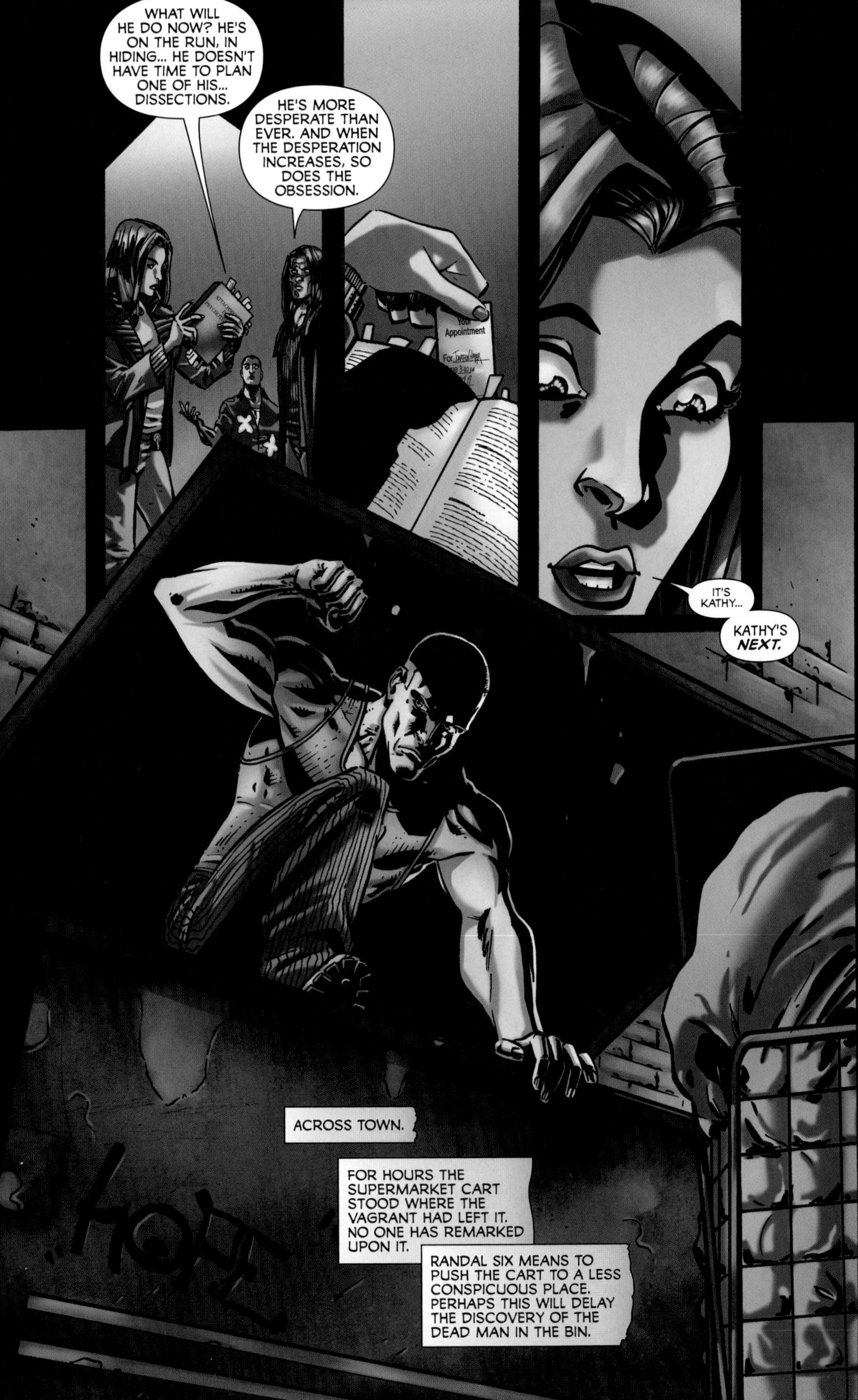
WHAT WILL HE DO NOW? HE'S ON THE RUN, IN HIDING... HE DOESN'T HAVE TIME TO PLAN ONE OF HIS... DISSECTIONS.
HE'S MORE DESPERATE THAN EVER. AND WHEN THE DESPERATION INCREASES, SO DOES THE OBSESSION.
Your Appointment
IT'S KATHY...
KATHY'S *NEXT.*
ACROSS TOWN.
FOR HOURS THE SUPERMARKET CART STOOD WHERE THE VAGRANT HAD LEFT IT. NO ONE HAS REMARKED UPON IT.
RANDAL SIX MEANS TO PUSH THE CART TO A LESS CONSPICUOUS PLACE. PERHAPS THIS WILL DELAY THE DISCOVERY OF THE DEAD MAN IN THE BIN.

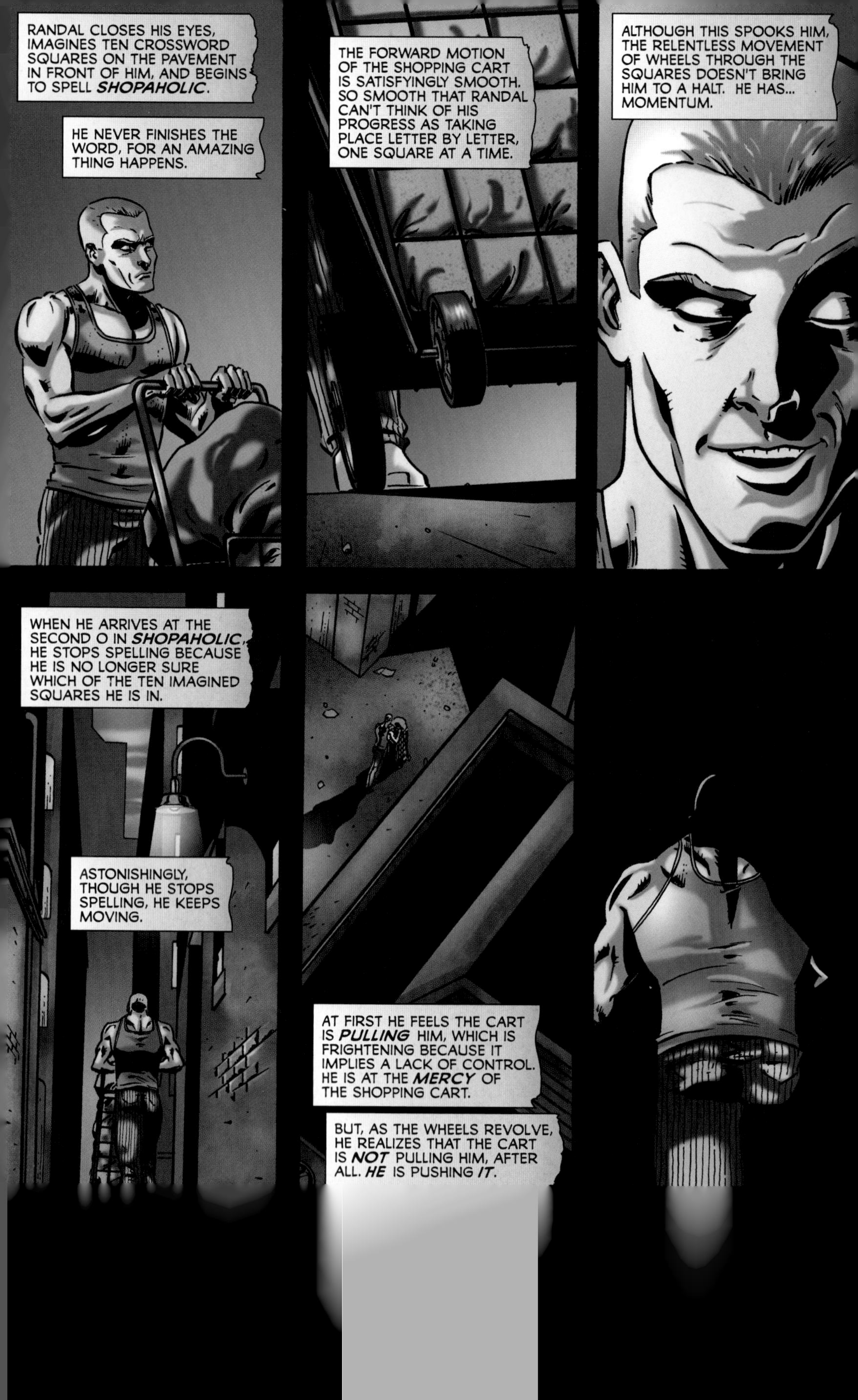
RANDAL CLOSES HIS EYES, IMAGINES TEN CROSSWORD SQUARES ON THE PAVEMENT IN FRONT OF HIM, AND BEGINS TO SPELL SHOPAHOLIC.
HE NEVER FINISHES THE WORD, FOR AN AMAZING THING HAPPENS.
THE FORWARD MOTION OF THE SHOPPING CART IS SATISFYINGLY SMOOTH. SO SMOOTH THAT RANDAL CAN'T THINK OF HIS PROGRESS AS TAKING PLACE LETTER BY LETTER, ONE SQUARE AT A TIME.
ALTHOUGH THIS SPOOKS HIM, THE RELENTLESS MOVEMENT OF WHEELS THROUGH THE SQUARES DOESN'T BRING HIM TO A HALT. HE HAS... MOMENTUM.
WHEN HE ARRIVES AT THE SECOND O IN SHOPAHOLIC, HE STOPS SPELLING BECAUSE HE IS NO LONGER SURE WHICH OF THE TEN IMAGINED SQUARES HE IS IN.
ASTONISHINGLY, THOUGH HE STOPS SPELLING, HE KEEPS MOVING.
AT FIRST HE FEELS THE CART IS PULLING HIM, WHICH IS FRIGHTENING BECAUSE IT IMPLIES A LACK OF CONTROL. HE IS AT THE MERCY OF THE SHOPPING CART.
BUT, AS THE WHEELS REVOLVE, HE REALIZES THAT THE CART IS NOT PULLING HIM, AFTER ALL. HE IS PUSHING IT.

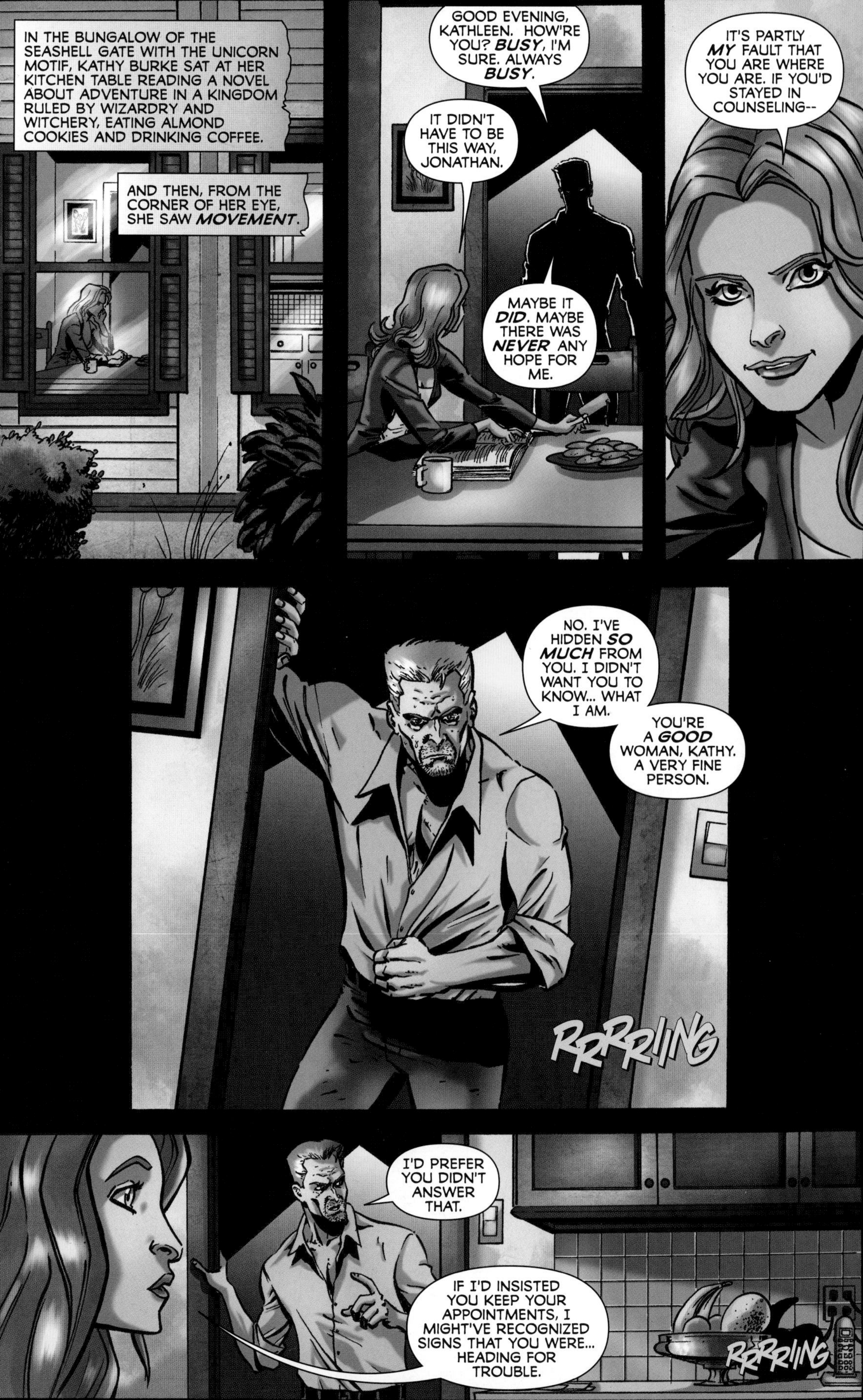
IN THE BUNGALOW OF THE SEASHELL GATE WITH THE UNICORN MOTIF, KATHY BURKE SAT AT HER KITCHEN TABLE READING A NOVEL ABOUT ADVENTURE IN A KINGDOM RULED BY WIZARDRY AND WITCHERY, EATING ALMOND COOKIES AND DRINKING COFFEE.
AND THEN, FROM THE CORNER OF HER EYE, SHE SAW MOVEMENT.
GOOD EVENING, KATHLEEN. HOW'RE YOU? BUSY, I'M SURE. ALWAYS BUSY.
IT DIDN'T HAVE TO BE THIS WAY, JONATHAN.
MAYBE IT DID. MAYBE THERE WAS NEVER ANY HOPE FOR ME.
IT'S PARTLY MY FAULT THAT YOU ARE WHERE YOU ARE. IF YOU'D STAYED IN COUNSELING--
NO. I'VE HIDDEN SO MUCH FROM YOU. I DIDN'T WANT YOU TO KNOW... WHAT I AM.
YOU'RE A GOOD WOMAN, KATHY. A VERY FINE PERSON.
RRRRIING
I'D PREFER YOU DIDN'T ANSWER THAT.
IF I'D INSISTED YOU KEEP YOUR APPOINTMENTS, I MIGHT'VE RECOGNIZED SIGNS THAT YOU WERE... HEADING FOR TROUBLE.
RRRRIING

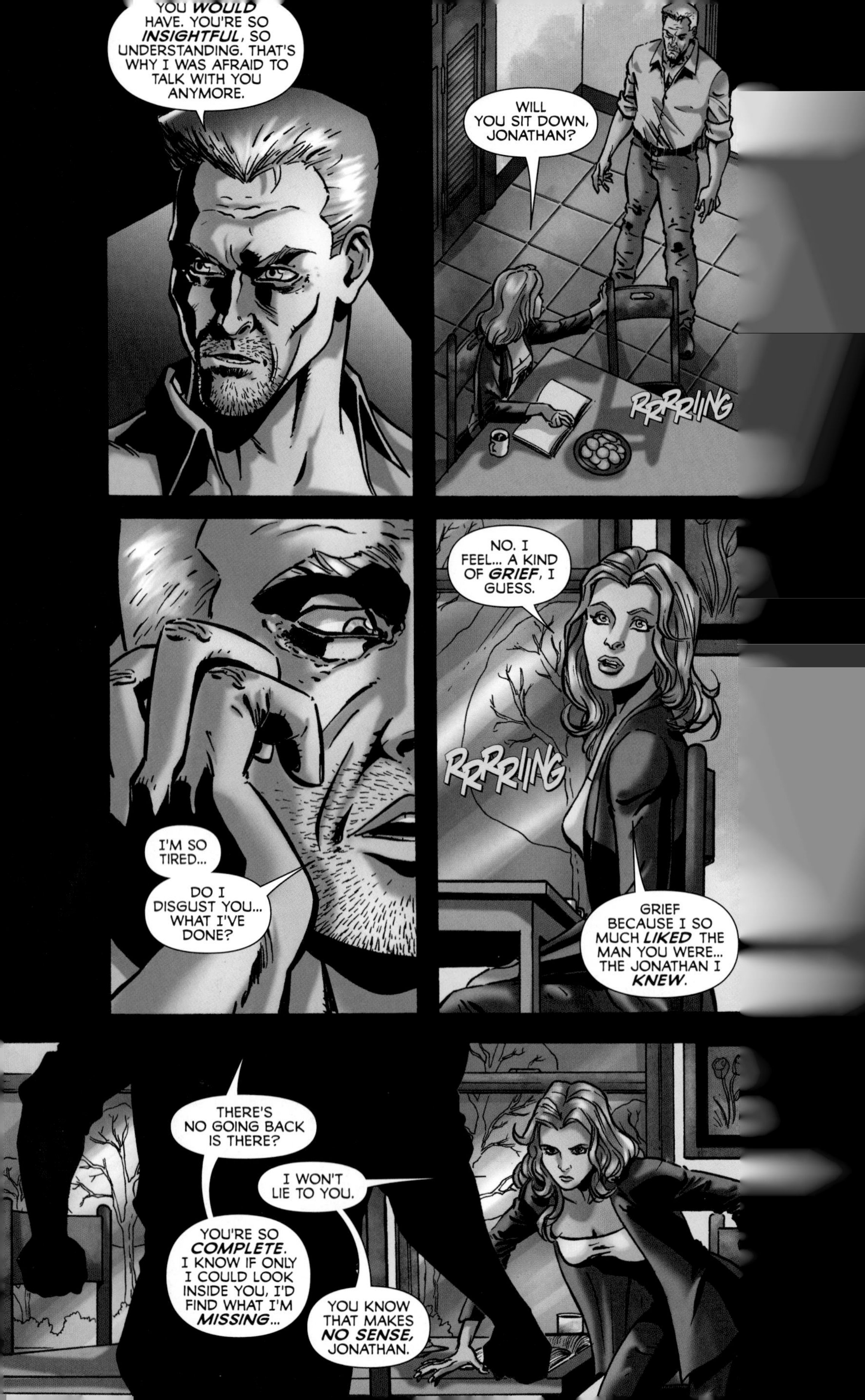
YOU WOULD HAVE. YOU'RE SO INSIGHTFUL, SO UNDERSTANDING. THAT'S WHY I WAS AFRAID TO TALK WITH YOU ANYMORE.
WILL YOU SIT DOWN, JONATHAN?
RRRRIIING
NO. I FEEL... A KIND OF GRIEF, I GUESS.
RRRRIIING
I'M SO TIRED...
DO I DISGUST YOU... WHAT I'VE DONE?
GRIEF BECAUSE I SO MUCH LIKED THE MAN YOU WERE... THE JONATHAN I KNEW.
THERE'S NO GOING BACK IS THERE?
I WON'T LIE TO YOU.
YOU'RE SO COMPLETE. I KNOW IF ONLY I COULD LOOK INSIDE YOU, I'D FIND WHAT I'M MISSING...
YOU KNOW THAT MAKES NO SENSE, JONATHAN.

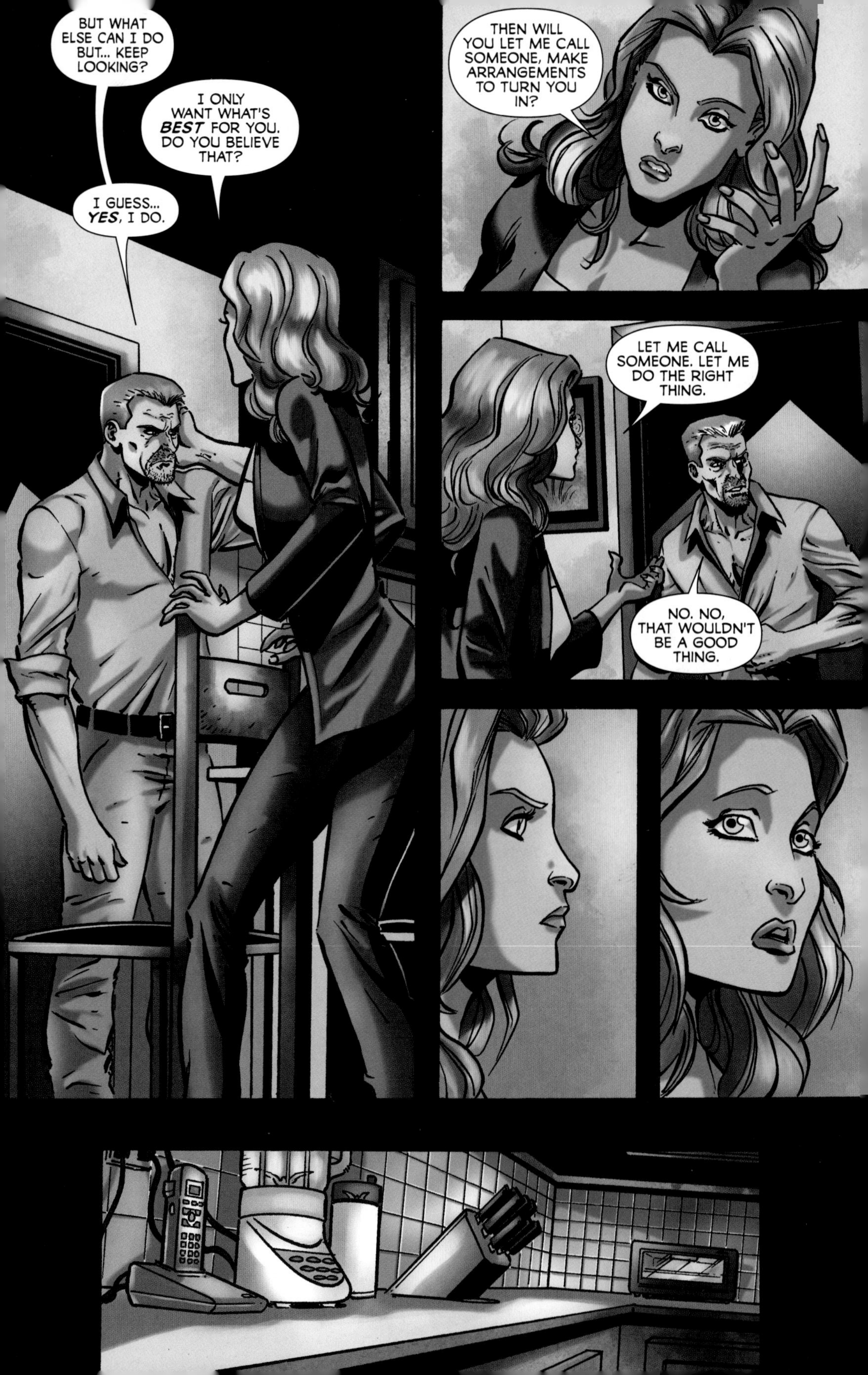
BUT WHAT ELSE CAN I DO BUT... KEEP LOOKING?
I ONLY WANT WHAT'S BEST FOR YOU. DO YOU BELIEVE THAT?
I GUESS... YES, I DO.
THEN WILL YOU LET ME CALL SOMEONE, MAKE ARRANGEMENTS TO TURN YOU IN?
LET ME CALL SOMEONE. LET ME DO THE RIGHT THING.
NO. NO, THAT WOULDN'T BE A GOOD THING.

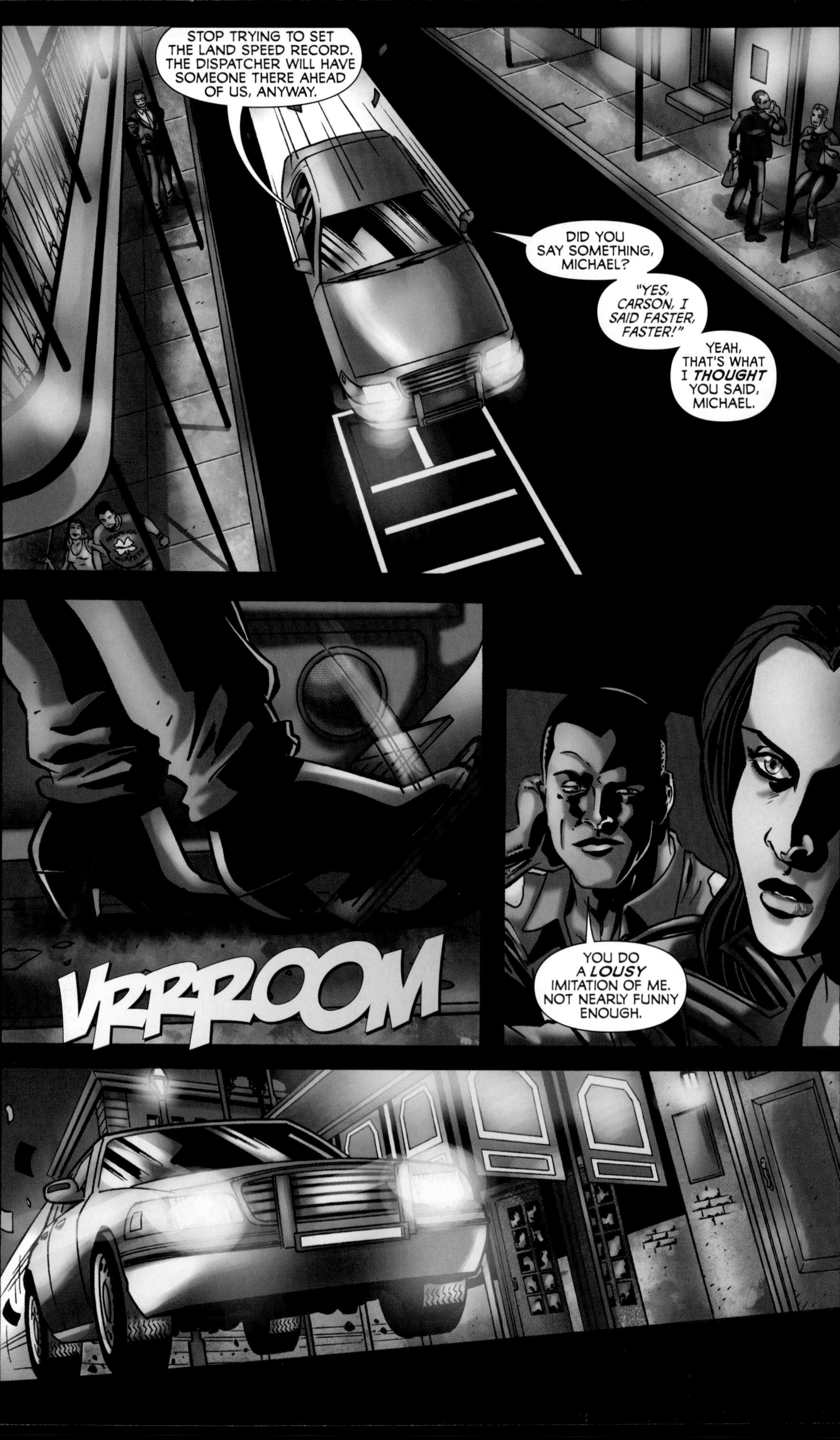
STOP TRYING TO SET THE LAND SPEED RECORD. THE DISPATCHER WILL HAVE SOMEONE THERE AHEAD OF US, ANYWAY.
DID YOU SAY SOMETHING, MICHAEL?
"YES, CARSON, I SAID FASTER, FASTER!"
YEAH, THAT'S WHAT I ***THOUGHT*** YOU SAID, MICHAEL.
VRRROOM
YOU DO A ***LOUSY*** IMITATION OF ME. NOT NEARLY FUNNY ENOUGH.

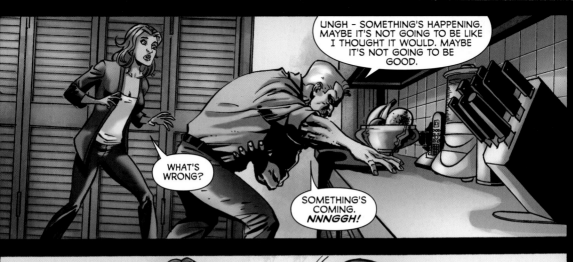

UNGH — SOMETHING'S HAPPENING. MAYBE IT'S NOT GOING TO BE LIKE I THOUGHT IT WOULD. MAYBE IT'S NOT GOING TO BE GOOD.

WHAT'S WRONG?

SOMETHING'S COMING. *NNNGGH!*

JONATHAN?!

I'M *SPLITTING*.

F-FATHER?

DETECTIVES!

OH, THANK GOD.

HARKER WENT OUT THE BACK--

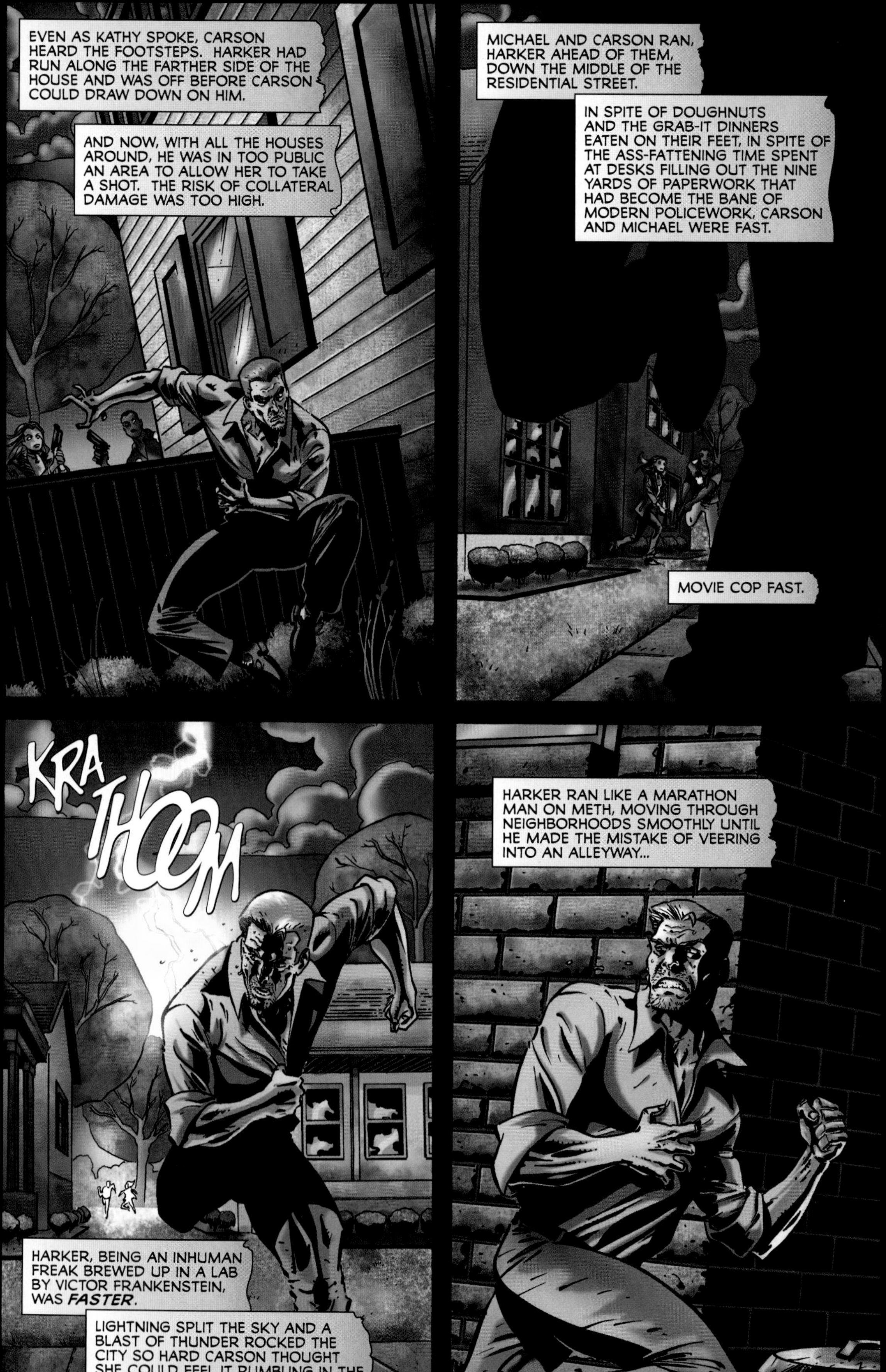
EVEN AS KATHY SPOKE, CARSON HEARD THE FOOTSTEPS. HARKER HAD RUN ALONG THE FARTHER SIDE OF THE HOUSE AND WAS OFF BEFORE CARSON COULD DRAW DOWN ON HIM.
AND NOW, WITH ALL THE HOUSES AROUND, HE WAS IN TOO PUBLIC AN AREA TO ALLOW HER TO TAKE A SHOT. THE RISK OF COLLATERAL DAMAGE WAS TOO HIGH.
MICHAEL AND CARSON RAN, HARKER AHEAD OF THEM, DOWN THE MIDDLE OF THE RESIDENTIAL STREET.
IN SPITE OF DOUGHNUTS AND THE GRAB-IT DINNERS EATEN ON THEIR FEET, IN SPITE OF THE ASS-FATTENING TIME SPENT AT DESKS FILLING OUT THE NINE YARDS OF PAPERWORK THAT HAD BECOME THE BANE OF MODERN POLICEWORK, CARSON AND MICHAEL WERE FAST.
MOVIE COP FAST.
KRA THOOM
HARKER, BEING AN INHUMAN FREAK BREWED UP IN A LAB BY VICTOR FRANKENSTEIN, WAS *FASTER*.
LIGHTNING SPLIT THE SKY AND A BLAST OF THUNDER ROCKED THE CITY SO HARD CARSON THOUGHT SHE COULD FEEL IT RUMBLING IN THE GROUND, BUT THE RAIN HELD OFF.
HARKER RAN LIKE A MARATHON MAN ON METH, MOVING THROUGH NEIGHBORHOODS SMOOTHLY UNTIL HE MADE THE MISTAKE OF VEERING INTO AN ALLEYWAY...

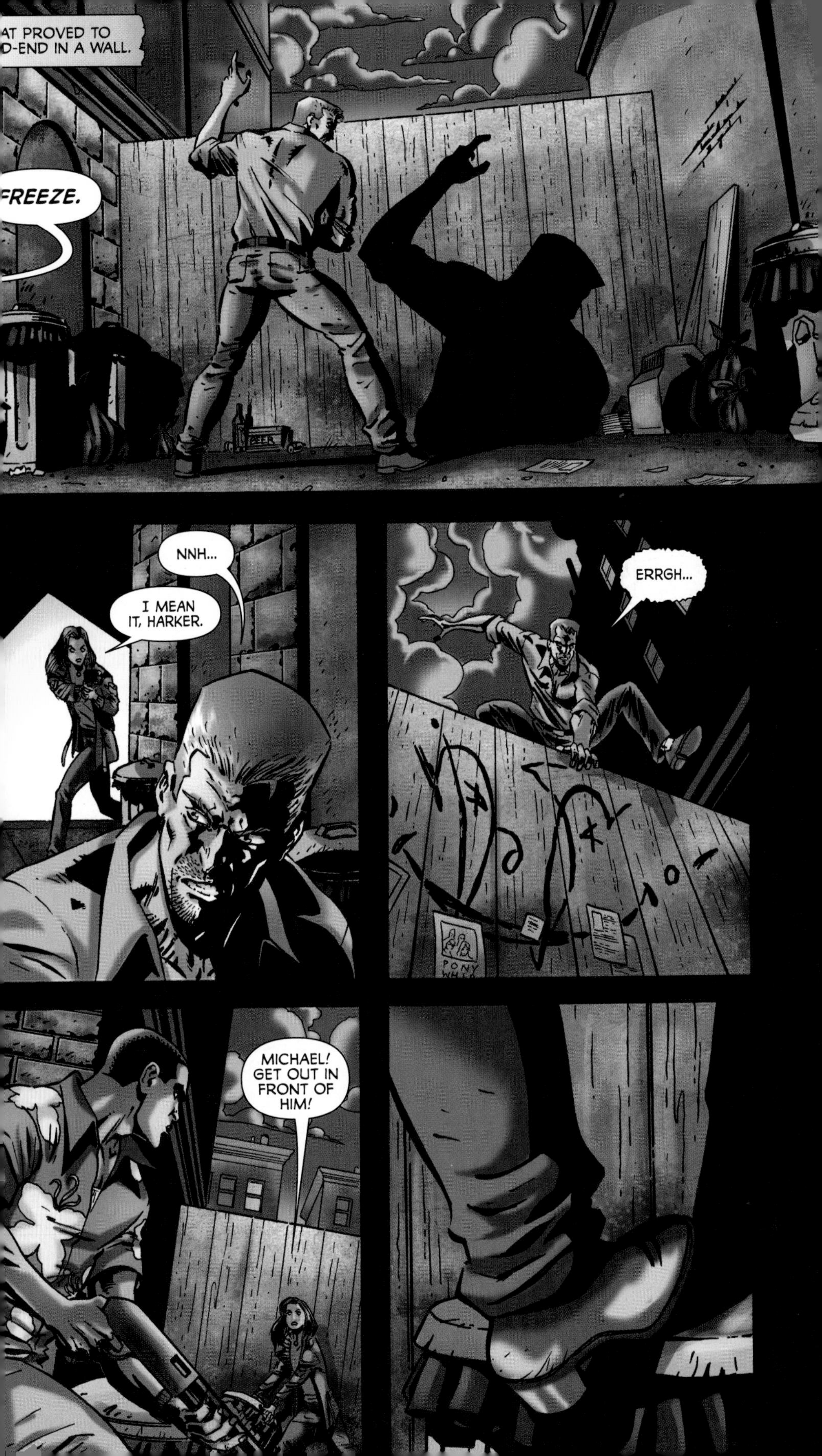
AT PROVED TO
D-END IN A WALL.
FREEZE.
NNH...
I MEAN IT, HARKER.
ERRGH...
MICHAEL! GET OUT IN FRONT OF HIM!

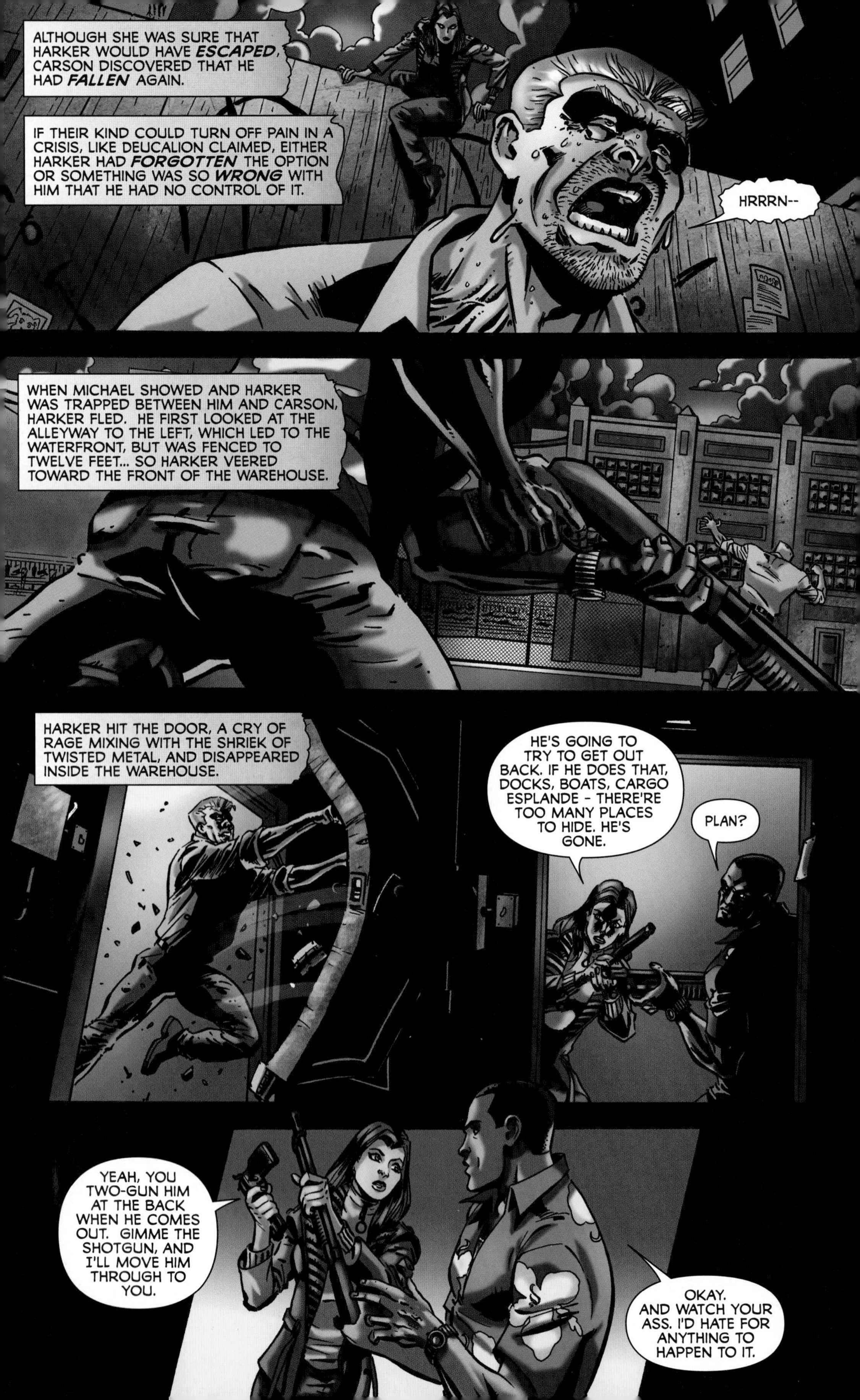
ALTHOUGH SHE WAS SURE THAT HARKER WOULD HAVE ESCAPED, CARSON DISCOVERED THAT HE HAD FALLEN AGAIN.
IF THEIR KIND COULD TURN OFF PAIN IN A CRISIS, LIKE DEUCALION CLAIMED, EITHER HARKER HAD FORGOTTEN THE OPTION OR SOMETHING WAS SO WRONG WITH HIM THAT HE HAD NO CONTROL OF IT.
HRRRN--
WHEN MICHAEL SHOWED AND HARKER WAS TRAPPED BETWEEN HIM AND CARSON, HARKER FLED. HE FIRST LOOKED AT THE ALLEYWAY TO THE LEFT, WHICH LED TO THE WATERFRONT, BUT WAS FENCED TO TWELVE FEET... SO HARKER VEERED TOWARD THE FRONT OF THE WAREHOUSE.
HARKER HIT THE DOOR, A CRY OF RAGE MIXING WITH THE SHRIEK OF TWISTED METAL, AND DISAPPEARED INSIDE THE WAREHOUSE.
HE'S GOING TO TRY TO GET OUT BACK. IF HE DOES THAT, DOCKS, BOATS, CARGO ESPLANDE - THERE'RE TOO MANY PLACES TO HIDE. HE'S GONE.
PLAN?
YEAH, YOU TWO-GUN HIM AT THE BACK WHEN HE COMES OUT. GIMME THE SHOTGUN, AND I'LL MOVE HIM THROUGH TO YOU.
OKAY. AND WATCH YOUR ASS. I'D HATE FOR ANYTHING TO HAPPEN TO IT.

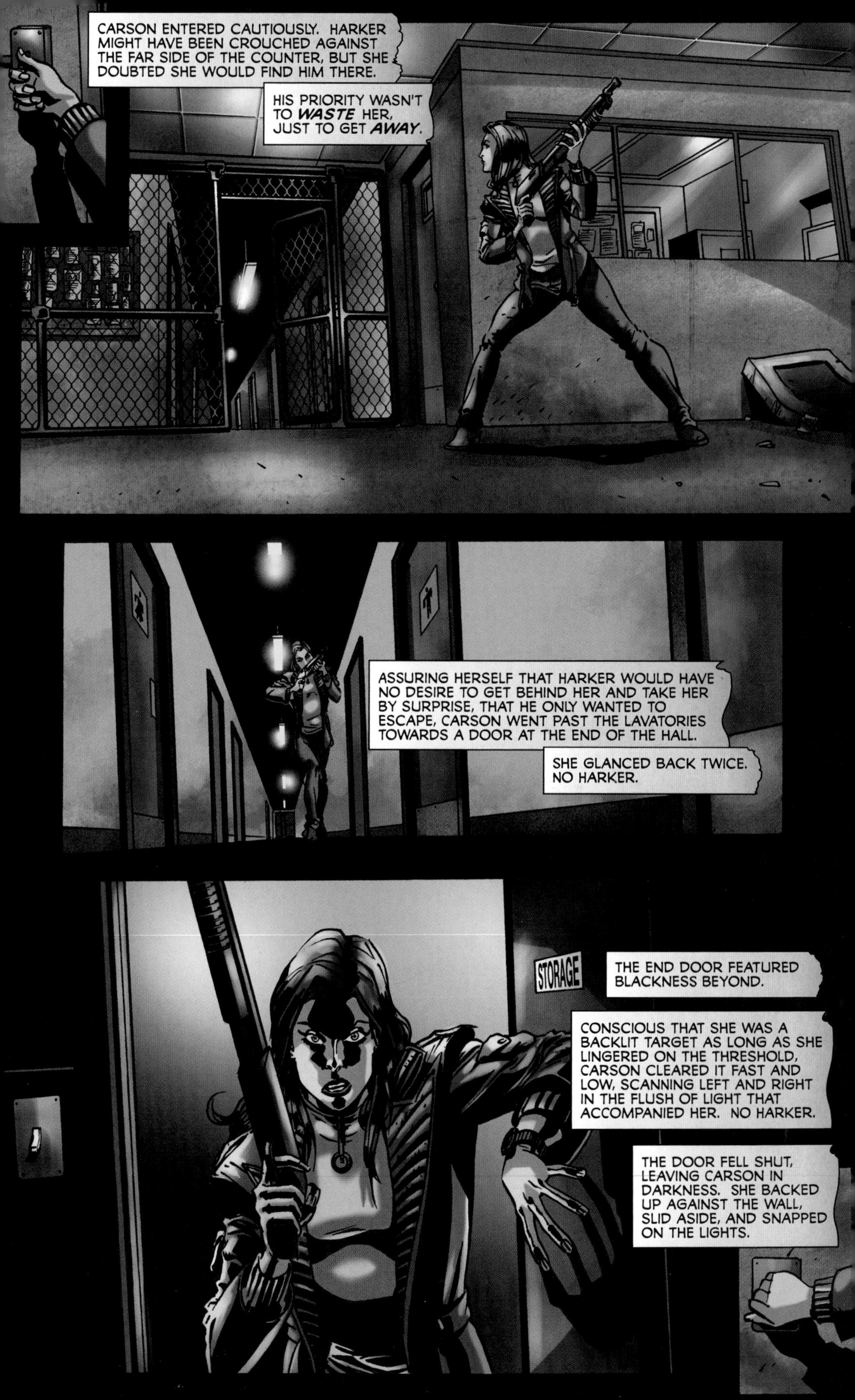

CARSON ENTERED CAUTIOUSLY. HARKER MIGHT HAVE BEEN CROUCHED AGAINST THE FAR SIDE OF THE COUNTER, BUT SHE DOUBTED SHE WOULD FIND HIM THERE.
HIS PRIORITY WASN'T TO *WASTE* HER, JUST TO GET *AWAY*.
ASSURING HERSELF THAT HARKER WOULD HAVE NO DESIRE TO GET BEHIND HER AND TAKE HER BY SURPRISE, THAT HE ONLY WANTED TO ESCAPE, CARSON WENT PAST THE LAVATORIES TOWARDS A DOOR AT THE END OF THE HALL.
SHE GLANCED BACK TWICE. NO HARKER.
STORAGE
THE END DOOR FEATURED BLACKNESS BEYOND.
CONSCIOUS THAT SHE WAS A BACKLIT TARGET AS LONG AS SHE LINGERED ON THE THRESHOLD, CARSON CLEARED IT FAST AND LOW, SCANNING LEFT AND RIGHT IN THE FLUSH OF LIGHT THAT ACCOMPANIED HER. NO HARKER.
THE DOOR FELL SHUT, LEAVING CARSON IN DARKNESS. SHE BACKED UP AGAINST THE WALL, SLID ASIDE, AND SNAPPED ON THE LIGHTS.

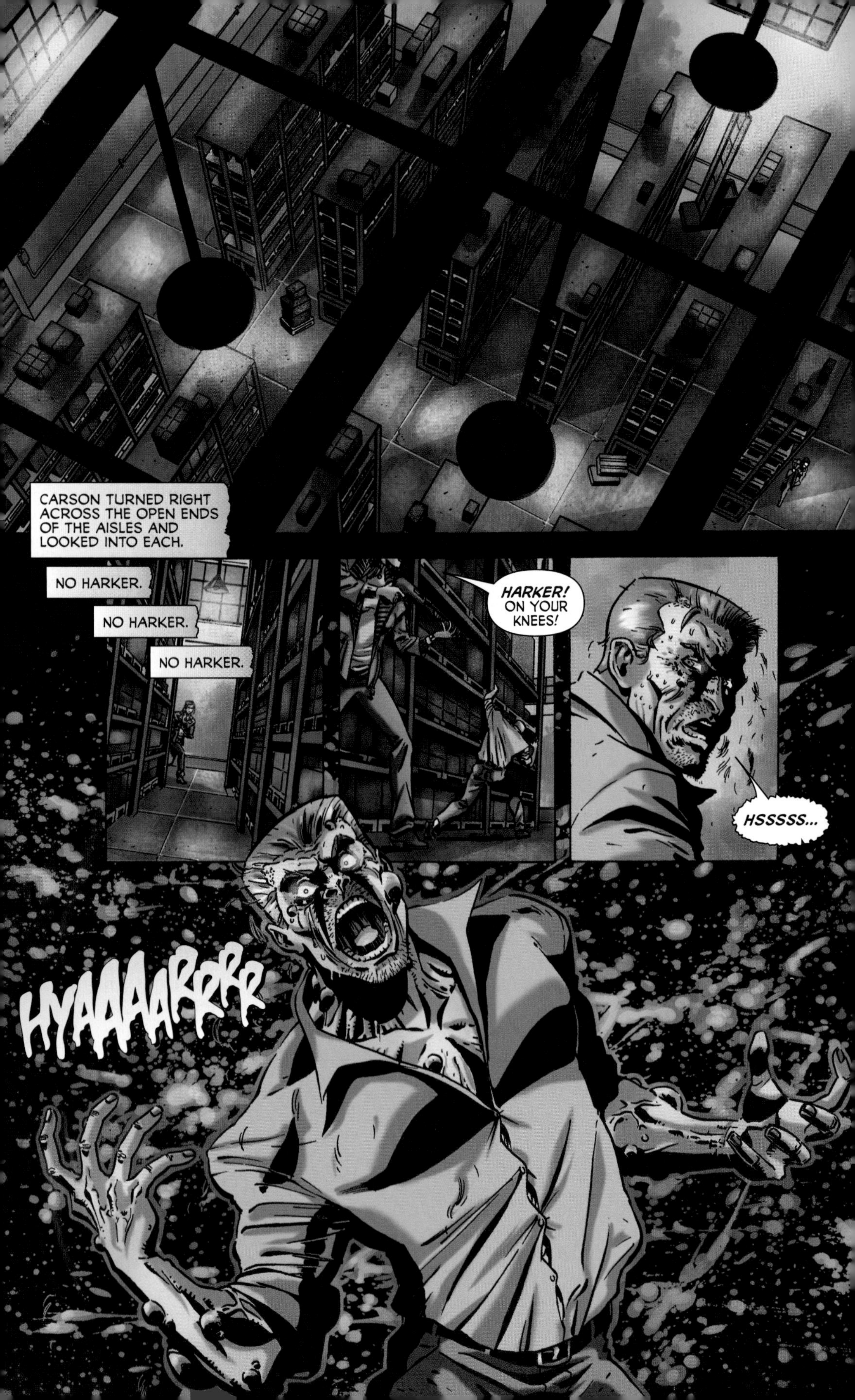
CARSON TURNED RIGHT ACROSS THE OPEN ENDS OF THE AISLES AND LOOKED INTO EACH.
NO HARKER.
NO HARKER.
NO HARKER.
HARKER! ON YOUR KNEES!
HSSSSS...
HYAAAARRRR

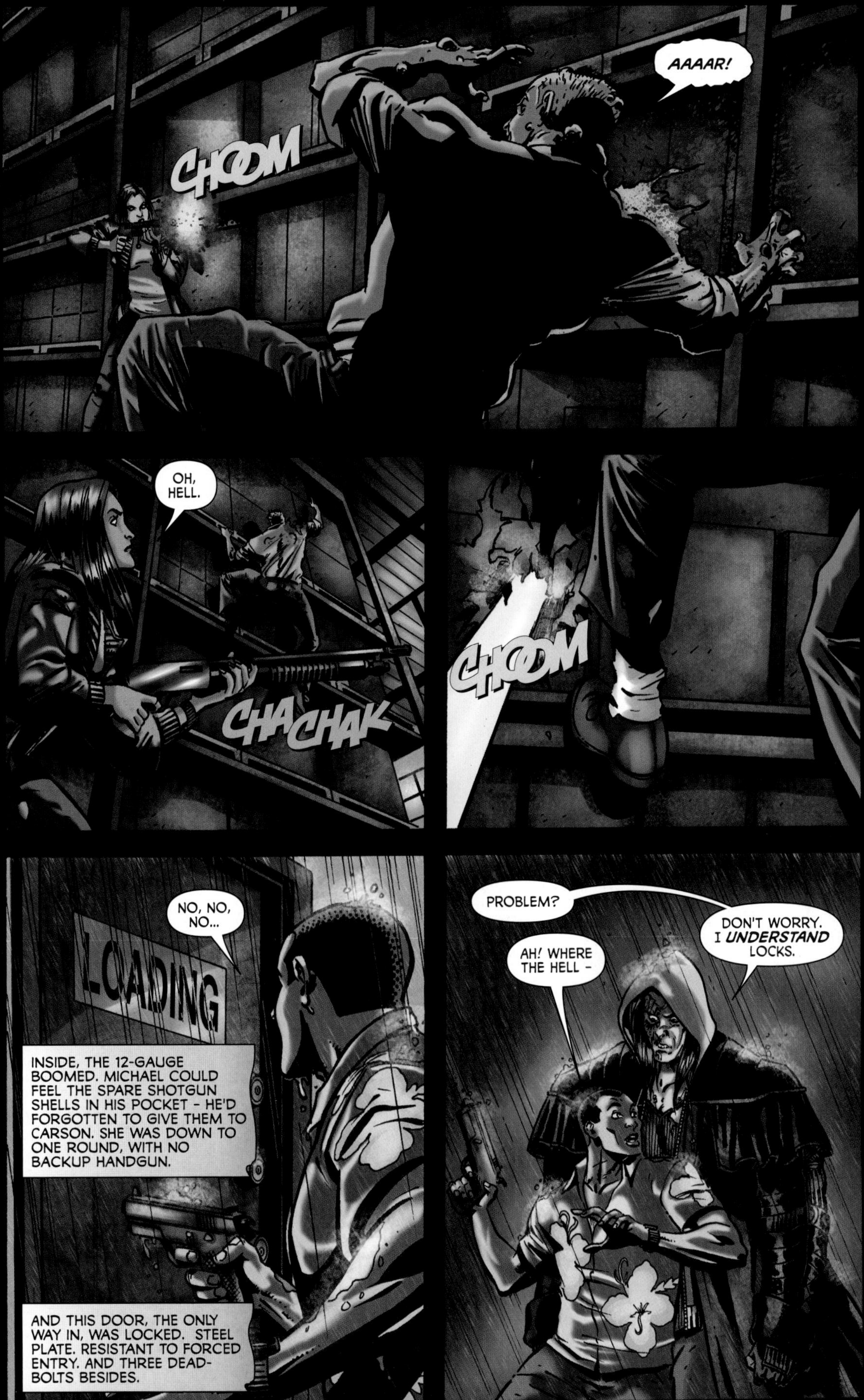
AAAAR!
CHOOM
OH, HELL.
CHACHAK
CHOOM
NO, NO, NO...
LOADING
INSIDE, THE 12-GAUGE BOOMED. MICHAEL COULD FEEL THE SPARE SHOTGUN SHELLS IN HIS POCKET - HE'D FORGOTTEN TO GIVE THEM TO CARSON. SHE WAS DOWN TO ONE ROUND, WITH NO BACKUP HANDGUN.
AND THIS DOOR, THE ONLY WAY IN, WAS LOCKED. STEEL PLATE. RESISTANT TO FORCED ENTRY. AND THREE DEAD-BOLTS BESIDES.
PROBLEM?
AH! WHERE THE HELL -
DON'T WORRY. I *UNDERSTAND* LOCKS.

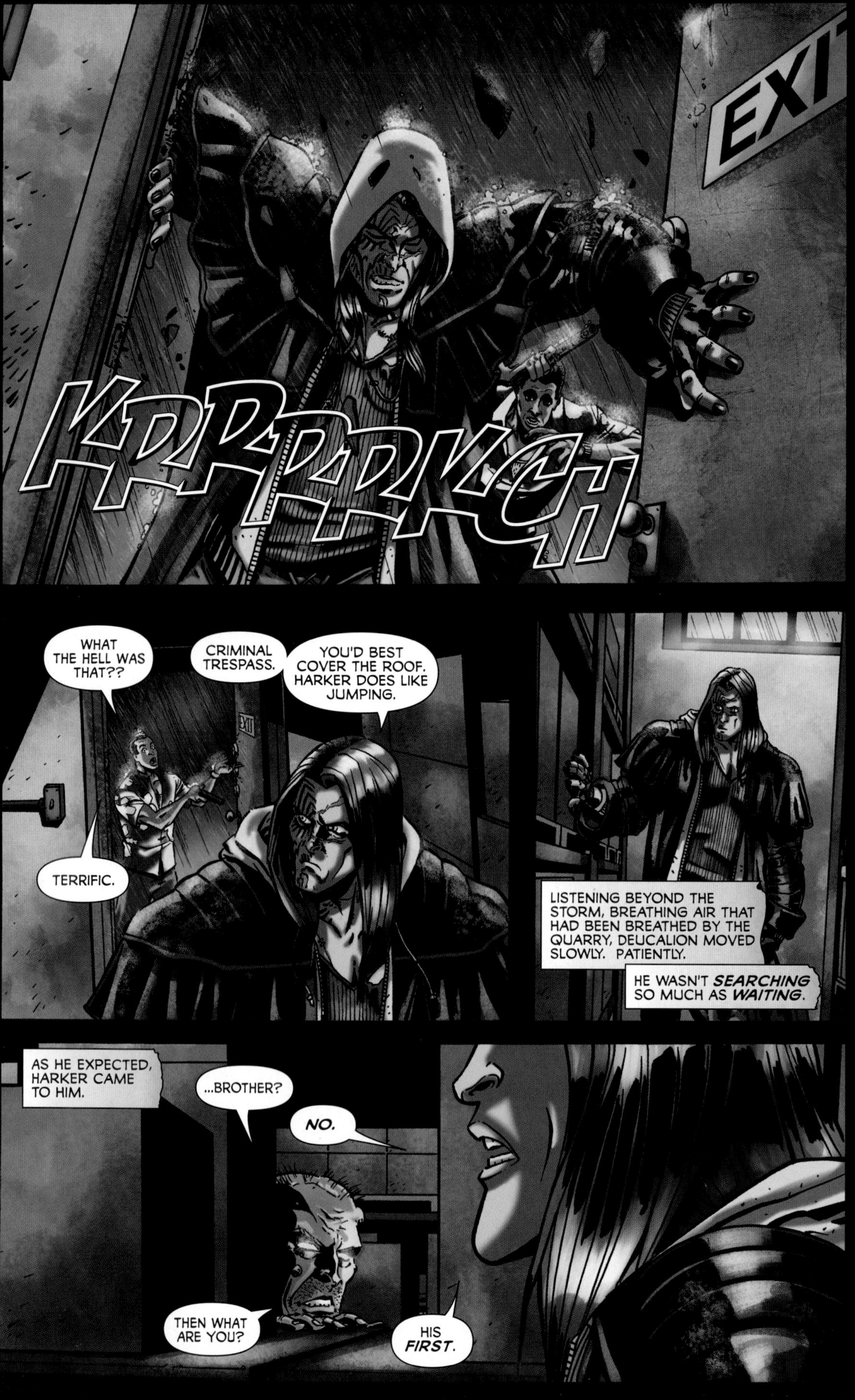
EXIT
KRRRRKCH
WHAT THE HELL WAS THAT??
CRIMINAL TRESPASS.
YOU'D BEST COVER THE ROOF. HARKER DOES LIKE JUMPING.
TERRIFIC.
LISTENING BEYOND THE STORM, BREATHING AIR THAT HAD BEEN BREATHED BY THE QUARRY, DEUCALION MOVED SLOWLY. PATIENTLY.
HE WASN'T *SEARCHING* SO MUCH AS *WAITING*.
AS HE EXPECTED, HARKER CAME TO HIM.
...BROTHER?
NO.
THEN WHAT ARE YOU?
HIS *FIRST*.

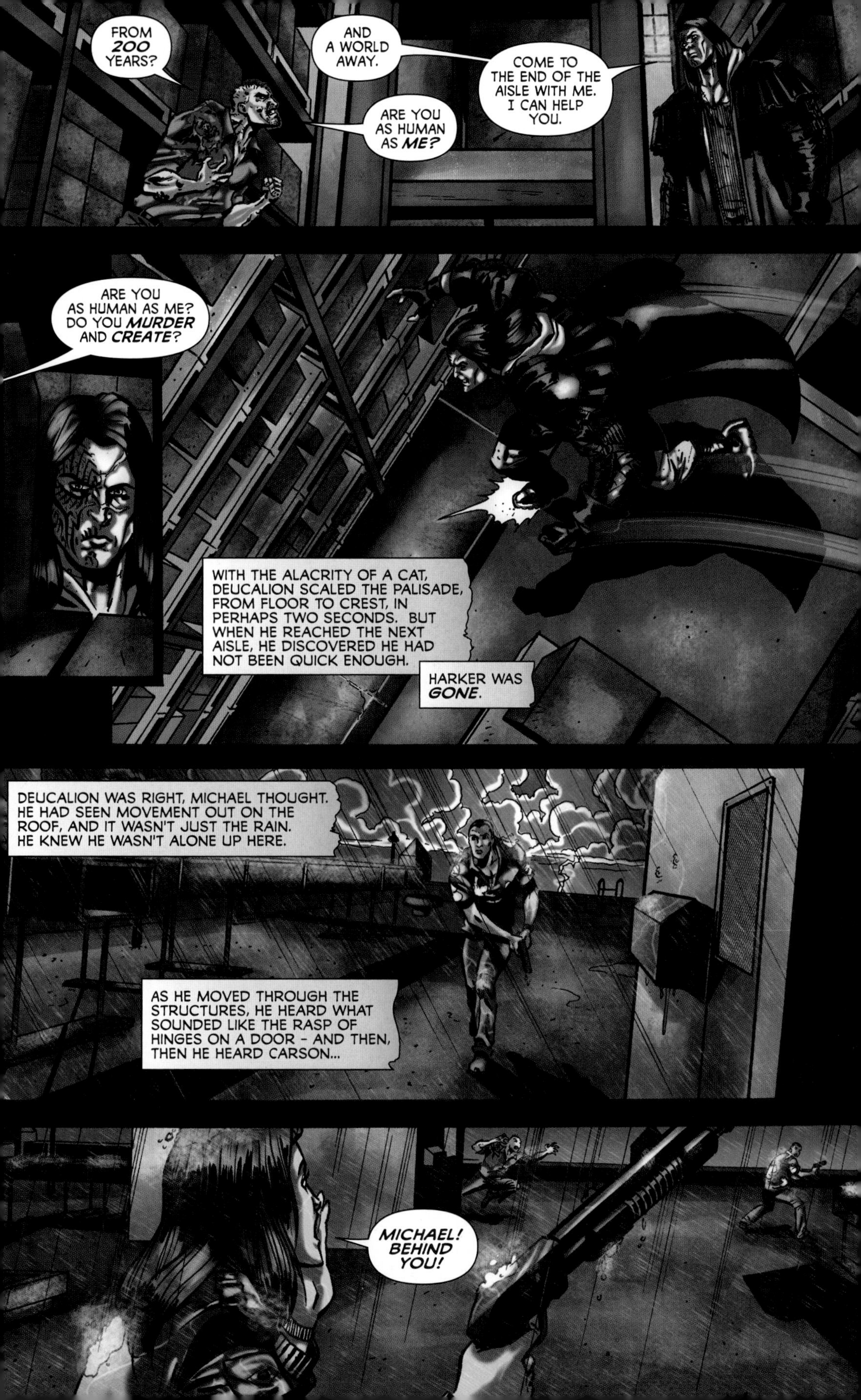
FROM 200 YEARS?
AND A WORLD AWAY.
ARE YOU AS HUMAN AS ME?
COME TO THE END OF THE AISLE WITH ME. I CAN HELP YOU.
ARE YOU AS HUMAN AS ME? DO YOU MURDER AND CREATE?
WITH THE ALACRITY OF A CAT, DEUCALION SCALED THE PALISADE, FROM FLOOR TO CREST, IN PERHAPS TWO SECONDS. BUT WHEN HE REACHED THE NEXT AISLE, HE DISCOVERED HE HAD NOT BEEN QUICK ENOUGH.
HARKER WAS GONE.
DEUCALION WAS RIGHT, MICHAEL THOUGHT. HE HAD SEEN MOVEMENT OUT ON THE ROOF, AND IT WASN'T JUST THE RAIN. HE KNEW HE WASN'T ALONE UP HERE.
AS HE MOVED THROUGH THE STRUCTURES, HE HEARD WHAT SOUNDED LIKE THE RASP OF HINGES ON A DOOR - AND THEN, THEN HE HEARD CARSON...
MICHAEL! BEHIND YOU!

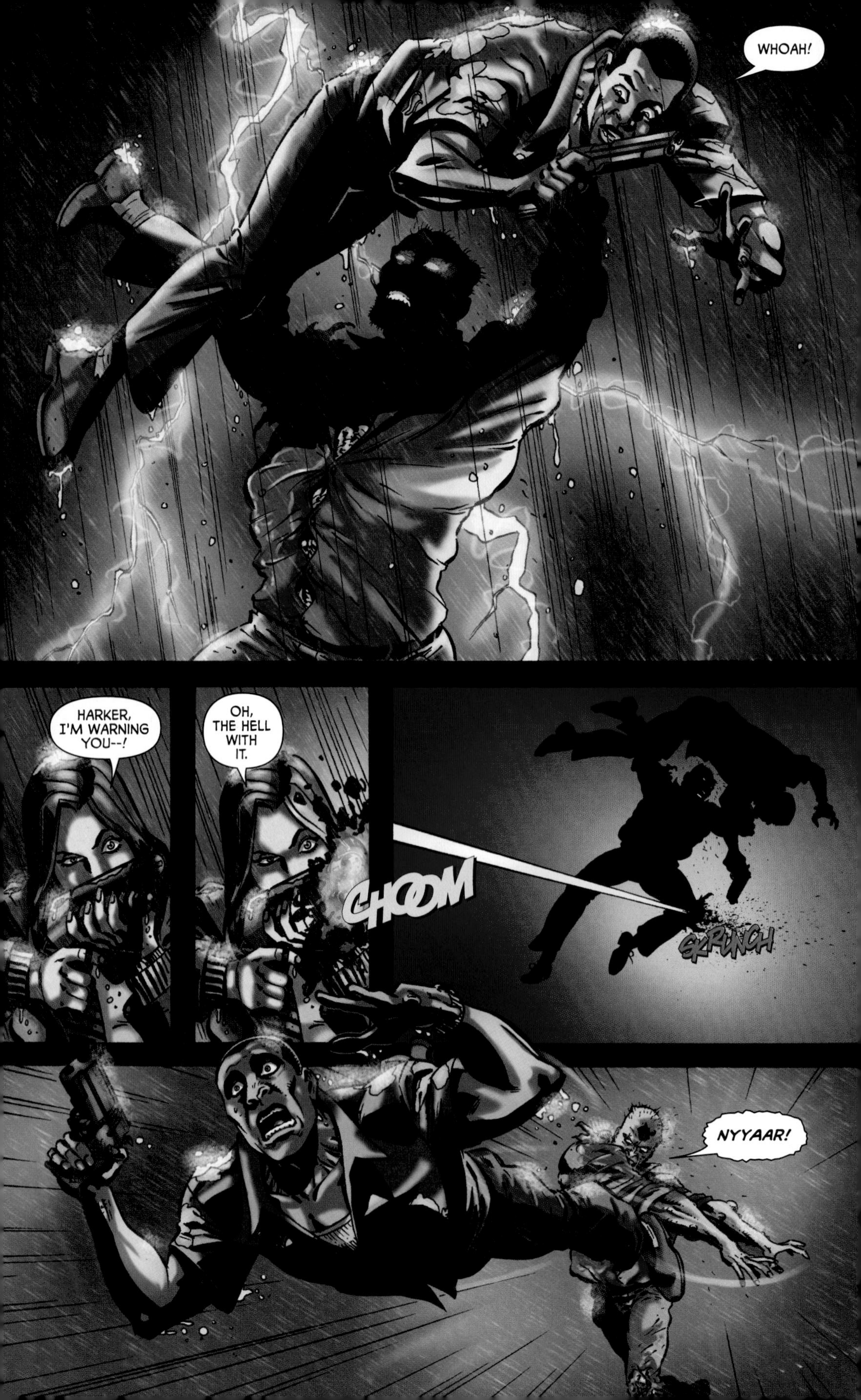
WHOAH!
HARKER, I'M WARNING YOU--!
OH, THE HELL WITH IT.
CHOOM
SKRUNCH
NYYAAR!

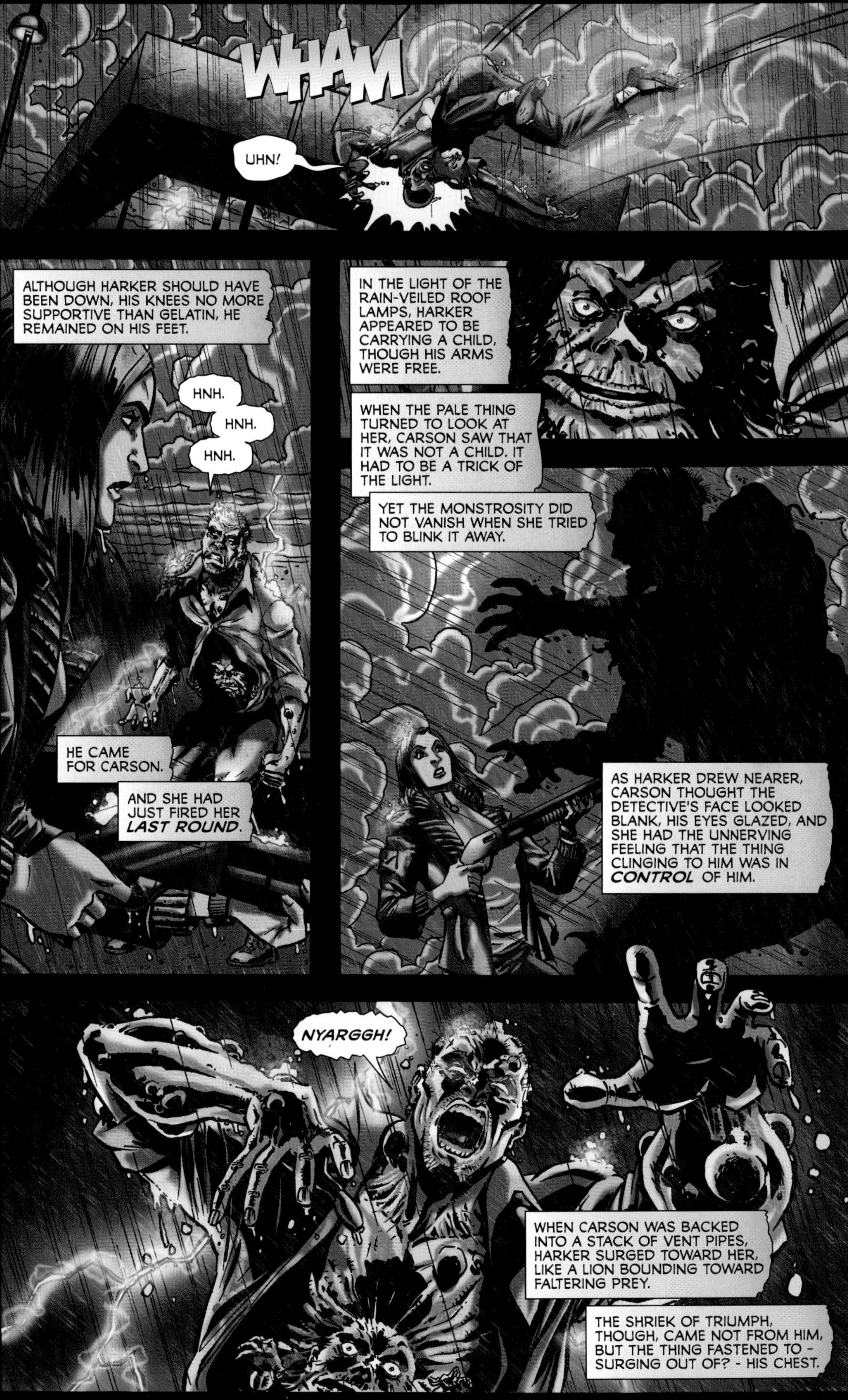
WHAM
UHN!
ALTHOUGH HARKER SHOULD HAVE BEEN DOWN, HIS KNEES NO MORE SUPPORTIVE THAN GELATIN, HE REMAINED ON HIS FEET.
HNH.
HNH.
HNH.
HE CAME FOR CARSON.
AND SHE HAD JUST FIRED HER LAST ROUND.
IN THE LIGHT OF THE RAIN-VEILED ROOF LAMPS, HARKER APPEARED TO BE CARRYING A CHILD, THOUGH HIS ARMS WERE FREE.
WHEN THE PALE THING TURNED TO LOOK AT HER, CARSON SAW THAT IT WAS NOT A CHILD. IT HAD TO BE A TRICK OF THE LIGHT.
YET THE MONSTROSITY DID NOT VANISH WHEN SHE TRIED TO BLINK IT AWAY.
AS HARKER DREW NEARER, CARSON THOUGHT THE DETECTIVE'S FACE LOOKED BLANK, HIS EYES GLAZED, AND SHE HAD THE UNNERVING FEELING THAT THE THING CLINGING TO HIM WAS IN CONTROL OF HIM.
NYARGGH!
WHEN CARSON WAS BACKED INTO A STACK OF VENT PIPES, HARKER SURGED TOWARD HER, LIKE A LION BOUNDING TOWARD FALTERING PREY.
THE SHRIEK OF TRIUMPH, THOUGH, CAME NOT FROM HIM, BUT THE THING FASTENED TO - SURGING OUT OF? - HIS CHEST.

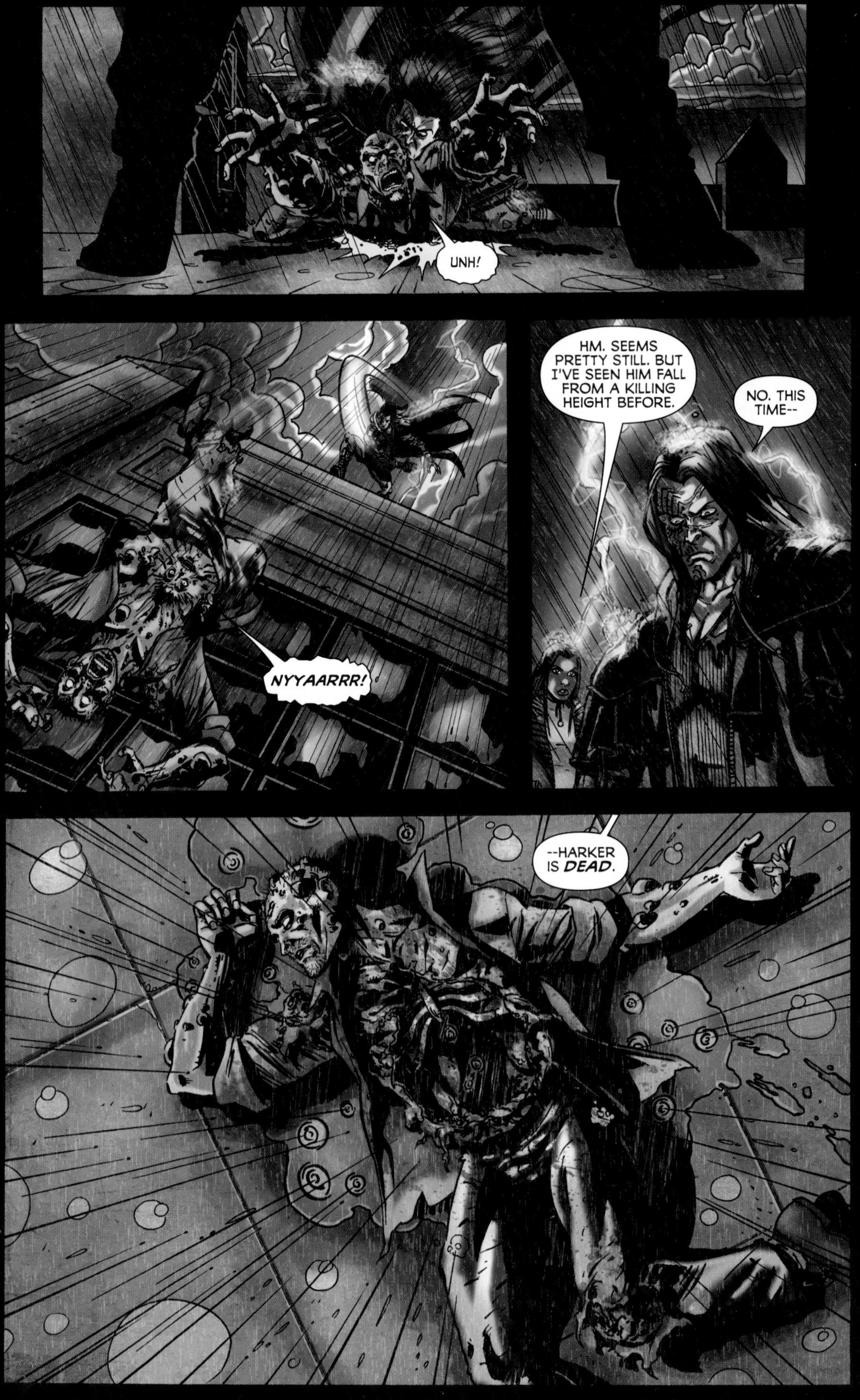
UNH!
NYYAARRR!
HM. SEEMS PRETTY STILL. BUT I'VE SEEN HIM FALL FROM A KILLING HEIGHT BEFORE.
NO. THIS TIME--
--HARKER IS *DEAD*.

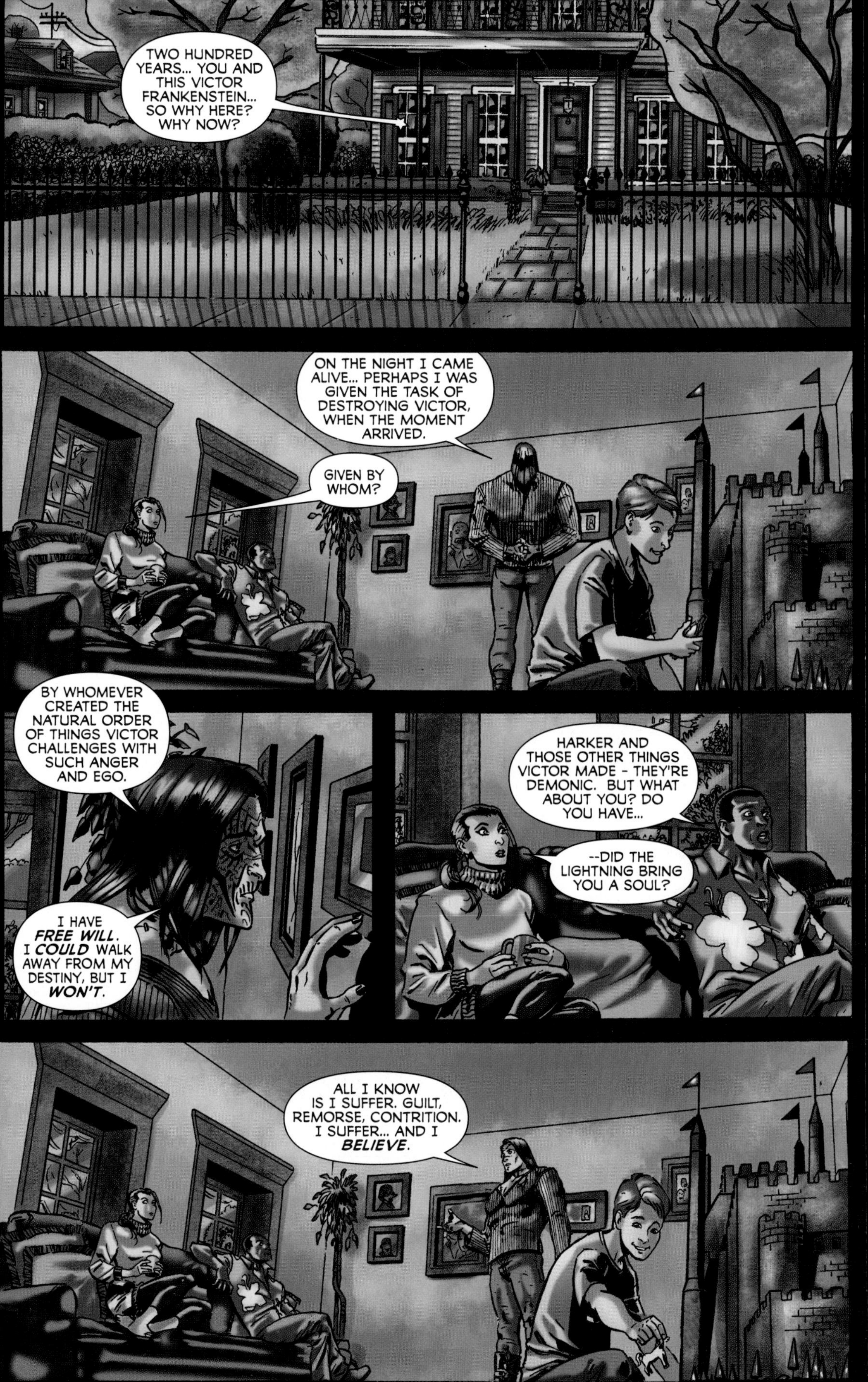

TWO HUNDRED YEARS... YOU AND THIS VICTOR FRANKENSTEIN... SO WHY HERE? WHY NOW?
ON THE NIGHT I CAME ALIVE... PERHAPS I WAS GIVEN THE TASK OF DESTROYING VICTOR, WHEN THE MOMENT ARRIVED.
GIVEN BY WHOM?
BY WHOMEVER CREATED THE NATURAL ORDER OF THINGS VICTOR CHALLENGES WITH SUCH ANGER AND EGO.
I HAVE ***FREE WILL***. I ***COULD*** WALK AWAY FROM MY DESTINY, BUT I ***WON'T***.
HARKER AND THOSE OTHER THINGS VICTOR MADE - THEY'RE DEMONIC. BUT WHAT ABOUT YOU? DO YOU HAVE...
--DID THE LIGHTNING BRING YOU A SOUL?
ALL I KNOW IS I SUFFER. GUILT, REMORSE, CONTRITION. I SUFFER... AND I ***BELIEVE***.

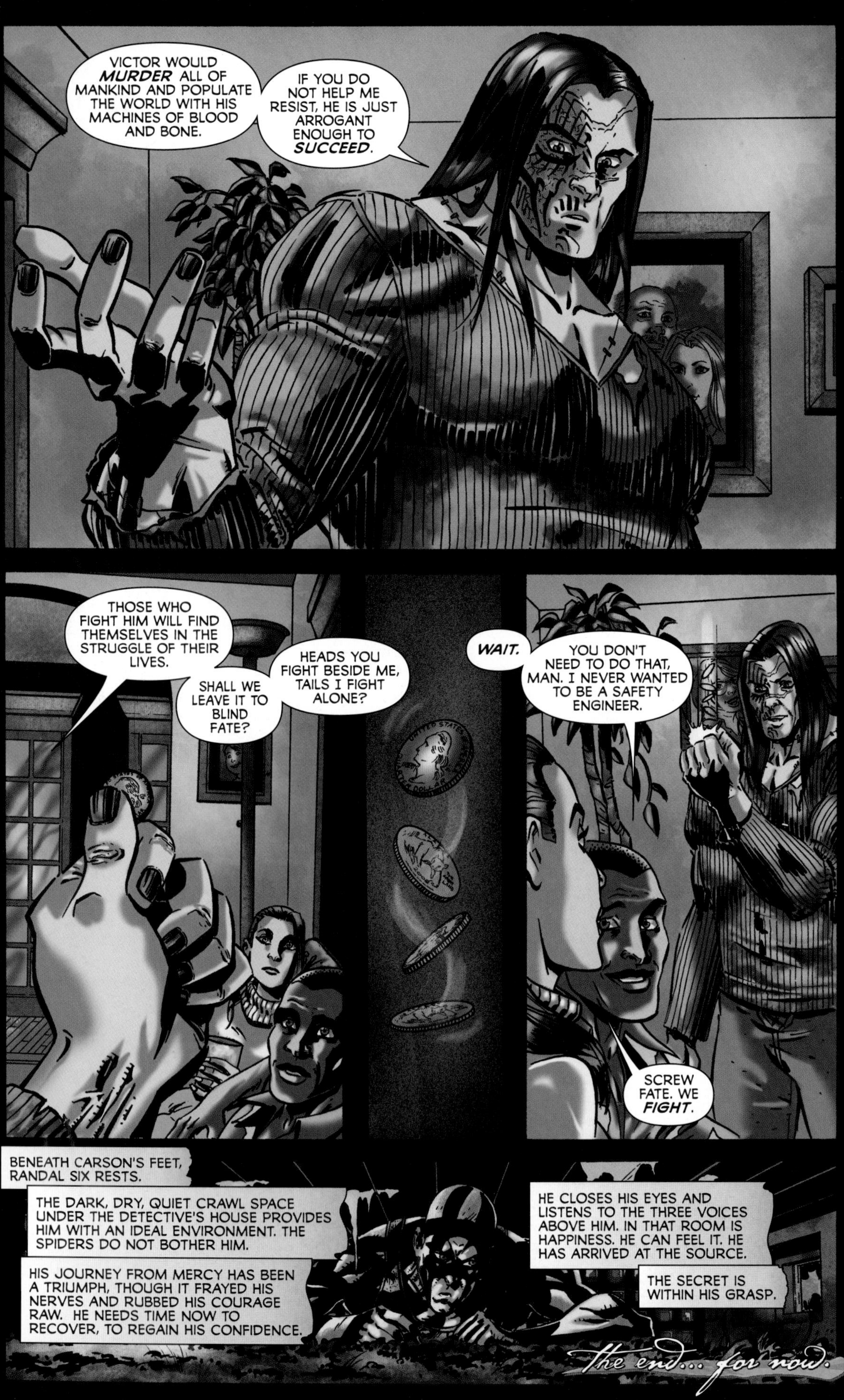
VICTOR WOULD MURDER ALL OF MANKIND AND POPULATE THE WORLD WITH HIS MACHINES OF BLOOD AND BONE.
IF YOU DO NOT HELP ME RESIST, HE IS JUST ARROGANT ENOUGH TO SUCCEED.
THOSE WHO FIGHT HIM WILL FIND THEMSELVES IN THE STRUGGLE OF THEIR LIVES.
SHALL WE LEAVE IT TO BLIND FATE?
HEADS YOU FIGHT BESIDE ME, TAILS I FIGHT ALONE?
WAIT.
YOU DON'T NEED TO DO THAT, MAN. I NEVER WANTED TO BE A SAFETY ENGINEER.
SCREW FATE. WE FIGHT.
BENEATH CARSON'S FEET, RANDAL SIX RESTS.
THE DARK, DRY, QUIET CRAWL SPACE UNDER THE DETECTIVE'S HOUSE PROVIDES HIM WITH AN IDEAL ENVIRONMENT. THE SPIDERS DO NOT BOTHER HIM.
HIS JOURNEY FROM MERCY HAS BEEN A TRIUMPH, THOUGH IT FRAYED HIS NERVES AND RUBBED HIS COURAGE RAW. HE NEEDS TIME NOW TO RECOVER, TO REGAIN HIS CONFIDENCE.
HE CLOSES HIS EYES AND LISTENS TO THE THREE VOICES ABOVE HIM. IN THAT ROOM IS HAPPINESS. HE CAN FEEL IT. HE HAS ARRIVED AT THE SOURCE.
THE SECRET IS WITHIN HIS GRASP.
the end... for now.

Bonus Sketchbook

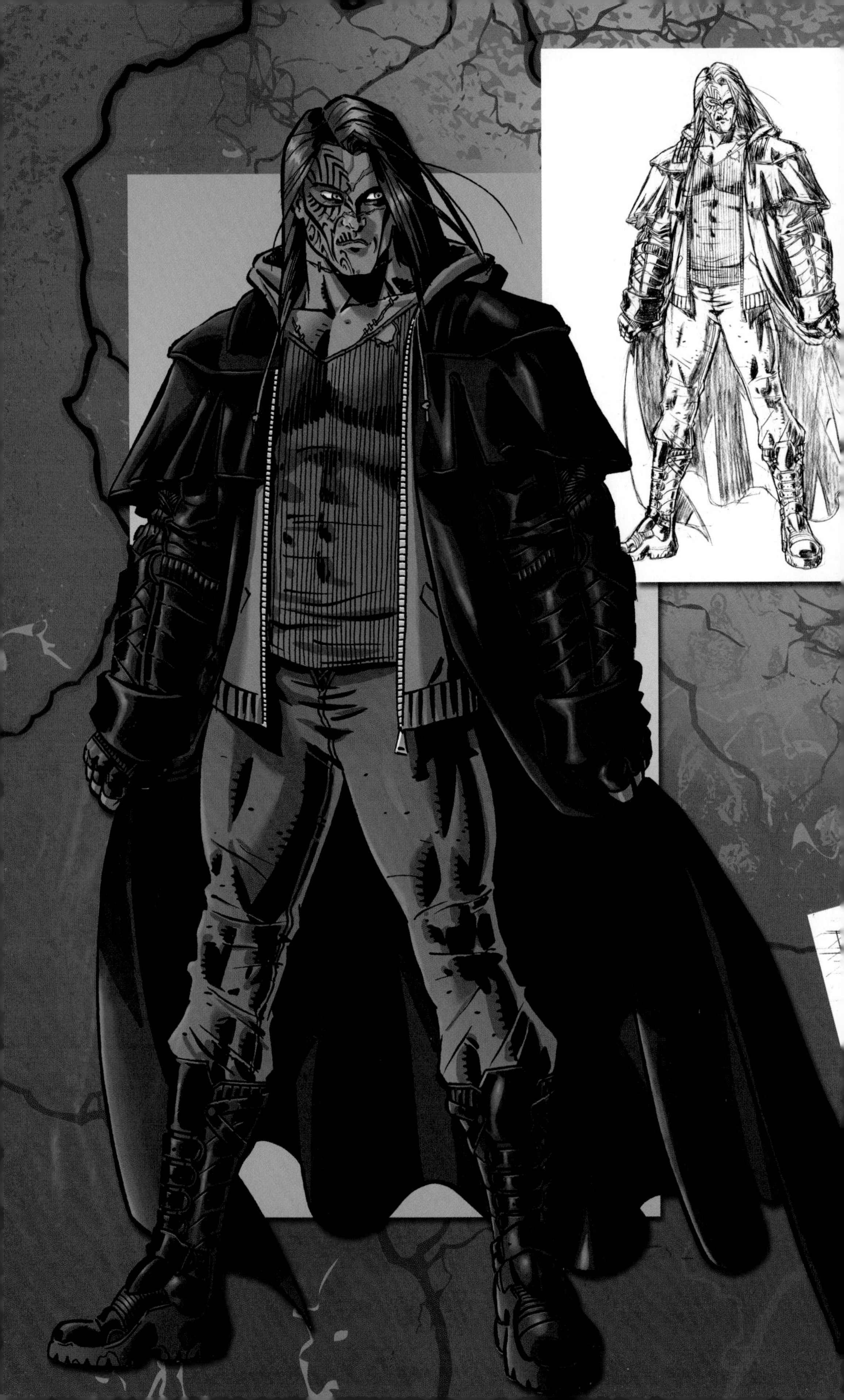

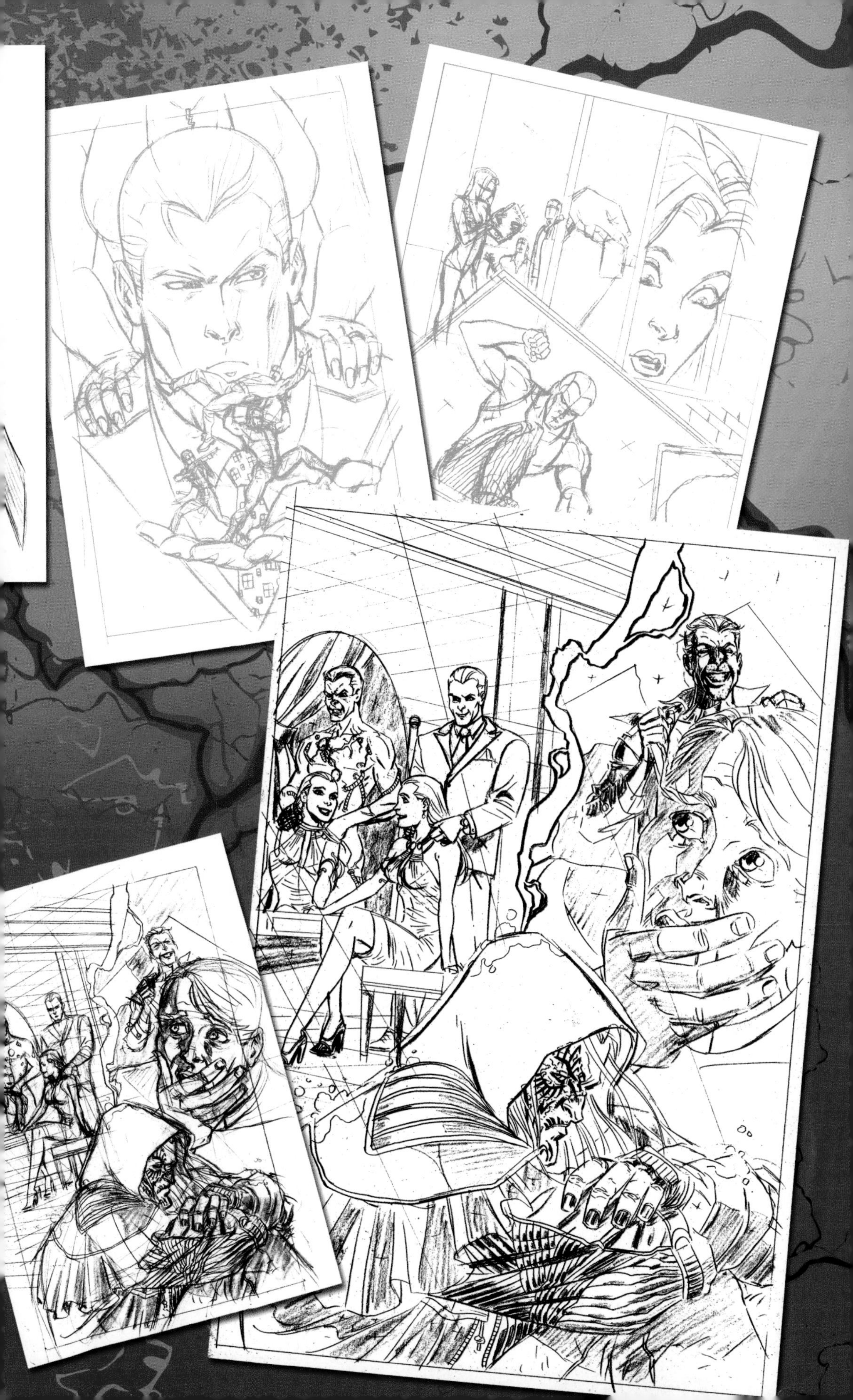

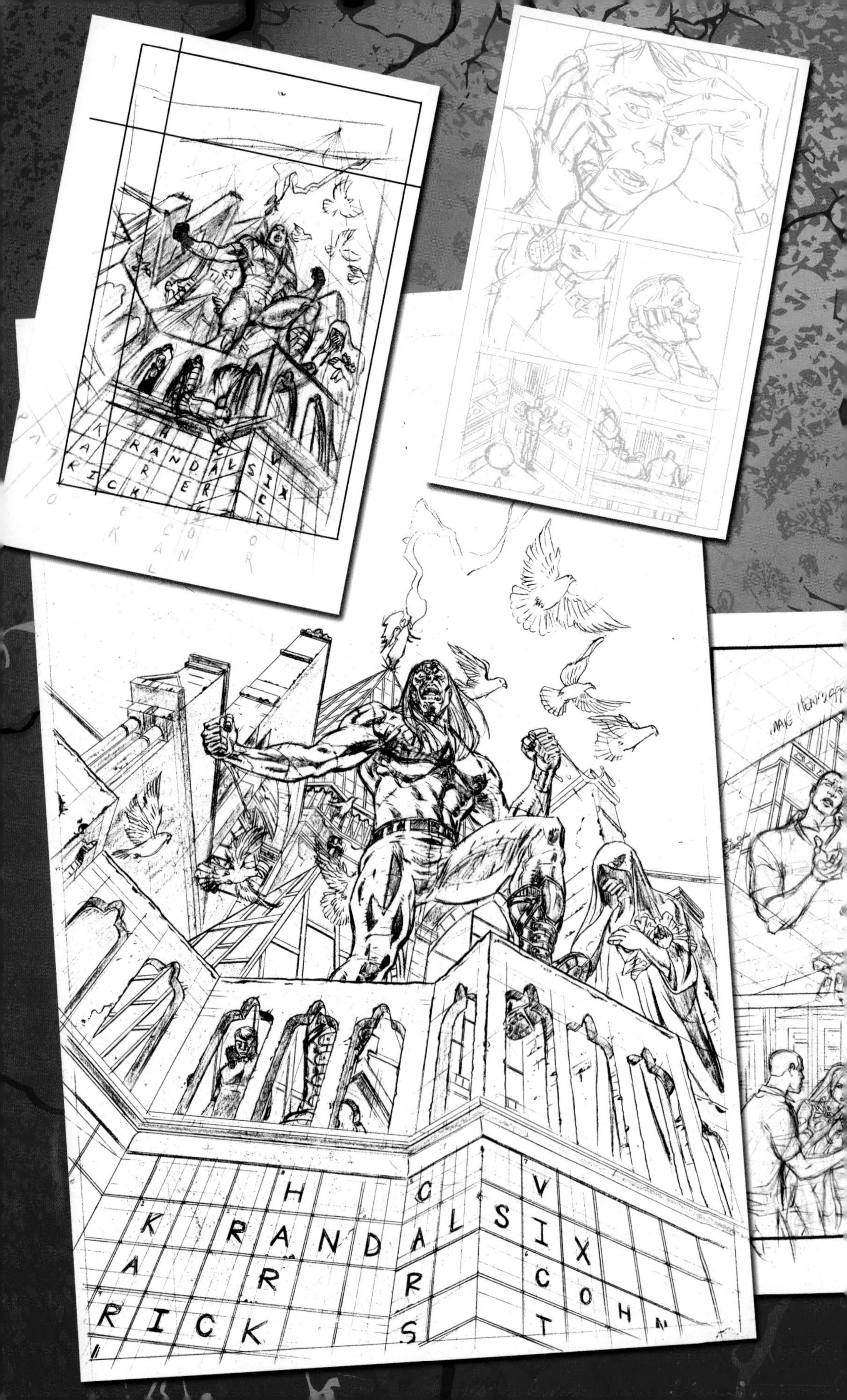
H C V
K RANDALSIX
A R R C O H
RICK S T

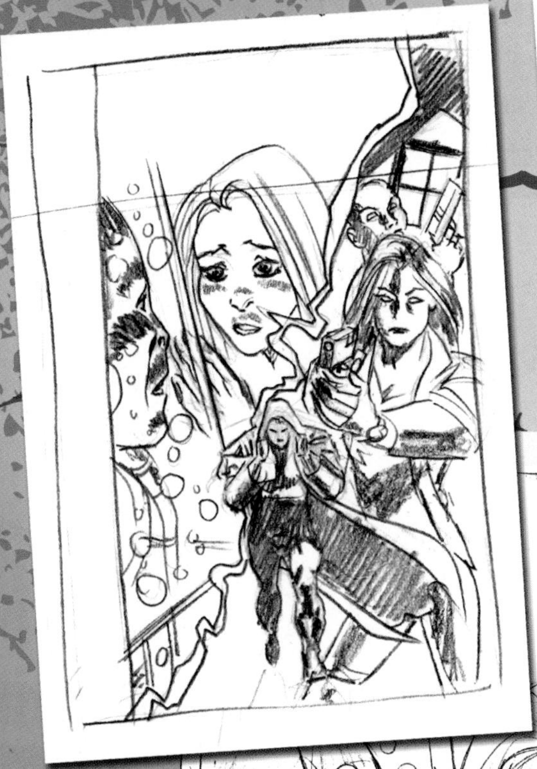
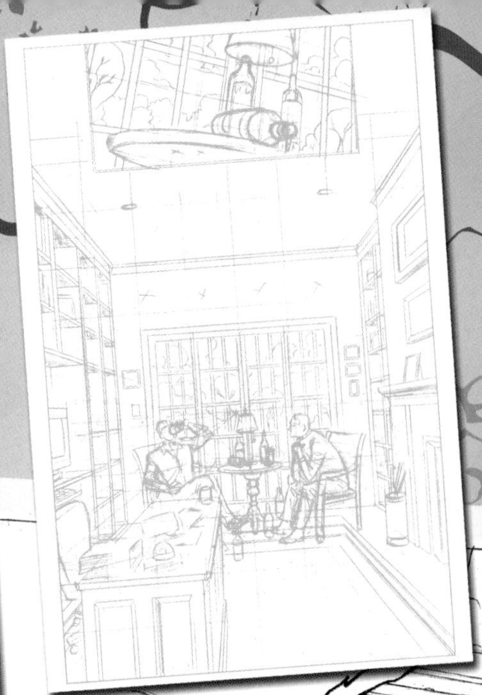
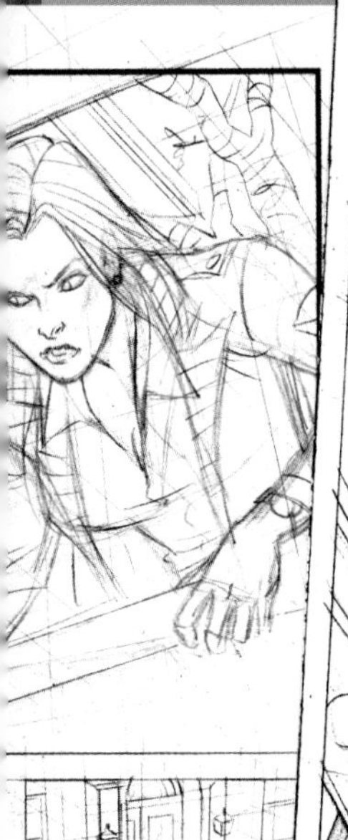
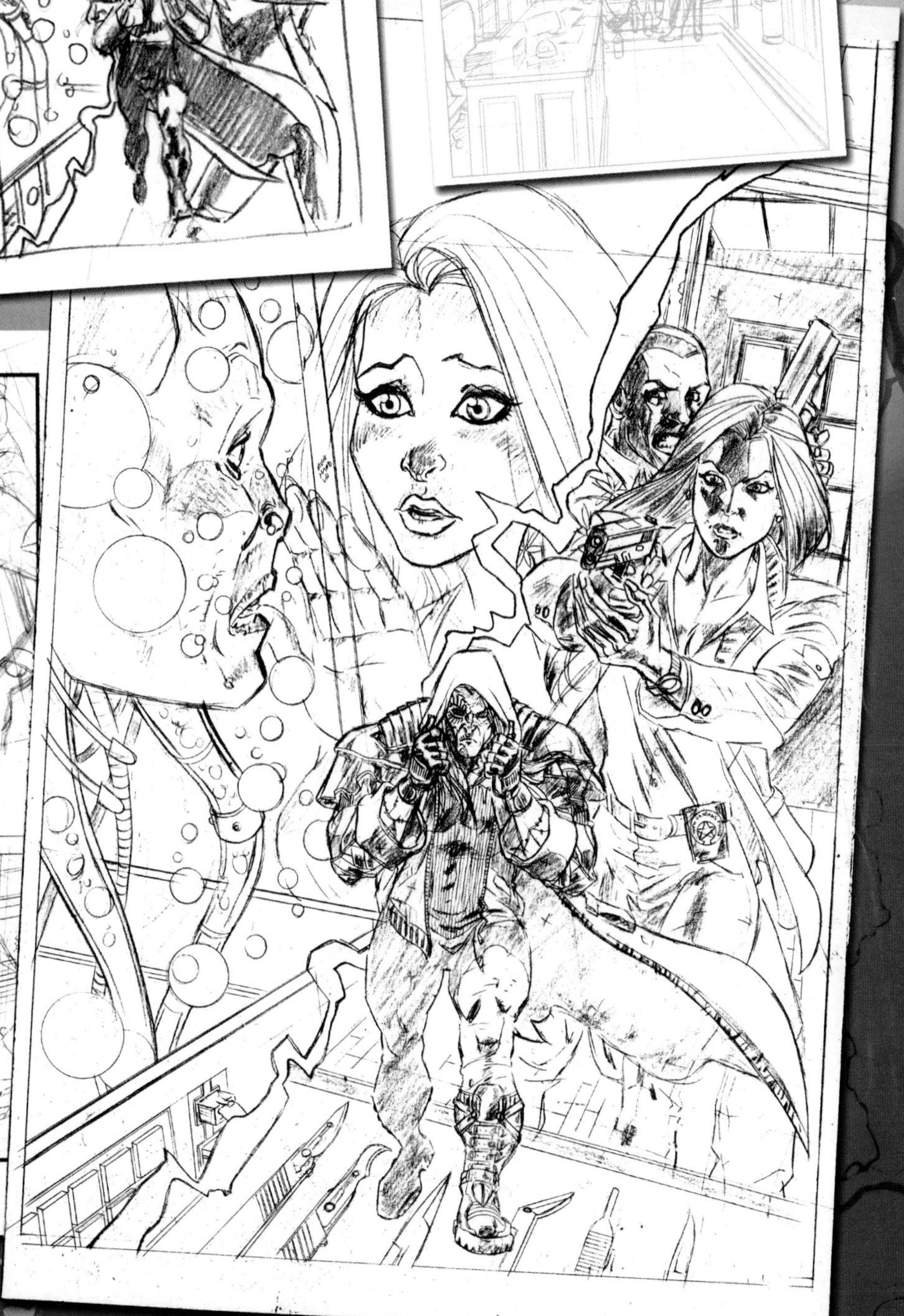

DEAN KOONTZ'S

FRANKENSTEIN™

Prodigal Son

volume two

DYNAMITE®
ENTERTAINMENT